WITH

THE
HENFIELD
PRIZE
STORIES

THE HENFIELD PRIZE STORIES

Edited by

John Birmingham
Laura Gilpin
Joseph F. McCrindle

WARNER BOOKS

A Time Warner Company

Warner Books, Inc., 666 Fifth Avenue, New York, NY 10103

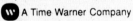 A Time Warner Company

Printed in the United States of America
First printing: January 1992
10 9 8 7 6 5 4 3 2

Library of Congress Cataloging-in-Publication Data

The Henfield Prize stories / edited by John Birmingham, Laura Gilpin.
Joseph F. McCrindle.
    p.   cm.
  ISBN 0-446-39304-5
    1. Short stories, American. 2. Literary prizes—United States.
I. Birmingham, John, 1951–   II. Gilpin, Laura, 1950–
III. McCrindle, Joseph F.
PS648.S5H38   1992
813′.0108—dc20   91-19096
                                  CIP

Cover design by Louise Fili
Book design by Giorgetta Bell McRee

ACKNOWLEDGMENTS

The editors are grateful for permission to reprint the following copyrighted material:

"Given Names," by Sue Miller. First published in *The North American Review*. Copyright © 1981 by Sue Miller. Reprinted by permission of the author.

"The Carnival Dog, the Buyer of Diamonds," by Ethan Canin, from *Emperor of the Air*. First published in *Redbook* (under the title "Abe, between Rounds"). Copyright © 1988 by Ethan Canin. Reprinted by permission of Houghton Mifflin Co.

"All Little Colored Children Should Play the Harmonica," by Ann Patchett. First published in *The Paris Review*. Copyright © 1984 by Ann Patchett. Reprinted by permission of the author.

"The Drowned," by Brad Owens. Copyright © 1992 by Brad Owens. Printed by permission of the author.

"The Doctor of the Moon," by Harriet Doerr, from *Stones for Ibarra*. First published in *The Ark River Review*. Copyright © 1978, 1981, 1983, 1984 by Harriet Doerr. Reprinted by permission of Viking Penguin, a division of Penguin Books USA, Inc.

"Horizontal Light," by Chris Spain, from *Praying for Rain*, published by Capra Press. First published in *The Antioch Review*. Copyright © 1988, 1990 by Chris Spain. Reprinted by permission of the author.

"Zorro," by Steven Barthelme, from *And He Tells the Little Horse the Whole Story*. Copyright © 1987 by the Johns Hopkins University Press, Baltimore/London. Reprinted by permission of the author and the publisher.

"Approximations," by Mona Simpson. First published in *Ploughshares*. Copyright © 1984 by Mona Simpson. Reprinted by permission of the author.

"Eye Water," by Jennifer Coke, from *Eye Water*. Copyright © 1992 by Jennifer Coke. Printed by permission of the author.

"The Letter Writer," by M. T. Sharif. First published in *Agni*. Copyright © 1988 by M. T. Sharif. Reprinted by permission of the author.

"The Sutton Pie Safe," by Pinckney Benedict, from *Town Smokes*. First published in the *Chicago Tribune*. Copyright © 1986, 1987 by Pinckney Benedict. Reprinted by permission of Ontario Review Press.

"High Bridge," by Fenton Johnson, from *Scissors, Paper, Rock*. First published (in different form) in the *Chicago Tribune*; then in *Turnstile*. Copyright © 1986 by Fenton Johnson. Reprinted by permission of the author.

"Pie Dance," by Molly Giles, from *Rough Translations*. First published in *The North American Review*. Copyright © 1984 by Molly Giles. Reprinted by permission of the author.

CONTENTS

CONTENTS

T H E

HENFIELD

PRIZE

STORIES

LIFT-OFF, LAUREL WREATHS, AND THE POWER OF "YES"

A DECADE OF THE HENFIELD PRIZES

by Allan Gurganus

"An American is insubmissive, lonely, self-educated and polite."

THORNTON WILDER

Let us begin with a stark and beautiful native fact:

> The power required to lift the American space launch be-
> yond Earth's atmosphere is nearly equivalent to the electri-
> cal wattage needed to light the Eastern Seaboard for those
> same minutes.

We rush to apply this to the ascent of a young writer. Consider
the hardship of pitching a student writer from the comforting gravitational field surrounding any college campus to that darker clearer
void called Adult Artistic Orbit.

Any writer's upsurge from a first story in the university literary
magazine (full of wince-making typos) to his/her finished inaugural
book—constitutes a sojourn just as arduous as any space launch's
climb. And much much slower. Such a lift-off requires comparable
planning, requires determination carried to the force of obsession,
requires many helping propulsive boosts. Such a voyage also demands—however briefly—a communal sacrifice. I mean the imperceptible dimming of an entire seaboard's lights. Which brings us to
the happy subject of the Henfield Foundation awards. Which brings
us to this various, lively sampling of rewarded stories. Each of these
tales won—just in the nick of time, I can promise you—that great
bonus to the trajectory of American literature, the Henfield Prize.

Yeats wrote: "There can be no literature without praise." By
praise he surely meant the lyric impulse: every writer's tendency to
face the pleasures and sensations of our gorgeous deranged world by
simply singing. And yet, Yeats's *praise* also suggests the nourishing
effects, the hope-giving levitation that positive criticism can offer
any writer, especially a beginning one. What an odd profession, to
insist that a writer find the world only by leaving it. In a culture that
so often undervalues mere pieces of white paper covered with mere
observations, mere passion, the Henfield Foundation has, over several decades now, made the world a bit more praiseworthy. Somehow

the foundation knew to advance financial and critical good faith to writers at exactly their first moments of skyward capability. Looking back on the major reputations the Henfield has already helped coax toward alighting, surely this organization deserves more than a footnote in the history of recent American letters. If there can be no literature without praise, those who praise literature first and best must occasionally warrant laurel wreaths all their own.

To understand the good done by this organization since 1980, and to hear the sorts of newborn writers that the Henfield has encouraged and engendered—we need to consider the difficulties of the launching pad.

To anyone outside this underfunded, dubious yet fully addictive profession, choosing to become a writer might seem simple as deciding upon ''Lawyer'' or ''Doctor.'' And yet, those other occupations mercifully set a task, a series of performances to accomplish. Once these are achieved, you actually ARE a lawyer, maybe not a good one, but there is the framed certificate to hang upon your rental wall, a credential and a fact. But when oh when does a literate person actually become a writer?

How long is the apprenticeship? There are few prodigies at fiction writing. One truism of musical composition and theoretical mathematical research: many pioneers, by age thirty, have already made their major contributions. Less true with fiction. Those in our literature who've made the greatest early contribution, often died very very young. They seem forewarned, they seem to compact a lifetime's achievement into, say, Stephen Crane's twenty-nine years or Flannery O'Connor's thirty-nine. But for many writers of sustained prose narrative, the actual job begins, the driver's license issued—at age forty. Only then does experience begin to come around a second or a third time: third marriages, third children, third major hurricane of a lifetime, third heavy-bodied stargazing visit to the launching pad.

For the past fifteen years I've earned my living as a college teacher of fiction writing. In my own way, I've been productively waiting to turn forty while funding my own slow learning. There are many reasons I've plied the teacher's trade: one is a personal fondness for eating at least two meals per day. Another benefit involves being close to the fervor of belief so plentiful in smart wide-open eighteen-year-olds. However tired a teacher might become year to year, there remains September's renewing moment of discovery. You give that first short assignment; you take the papers home and—avid talent scout—you fall upon them with the nerve of Cortez and the material attention of the Wright Brothers. You are a discoverer and there, among the good ones, the okay ones and those already bent on shortcut, you refind the reason that you do what you do. Somebody's first story is—well, fetal, and yet it has all its parts; it is already complete, imagined, and it jump-starts your own capacity for belief, for craft.

My central joy in teaching is watching/coaching intelligent and volatile young people discover their own gift for voices, their own abiding need to define themselves via empathizing with others. Year after year, I've seen them understand their own sweet surging drive to Tell. Which means, of course, their assuming that remarkable component requirement: listening professionally, listening with the acuity of an animal listening (as fearful as respectful) to another animal.

Since our culture remains somewhat underwhelmed by a glorious prose style, dubious of any story that shows what we need to know instead of what we've been lead to lazily assume, any teacher of fiction writing must occasionally feel guilty. How dare we profess a profession that—in the eyes of our brusque commercial society—offers so few outward rewards? Into my classroom, I've seen rangy young medical students wander. Here comes a third-generation doctor from a family that values this holy calling above all else. In he strolls, planning one last fling at the Liberal Arts; then suddenly—within spitting distance of hanging out his healer's shingle—this kid finds his true calling. I've learned—as a general practitioner myself—to recognize the signs: early warnings of incoming scrivener's madness—insomnia, excitability, a tendency to mutter possible perfect sentences half-aloud, the accompanying volume of Chekhov's stories almost completely underlined in blue ballpoint. How can I justify this new kind of Organic Chemistry? Writing novels might be just as inwardly rewarding as healing the halt and the lame, but it is infinitely less remunerated. Can so private and far-flung an Orbit even be called an adult activity?

Chekhov, in his greatest story, "The Lady and the Little Dog," provides us with one of literature's most familiar and endearing adulterers. In this gentleman's split between his dreary married existence and his passionate clandestine affair, he might well embody the interior schism of the writer: "He led a double life: one for all who were interested to see, full of conventional truth and conventional deception, exactly like the lives of his friends and acquaintances; and another which went on in secret. And by a strange concatenation of circumstances . . . quite by accident, everything that was important, interesting, essential, everything about which he was sincere and did not deceive himself, everything that made up the quintessence of his life, went on in secret, while everything that was a lie, everything that was merely the husk in which he hid himself to conceal the truth, like his work at the bank, . . . his discussions at the club, . . . his going to anniversary functions with his wife—all that happened in the sight of all. He judged others by himself, did not believe what he saw, and was always of the opinion that every man's real and most interesting life went on in secret, under cover of night. The personal, private life of an individual was kept obscured."

During a bout of self-reproach for indoctrinating the young into the mysteries of fiction while depriving them of decent livelihoods, I first heard about the Henfield Prize.

At Sarah Lawrence College, at the end of every school year, we coffee-drinking teachers of writing gathered to nominate students for what was simply, fondly, and familiarly called The Henfield. Each of us came prepared, having read the best stories by each other's most serious (read "playful," read "airborne") students. In this way we came to know what excitement had transpired all year long in other classrooms; we discovered those young writers we would most like to "work with" next semester. To understand how much the Henfield Prize has already given to American letters, it is necessary to understand how few rewards are offered for young artists at the very start of their long rides upward.

Part of the particular genius of the Henfield and its benefactor, Joseph McCrindle, is having noticed how many prizes are offered for persons who've completed a first novel or collection of stories. Awards exist for writers of their fifth books; for North Carolinian poetry-writing carpenters over the age of forty. But all these rewards demand—A Book. Everybody loves the already airborne. But who will endorse and help lift those making their maiden vertical voyages?

What other foundation has understood the harrowing, winnowing, Darwinian process that stretches between a bright start as an undergraduate writing student and the advent of that first annealed grownup work of art? Such an expanse can constitute a wasteland. Call those who survive to achieve book-length flight the surviving fittest. It helps if you enjoy rejection slips. My own extensive collection numbers not in the hundreds but, bruised badge of honor, source of grumpiness on rainy days, the thousands. Getting one's work aloft takes nothing less than a gyroscopic sextant called Obsession; it takes a lot of help from your friends; it takes such unbidden acts of philanthropy as the Henfield's, such stabilizing jolts of confidence and affirmation. The United States spends less on the arts than any other industrialized Western nation. And yet, go to a gallery in Amsterdam, you'll find instant clones of last month's work exhibited in Manhattan. Browse through any Belgian bookstore and find endless translations of young American writers. Independence must make for a kind of stamina and force. But it's hard to put in forty hours a week at your listed work, the job you state on your IRS form—and all to support your true and secret life, your hidden life as a burgeoning writer.

If lawyers were required to work in more menial jobs for two decades prior to trying their first case—the yellow pages under "Attorney" would be slimmer by far, and our world might prove less apt to sue. Ours is a nation that pays beginning garbage collectors more than veteran teachers. And it even pays teachers more than the most dogged vet writers. Still, bushed after a regular job, millions of Americans retreat to that preferred terrain, their unsold manuscripts in progress, the zones of perfect justice that these unsung writers conceive, sustain, and nightly love toward reality. The miracle is that anyone ever achieves narrative imaginative lift-off. So, it is into this stubborn gravitational down-pull that the Henfield wisely offers its annual aerial encouragement.

T. S. Eliot wrote, in the launching issue of the original *Transatlantic Review*, "Good literature is produced by a few queer people in odd corners; the use of a review is not to force talent, but to create a favourable atmosphere. And you will serve this purpose if you publish, as I hope you will find and publish, work of writers of whatever age who are too good and too independent to have found other publishers.'' In 1959, Joseph McCrindle wisely revived the defunct *Transatlantic Review*. The magazine, funded by the Henfield Foundation in its early days, took Eliot's advice to heart. It discovered the most venturesome and intriguing artists of our age. McCrindle privately recalls that, after *Transatlantic* issues featuring unfamiliar early works by those anarchic erotic rogues William Burroughs and Alfred Chester—McCrindle's own all-too-respectable parents ceased mentioning the magazine. Till then, they had proudly given subscriptions to their friends. From the start, McCrindle remained loyal to Eliot's credo of discovery. Thank God for those ''few queer people in odd corners . . . too good and too independent to have found other publishers.''

Joseph McCrindle is a very modest man of rare discernment, wide sympathies, and considerable generosity. Just as John Quinn has been recognized for the ways he enabled and eased the groundbreaking work of Pound and Joyce in Paris in the twenties, McCrindle will be counted among the great allies of fine writing in our sad century's second half. No one alive has done more good for more good writers. (And I will endeavor to prevent his blue-penciling away this obvious fact.)

In 1980, the first Henfield Prizes were given, applicants culled from more than twenty invited colleges. Along with Mr. McCrindle, Laura Gilpin and John Birmingham have annually faced the daunting task of finding the most gifted of this year's undergraduate and graduate writing students and awarding them accordingly. Many another foundation gives prizes on the basis of how much critical attention a small cadre of established writers has received in a given year; it is possible for any pundit with subscriptions to a few crucial periodicals to predict in advance ''whose year it is.'' How much more difficult and interesting to pore over manuscripts by unknown authors, a bumper crop of these new and ancient voices. How much more Jeffersonian and how infinitely closer to the true spirit of literature. The conventionality of the traditional New York publishing cannot be overstated. ''We always do things this way'' is the industry's watchword—a phrase roughly as considered and humane as ''Because I said so and because I'm the Daddy, that's why!''

Given the industry's love for a sure thing only, how necessary and profound the Henfield's mission of helping the freshest voices find their way up, first into our general hearing, then into our general view.

The present volume contains stories by those who—since first being rewarded by the Henfield Foundation—have become well-known, and those who should, and those who certainly will. Present readers and future scholars will note the appearance of fiction by Ann Patchett, Brad Owens, Walter Mosley, Steven Barthelme, Mark Dewey, Emily Hammond, Suzanne Juergensen, David Lipsky, Daniel Mueller, Michael Drinkard, Jonathan Ames, M. T. Sharif, Jennifer Coke, Lauren Belfer, A. M. Homes, Molly Giles, Chris Spain, and Fenton Johnson. Most all the stories were unpublished when the writers won their prizes. Sue Miller was in the first group of 1980 winners; her work presented here went on to become part of her widely praised first novel, *The Good Mother*. Pinckney Benedict is the only writer to win the award twice. "Approximations" by Mona Simpson, later reappeared as a chapter of her admired and forceful novel *Anywhere but Here*. Ethan Canin's short fiction has managed, with his popular and acclaimed collection, *The Emperor of Air*, to win a large following both for his own sympathetic stories and for that blessed form in general. (It must be remembered that the short story is, thanks to Poe, Hawthorne, and Washington Irving, credited as a particularly American form. It belongs alongside those other American-invented art forms: jazz, the musical comedy, and, less commonly acknowledged, yes, striptease.)

One of this collection's notable writers went on to write *Stones for Ibarra*. Harriet Doerr, born in 1910, was in her early seventies when the three Henfield readers came upon her story; it was soon to be a chapter of her first novel, winner of the National Book Award. We remember Eliot's admonition to find "writers of whatever age." Doerr's gift, belatedly revealed and justly celebrated, heartens all of us who work slowly but, we hope, deeply and well.

This collection's fine range of writing, the breadth of sympathy shown by the Henfield judges, bespeaks an undoctrinaire vision of what fiction can still offer us all. These separate stories depend upon no single "school." If the assembled tales have anything in common, that might be a sense of life, an attention to the beauty of language in motion, language in the service of some larger idea of human possibility. It is this very openness to the new—new talents, new subjects, new styles—that continues to render the Henfield so valuable and necessary. In our age of government arts-funding cuts, with the vigilante protectors of decency patrolling the few works that are rewarded, private grants like the Henfield Prize Awards take on a whole new meaning and force. Private generosity becomes a public act of faith in a culture that can always fund short-term wars but that ignores the creation of long-range masterpieces.

A student of mine won the Henfield Prize a decade ago. Ann Patchett's story is included in this distinguished company, ranking as a favorite among the hundred past winners. I concede that, as this story's godpoppa, I feel very proud. I was about to attempt an act of ventriloquy, about to imagine what the prize must've meant in overtaking my very young and gifted student. Then, trusting Ann's continuing agility with her own story's story, I tracked her down by phone; I found her finishing a first novel (*The Patron Saint of Liars*, forthcoming from Houghton Mifflin) at the Fine Arts Work Center in Provincetown. Never shy to give ex-students new assignments, I asked Ann to put in a full day's work on her novel; and then would she write—very quickly, in a single sitting, mailed to me posthaste—her impressions and memories surrounding that early story and the lingering effects of the prize it won? She sent this letter:

In the fall of 1982 I took my first fiction writing class (at Sarah Lawrence College). Allan Gurganus taught it and the rule was a story a week, which I believed, at the time, meant a new story every week. I worked at that class like trigonometry, inorganic chemistry. I killed myself for a story a week. Over Christmas break I wrote, "All Little Colored Children Should Play the Harmonica," in part because I'd bought my stepfather a harmonica for Christmas, but mainly to address the problems of talent. I figured if I had a narrator who was a young black boy in the 1940's who played the harmonica, no one would realize that it was specifically my problem I was wrestling with. (And I'll add that no one did figure it out. People still ask me how I came to know so much about black musicians.)

When I came back for second semester something in me

had snapped. I couldn't keep up anymore. I couldn't find a new story a week. Through panic, I began to learn the art of rewriting. I reworked that same story from vacation and hoped Allan wouldn't notice that I wasn't producing new work. But what I found was that he meant a full story's worth of effort every week, and that newness could be achieved through finding depth as opposed to constantly searching out different ground. We tirelessly went through that story, again and again. I learned that there were an endless number of things for me to think about, talk about, and most importantly, see through to their natural conclusion, in those eighteen pages. If I had been a gymnast, Allan would have been spotting me. I was doing the tricks, jumps, and turns, but all with safety cords, all with a hand that knew the exact moment to press my back gently in the right direction. You may or may not be able to teach someone how to write, I'm not sure about that. But you can teach someone how to rewrite, or how to think things through.

When the story won the Henfield Prize I was nineteen years old. It was summer and I was at Harvard, and I remember running to tell my friend who threw the glass of Coke she had in her hand against the wall so as to pick me up and swing me around. It was a small transfiguration, one of the truly pure joys in my life, because it was the first. When other prizes or publications came later, I had friends who were writers. I knew people who didn't win, and so I kept my happiness to polite levels. The Henfield was only goodness. Later that night, however, I felt a huge wave of fear, because now I was on the path of doing something, instead of just hoping I'd do it. It was as if my fondest wish had been said aloud and now I've had to live up to it. Living up to that promise is something I still think about, trying to do the best work possible without excuses.

Whoever set up the rules of receiving the money must have known me. It had to be spent in a year to enrich your writing in some way. If I hadn't promised to spend it, I would have saved it for the orthodontia of childen I still do not have. Instead, I went to Europe. Hitchhiked through

Denmark, sat in cafés in Paris, walked the rubble in Northern Ireland. I went out into the world to find stories and found them.

Things were very hard after that for a long time. I kept on writing. I knew how to do that, but I hadn't learned to be the hand on my own back. My stories were imaginative but thin. Alone, I couldn't seem to pound them into fighting shape, make them strong enough to survive the world without me. The only thing stronger than my desire for a good story was my desire to uphold the good manners my mother taught me, and I never sent Allan a story to read once I left his class; to this day I sometimes long to do so. He had shown me how, had taken me all the way through one time, and now I would have to fall and get up and fall and get up, until I learned how to do it alone.

I think confidence is the single thing a writer needs most. The Henfield Award gave me confidence. It existed in the world, a truth, and I will be proud of it forever. It gave me proof, for myself alone, that the talent was there, and that I would only have to keep mining to find it again. It makes me think I had it easy, because so many fine writers have mucked through their dry periods without such a gift in which to take solace.

I am still writing. I am still wanting to be better than I am. I am still proud of the good work I have done. And I am thankful for a teacher who taught me how to do for myself instead of doing for me, and for a prize that said I had done well.

Colette's most poignant work begins with the artist's mother standing at a garden gate, wiping hands onto her apron just at suppertime; she keeps calling into the evening air, a question of sweet terrible sadness, "Where are the children? Where are the children?"

Looking over the field of American literary reputation, we need to constantly ask the same question. We want to know which artists have brought Chekhov's secret life into a public narrative form that remains so useful to us all. Who are the new heroes? We know all too well the graying eminences, the automatic prize-winners, many of whom have not written a fresh, true page in decades. We can turn for the real answer to one preeminent organization. It has assured that our younger generation—of all ages—will be encouraged, housed, stimulated, and acknowledged when acknowledgment is most needed, exactly when it is generally least available. If there can be no literature without Praise, there needs to be a particular branch of literature dedicated to praising the Praisers of Literature. Let that start here. A laurel crown for Mr. McCrindle, his astute and passionate fellow readers, and for the laurel-awarding Henfield itself.

And now, fellow reader, we face the pleasure of rediscovering a decade of gifted discoveries, permanent gifts. How hard is it for a student fiction writer to become a published author whose works achieve the American literary canon?

> The power required to lift the American space launch beyond Earth's atmosphere is nearly equivalent to the electrical wattage needed to light the Eastern Seaboard for those same minutes.

Now, for the joy known only to discoverers. Imagine that you are yourself a Henfield judge. Imagine you are the very first to ever hear these richly individuated full-blown stories. Imagine it is your joy and power to say simply, "Yes, that. Yes, more of that, please. Come forth, ye new and ancient voice."

Then know that just such a "Yes" rests wholly in your power. Many such "Yesses," latent accelerators, wait right here in your hands. Yeats, as usual, is correct. There can be no literature without Praise. There can be no upward surge without a sufficient sacrificial earthbound send-off. Let us then acknowledge how many brilliant maiden voyages have been steadied, bettered, boosted by the Henfield's sweet supplementing velocity. "Yes" at just the right moment is "Yes" spelled in thunder.

Four, three, two, one, "yes," contact . . . . . . blast-off.

Now, the difficult ascent begins!

GIVEN NAMES
by Sue Miller
(Boston University)

My aunt's last words were characteristic. My uncle, her brother, to whom she had spoken them, repeated them compulsively to everyone who would listen at the memorial service a week later. My aunt had drowned. She had been drunk, which was not unusual for her, and she and my uncle were rowing home together in the dark from a family picnic. She objected to the way he rowed. "My God, Orrie, look at you, batting at the water in that half-assed way," she had said. "Jesus, put a little life into it. I could *swim* home faster than this."

Orrie said she sat still for a minute after this, and the only sound was of the oars slipping in and out of the black water. Then she stood up, kicked off her shoes, and dove in.

The boat rocked violently after she sprang off. My uncle thinks he might have jerked his hand off the oar to pull back from her splash, or maybe just the rocking bounced the oar out of the oarlock and his hand. It slid off into the water at any rate, and he spent several minutes retrieving it. My aunt floated on her back near the boat briefly, and he said he spoke sharply to her, told her she was "a damn fool or some such thing." She laughed at him and blew an arc of water up into the moonlight, "a great jet" he called it, then rolled over and swam off. By the time he got the oar back into the oarlock, he could barely hear her in the distance. He tried to row in her direction. He said he would row for a few strokes, pulling hard for speed, then coast and listen for her. By the third or fourth interval he knew he'd lost her. All he could hear was the gentle rush of water against the bow of the coasting boat. He rowed around in wide circles in the moonlight for a while, and then he had to row home and tell his parents. She was forty-two. They found her two days later.

The rowboat wasn't used until three days after that when my grandparents headed into town to retrieve her ashes. As my grandfather carefully handed my grandmother in, she spotted Babe's Papagallo shoes in the stern of the boat where she'd kicked them off before her dive. At this my grandmother, who'd taken it all "like a brick, a real brick" in my uncle's words, became hysterical. She began to scream rhythmically, steady bursts of sound. When my grandfather tried to loosen her hands from the edge of the boat, she hit him several times. She broke his glasses. Dr. Burns had to be summoned from his cottage across the lake to administer a sedative. "My baby, my baby," she whimpered, until she fell into her chemical sleep.

My aunt was my mother's youngest sister, my grandparents' youngest child. She had been an afterthought of one sort or another; everyone always had known it. But no one had ever dared to ask, and so no one knew, whether she was a mistake, or one last yearning look back at a stage in their lives already well past for my grandparents. My mother was twenty-two years older than her sister. She told me once that she had at first thought her mother was joking when she said she was going to have another child; and then was ashamed and embarrassed by it. She said it ruined her senior year of college.

They were full of nicknames in my mother's family. The brother who rowed home alone in the moonlight had been christened Frank Junior. But because of a prematurely lugubrious nature, he was called Eeyore as a boy, short for Junior. That eventually became Or, which grew back again into Orrie.

My aunt's name was Edith, but she was "the baby" while she grew up, and this shortened easily to Babe. My mother was Bunny, and the two middle sisters were Rain and Weezie, for Lorraine and Louise.

They were a handsome, high-strung group, dominated by my grandfather, who was at once expansive and authoritarian. His parents had been immigrants. As a young man he had patented a wear-resisting heel for shoes, then sold the patent to B. F. Goodrich, and learned to make money from money. Each of the daughters had, in turn, married a man of great business promise, but somehow each one got stuck as a middle-level executive, none so gloriously successful as my grandfather.

My grandmother seemed overwhelmed in their company. In the few remaining pictures of her alone, without the family, she is a radiant debutante, a smiling, confident bride. But in even my earliest memories she is mostly just a silent presence; a cool hand on my forehead through a feverish night, or someone to make intercession with Grandfather over a minor infraction of the rules; but of herself, inexpressive.

I was the oldest grandchild, five years younger than my Aunt Babe. I spent every childhood summer with her on the lake where my grandparents had their summer home, and where she died. In her isolation Babe befriended me. Reciprocally, I adored her. I had no siblings. I was dominated completely by my mother, and Babe seemed the ideal older sister, glamorous, strong, and defiant.

My grandparents' summer home was really what used to be called a camp, of several buildings on the far shore of an inland lake in Maine. The road ended on the near side, so the first people to open camp in the summer had to bushwhack their way around the lake, open the shed, and lower the leaky rowboats into the water; then return for the boxes and trunks and whining, dusty children. Subsequent arrivals would park and honk their horns, one long, three short. There was always some eager cousin waiting to row across and fetch them.

My grandparents' summer home had no electricity, no running water, no telephone. We used only canoes or rowboats for transportation. There was an unspoken contempt for those weekend families across the lake, whose clusters of electric lights twinkled merrily at us after dark while we huddled around kerosene lamps; who polluted the lake with motorboats, and had names on their cabins like Bide-a-Wee, or Cee-the-Vue. In the last several years, because they are old now, and made more uncomfortable by the camp's inconveniences, my grandparents have paid to have electric wires run around and bought a small power boat. On the night Babe died, my younger cousins were using the power boat to ferry the rest of the family home.

There were four separate family cottages at camp, but most of us cousins slept together on the sleeping porch of the large main house, the only one with a kitchen. Each child had an iron hospital bed, and we were grouped by families. Since I was an only child and Babe an aberration, we slept together. Babe had rigged up a curtain to separate our corner of the porch from the rest. She didn't mind my hanging around watching her paint her toenails or curl her hair. But if one of the younger cousins poked a head under the curtain, she was harsh. "No brats!" she'd snap.

In the early morning the sunlight reflected off the lake onto the whitewashed ceiling of the sleeping porch. As the air began to stir, the motion of the ripples increased until the ceiling shimmered with golden lights. I lay still and watched them—watched my beautiful aunt sleep—until my grandmother arrived from her cottage to the kitchen. With the smell of coffee and bacon, the squeak of the pump by the kitchen sink, I'd get up, easing my weight slowly off the steel mesh which supported my mattress so as not to disturb Babe, and go to help Grandmother make breakfast for the fifteen or twenty cousins and aunts and uncles who would rise when she rang the bell.

The buildings were all painted white, with dark green trim. Years later, newly divorced, with a one-year teaching appointment in the midwest, I chose those colors to paint my daughter's bedroom; and it was only as I recognized their source in the finished job that I realized how frightened and homesick I was for something familiar and safe.

My mother always sent me to my grandparents' for the whole summer. She herself would come up only for a month or so. My father stayed in Schenectady for all but the two weeks GE allowed him. He seemed uncomfortable when he did come up, as did the other brothers-in-law. They spent their time growing beards and fishing. The walls of the main house were dotted with birch bark reproductions of record catches, traced by the men in an unspoken competition that had developed over the years.

The sisters grew more expansive and thick as thieves as the summer wore on, seeming to pull away from us children. They told secrets, laughed at private things, often made fun of Uncle Orrie's wife, who clearly was never to be one of them. In general they seemed transformed into people we had never known, could never know. Into girls, in a sense, but girls whose club was private and exclusive and cruel.

Babe was, of course, not a part of the club. But she was also clearly not one of us cousins. Her singular status was a constant irritant to my aunts and my mother. They wanted someone to be in charge of Babe, her appearance, her language, her behavior towards the nieces and nephews. They turned in vain to my grandmother. She was, in her silent way, almost proud of Babe's eccentricities. She'd say, "Oh, that's just Babe's way." Or, "But you know, dearest, *I* can't do a thing with her." Neither could they, so she existed in a no man's land, nobody's child, nobody's mother.

She was sometimes a leader of the cousins, and sometimes tormented them. I was honored to be her ally in whichever direction she went. I felt I had no choice, and didn't want any. To be more than just myself, to be like her, that was the opportunity she offered me. Even now I feel I would have been a fool to say no. And when I occasionally tried, she made me ashamed of myself. "But, Babe," I'd say, "Aunt Rain *said*—"

"You want to grow up to be a creep like Rain?" she interrupted. "The most exciting thing she's done in the last ten years, she finished that thousand-piece jigsaw puzzle last week?"

And so I was her accomplice, for instance, when she decided we should haunt the outhouse. It was an ideal spot, in some ways. The path out to it was curved and tortuous. Roots leaped up from its surface to trip you. Industrious spiders could spin a web in the tiny building in the span of an hour to catch at your face as you stepped into the dark, reeking room. I was always terrified of animals biting me from below, and could never resist turning my flashlight into the hole to check for them; the sight of the lime-sprinkled turds of three generations invariably caused my stomach to clench.

Babe and I alternated stationing ourselves behind the building in the evening, just as the cousins were trooping out one by one with their flashlights for their last visit of the day. She was good at animallike noises. I was less inventive and would merely scratch at the walls, or throw pebbles from a little distance once the cousin was settled inside.

Soon several of the cousins stopped going to the outhouse at night. Peering around the corner of the building, I could watch their approach, the tiny pajamaed figures stumbling along with the little circle of light dancing in front of them on the path. Now I would watch the light beam swerve off the path, stop, and then I could hear the steady stream of piss hitting the forest floor.

It was not long before the first shit was found. "Distinctly humanoid," Aunt Rain pronounced, and there could be no arguing. It suddenly occurred to several others that the traces of deer or bear they'd thought they'd seen could have been humanoid also. Grandfather organized an inspection tour of suspicious droppings. Then a family council was called.

There were seven children at camp that summer, including Babe and me. One, Agatha, was exonerated because she wore diapers.

My grandfather, as usual, took over the actual administration of the punishment. Some person or persons, Grandfather said, had been doing number two around camp. There was no excuse for this as everyone knew the rules, that in an emergency or if you woke at night, you could do number one outside, but for number two you had to go to the outhouse. He wanted the guilty party or parties to speak up. If they didn't, they would have to bear the additional guilt of knowing they caused all of us to be punished equally. We would wait.

In the distance the loons called tragically to each other. My grandfather was reading. My aunts' voices in the kitchen rose and fell as they prepared supper, and the water lapped steadily on the tiny rocky beach where the rowboats were pulled up on their rotting slips.

There was a little whispering among the seven-year-olds. My grandfather's eyes did not rise from the page, but his voice was sharp. "There will be no collusion!" The profound silence fell again. Grandmother brought him out a cup of tea and looked worriedly around at us all, her eyes resting an instant longer on Babe and me than on anyone else. Finally, after about fifteen minutes, one seven-year-old capitulated. "I did some of 'em, Gramps." He could barely be heard. A rush to confess followed, and three of the boys admitted responsibility.

Their punishment was twofold. They had to clean up all the piles. (They were heard grumbling, "Geez, we didn't do *all* these!") And they had to scrape and repaint the peeling, stinking outhouse, inside and out. Babe claimed she felt no remorse and curled up on her bed with *Jane Eyre,* but I went out several times and helped them. Once my grandfather, coming out to check on the work, caught me wielding the scraper and gave me a hard look, but nothing was ever said.

If the cousins ever guessed Babe's part in this or other misfortunes that befell them, it didn't alter their feelings for her. She was their heroine too. She was a born teacher, Babe, and she bound them to her through crime and her own special insights into the adult world. She swiped food regularly, and kept a supply in the icehouse which she sometimes shared. She pilfered cigarettes and taught us all to smoke. We had a meeting place, a dappled clearing far back in the woods; and I can see her now sitting on a rock, puffing a Pall Mall, her fuschia toenails glimmering on her dirty bare feet, and pronouncing all the aunts and uncles, our parents, a bunch of fucking assholes. She didn't even cough.

Another time she pulled down her pants and showed us where the hair was going to grow when we were as old as she was. We thought it was disgusting, ugly. We hoped she was wrong, that it wouldn't happen that way to us. But we adored her for doing it.

The few years after this Babe grew more remote from me. Her adolescence fell like a shadow between us. She was simply gone a good deal of the time, off with young men in power boats from the other side of the lake where the houses clustered close to the shoreline. They would come swooping into our inlet to get her, shearing off endless cotter pins on the unmarked rocks which studded it, and then hover helplessly fifteen feet from shore. We had only rowboats, so no need of docks. Sometimes I or a cousin would row her out the little distance, but often she waded out, holding a bundle of dry clothes out of the water with one hand, swimming the last few feet awkwardly. She often came back after dark, and occasionally so late that she swam in quite a distance, theoretically so that the noise of the boat wouldn't wake the family. The lake was so still at night, though, that I'm sure my grandparents lay in their beds listening, as I did, to the dying whine of the motor's approach, the murmur of voices, laughter, carrying over the still water, and the splash as she dived in. Her teeth sometimes chattered a long time after she slid under the layers of covers on the cold sleeping porch. Later I wondered if she was thinking of all those nights when she dove out of Uncle Orrie's rowboat.

My grandfather was always angry at her now, but his methods of punishment had no effect on Babe. He was stony with her. I heard him talk more than once of her betraying his trust. He withdrew from her his charm and warmth, of which he had a considerable supply. She simply didn't care. Occasionally he would force her to stay home in the evening. She would pace around the sitting room of the main house, where we all passed evenings together, occasionally stopping to try and fit a piece into whatever the ongoing puzzle was, sighing, picking up and putting down whatever book she was reading. She made everyone nervous, and we were all just as happy, in truth, to have her gone.

The two summers after this, my mother enrolled me in music camp, so I saw Babe only for a week or so at the ends. When I again spent all summer at my grandparents', she was nineteen, in college, and I was fourteen. From the start of the summer she was preoccupied and dreamy. She wrote long letters daily, and usually made the trip into town herself to get the mail in my grandparents' old Packard. Sometimes I accompanied her, as she seemed to be at a stage again where she didn't mind my presence. Once or twice we sat in the car for a long time listening to popular songs on the radio while the battery ran down. There was no radio allowed at camp.

She seemed plumper, softer, tamed. Yet, mysteriously to me, she still seemed to create a furor in the family. There was constant tension between her and my grandfather and aunts. Sudden silences would fall when I or the cousins came around. Yet her behavior by contrast with previous summers seemed impeccable.

I was myself preoccupied because of the music camp. Somehow, it was clear to me, the decision had been made that I was not, as my mother had hoped, musically gifted. My teacher's attitude had shifted during the previous year, from that of rigorous demand to a kind of tensionless approval. I knew she and Mother had talked. I would not go to the camp again. Mother said it seemed a waste of money, when I could have such a good time at my grandparents'. I don't remember that the decision about music had ever been mine, but I had accepted it and wanted to be good. Now I felt that my life as a serious person was over.

Near the end of August, Babe and I went on a picnic together to Blueberry Island. I swam briefly, feeling my usual anxiety about brushing against unfamiliar rocks or trees in the strange water. Babe lay in shorts and a man's shirt, with sleeves rolled up, and sunbathed.

I came out of the water and dried off. Babe sat up. We chatted briefly, about my mother, about how disappointed she was in me. Babe offered the theory that she probably lost interest in my musical career when she discovered you didn't wear little white gloves to play in concerts. I went down to the rowboat we'd pulled up onto the shoreline and brought back a sweatshirt for myself, and two blueberry pails. We walked into the center of the small island, screened from the lake by trees and brush, and knelt down to pick the berries. After a while, I asked Babe why everyone seemed so angry at her, why all the doors kept slamming shut on family conferences. Babe's lips and teeth were stained blue and she leaned back on her heels and said, "You might as well know now, I guess. I'm going to have a baby. I'm almost three months pregnant. They're all in a twit. They *hate* my boyfriend, he's not res*pect*able enough. They think I'm too young. Daddy brought me up here this summer to get me away, to bring me to my senses he said. They want me to go to Europe next year." Tears began to slide down her face. "All I want is just to be with Richard."

I was stunned and appalled and thrilled, just as I had been when she had shown us the secrets of her adolescent body. I remember I asked her why she and Richard didn't run away, and she said he had no money. He needed to finish college. He was ambitious and poor, and besides, he didn't know she was pregnant.

I asked her how *she* knew, and, eternally the teacher, she wiped her nose on her sleeve and carefully explained to me the way. Then she said she also knew almost right away by her body, how it looked and felt, and that was how Aunt Wizzy had found out about it—by seeing Babe naked and guessing.

"How *does* it feel, Babe?" I asked, knowing she would tell me.

She smiled. "Oh, wonderful. Kind of ripe and full. Like this." She held up a fat berry. Then she put it between her teeth and popped it and we both laughed. A sudden shy silence fell between us. Then she said, "Do you want to see?"

"Sure," I said, trying to sound casual.

Babe stood up and stepped out of her shorts and underpants. The big shirt covered her to midthigh. She unbuttoned it ceremoniously, top to bottom, and took it off. Then undid her bra and let it drop. I was silent, embarrassed and aroused. Babe was beautiful. She had been beautiful even at my age, but now she looked like a woman to me. If her waist had thickened at all, it was just slightly, but a kind of heaviness seemed to pull her belly lower so it had a curve downward, and her thick fleecy hair seemed tucked underneath it. But her breasts were what most stirred me. They were still smallish, but they seemed fat, and the nipples had widened out like two silver dollars. She looked down at herself with satisfaction, and began, unself-consciously, to explain the sequence of changes she was going through. I remember she held one breast fondly and set two fingers gently across the pale disc in the center as she talked. If Norman Rockwell had ever gone in for the mildly erotic, he might have found a subject in us: Babe, beautiful anyway, and now lush, standing in a pool of discarded clothing, representing a womanhood I felt was impossible for me; and me, all acute angles, caught on the edge of pubescence, gaping at her in amazement. She smiled at me.

"Do you want to feel?"

I nodded, though I wasn't sure what I wanted. She stepped towards me, reaching for my paralyzed hands, and raised them to her breasts. Her skin was softer even than it looked. My skinny brown hands, laced with tiny white scratches from the blueberry bushes, the nails clipped short out of habit for piano practice, seemed hard, male, by contrast with her silken perfection. Her voice was excited, telling me—what? I can't remember. She moved my hands down to her waist, then to her abdomen. I felt her fur brush against my fingertips, dry, and yet soft. As soon as she loosened her grip on me, I pulled my hands back.

When we returned, my grandmother uncharacteristically kissed Babe to thank her for the berries. She cooked them in pancakes for everyone the next morning, and suddenly the whole family, with their blue teeth, seemed part of Babe's secret to me. Except my grandfather. His breakfast was invariable, grapefruit and poached egg on whole-wheat toast; his smile stayed impeccably his own.

Less than a week later, Babe left, abruptly and tearfully, for Europe, accompanied by Aunt Rain. I rowed them across, facing my grandfather in the stern of the boat. He was to drive them to the train station in town. They each had only a small suitcase, but my grandmother was going to ship Babe's things to her later. As we

walked up the path to the road where the car was parked, my grandfather pointed out places where it was growing over and suggested
I bring the scythe with me when I rowed back to pick him up again.

Babe hugged me hard, and kissed me once, on the mouth, as
though it were Richard she were saying good-bye to, not her niece.
I noticed I was taller than she, and the taste of her tears stayed in
my mouth until I swallowed. I waved to the retreating car until all
I could see was the dust settling behind it.

That fall and winter I waited for news of Babe's baby. From the
family came reports of her adventures in Europe. She was doing
well in school in Switzerland. She had enjoyed learning to ski in the
Alps. She stayed with friends of the family in Paris at Christmas.
She sent me a card from Paris. It showed the Madonna and Child
on the front—the child a fat, real, mischievous boy, penis and all.
Inside it said "Noël." She had written on the back: "Life goes on,
Europe isn't quite all it's cracked up to be, but the wine is wonderful,
and I go through the days here agreeably, as I'm supposed to, a
Jack-O'-Lantern's grin carved on my face. Keep up the good fight.
Love, Babe."

In the spring, striving to sound casual, I finally asked, "Mother,
was Aunt Babe ever going to have a baby?" She was sewing, and
she looked up for a minute over the edge of her glasses. Her mouth
pulled tight, and then she smiled.

"Of course not, dear, Aunt Babe's never even been *married*. You
knew that."

I recall that I blushed uncomfortably. My mother looked at me
sharply, but then turned back to her sewing and nothing more was
ever said.

My life went on also. My body changed in some of the ways Babe
had promised, and I grew more comfortable in it, though not as
comfortable as she would once have liked me to be. She seemed to
shun most family gatherings. On those infrequent occasions when I
did see her, she was usually fortified by a fair amount of booze and
a new man. For a while after college she had a job in an art gallery
in New York, and later at the Whitney Museum. Over the years I
have drifted away more from the family, but apparently Babe had
begun to effect a ginger reconciliation. The family party which was
the occasion of her death was my grandparents' sixty-fifth wedding

anniversary. I was absent, but I did make it a point to come to Babe's memorial service the next week.

We were lined up in generations in the church, my mother and aunts in the row in front of me and the other cousins. I could watch my grandparents sharing a hymnal in the front row, the one ahead of my mother. It seemed a reminder of our mortality, this arrangement; the blonde and jet black of my row giving way to the gray of our parents, and then to the yellowish white of Grandmother and Grandfather and the two extant great-aunts. My grandfather's voice sang out bravely and joyously the words to the hymn. My grandmother, I noticed, did not sing at all. The eulogy was short and somewhat impersonal, focusing on the untimely nature of Babe's passing instead of saying anything about who she was.

My mother and her sisters seemed to be crying occasionally in the church, but in the car on the way to the family luncheon, Mother expressed what seemed like resentment over my grandmother's grief for Babe. "After all," she said, "it isn't as though Babe were the one who did *anything* for her or Daddy all these years."

For a little while, there was a kind of deliberate sobriety to the luncheon, but shortly after the fruit cup the aunts began to chatter, and my cousins to compare house purchases, pregnancies, and recipes. Only Orrie, sitting on my right, who couldn't stop telling his awful story over and over; and Grandmother, stony at the end of the table, seemed affected.

I had to leave early. I'd left my daughter with friends overnight, and needed to catch the afternoon plane home. I went around the table, whispering good-byes to those who might be hurt if I didn't—my mother, grandfather, and the aunts; then I stopped at my grandmother's chair, and knelt next to her. She swung her head slowly towards me like someone hearing a distant call. I realized she was still strongly sedated.

"Gram?" I said. "It's Anna. I came to say good-bye to you. I have to go." I spoke clearly and slowly.

She reached out and touched my face in a kind of recognition. "Say good-bye," she repeated.

"Yes, I have to go. I'm sorry I can't stay longer. But I wanted just to come, to remember Babe today." She kept nodding her assent.

"Edith," she said mournfully.

"Yes, Edith. I was so sorry, Gram." She nodded.

"I'm going now Gram. Good-bye." She stopped nodding as I leaned forward to kiss her. Her hand clutched at mine. Her grip was bony and tight.

"Don't go," she whispered.

"I'd like to stay, Gram, but my plane . . ."

"Don't leave me." I looked at her face. It stayed inexpressive, but tears sat waiting in her eyes. Impulsively I put my free arm around her and held her. "I can stay just a minute, Gram," I said, patting her back.

She whispered in my ear, "Don't leave me alone."

Her body felt empty but for the frame of bones. I held her until her hand loosened its grip on mine. When I leaned back away from her, her face was completely blank again. I kissed her cheek. "Good-bye, Gram."

I sat alone on the plane. I ordered a drink, but even before it arrived I had begun to cry. The stewardess was concerned; asked me if I were all right. I assured her I would be, I had just been to a funeral. As I sipped the drink and stared out into the blank sky, I realized that I had never before heard anyone in the family call Babe by her christened name.

THE CARNIVAL DOG, THE BUYER OF DIAMONDS

by Ethan Canin
(University of Iowa)

What's the one thing you should never do? Quit? Depends on who you talk to. Steal? Cheat? Eat food from a dented can? Myron Lufkin's father, Abe, once told him never get your temperature taken at the hospital. Bring your own thermometer, he said; you should see how they wash theirs. He ought to have known; when he was at Yeshiva University he worked as an orderly in the hospital, slid patients around on gurneys, cleaned steelware. Myron knows all his father's hospital stories and all his rules. On the other hand, there are things you *should* do. Always eat sitting down. Wear a hat in the rain. What else? Never let the other guy start the fight. Certain inviolable commandments. In thirty-two years Myron Lufkin had never seen his father without an answer.

That is, until the day five years ago when Myron called home from Albert Einstein College of Medicine and told his father he had had enough, was quitting, leaving, *kaput,* he said. Now, Myron, living in Boston, sometime Jew, member of the public gym where he plays basketball and swims in the steamy pool after rounds, still calls home every other week. The phone calls, if he catches his father asleep, remind him of the day five years ago when he called to say that he was not, after all, going to be a doctor.

It was not the kind of thing you told Abe Lufkin. Abe Lufkin, a man who once on Election Day put three twelve-pound chains across his chest and dove into San Francisco Bay at Aquatic Park, to swim most of the mile and three-quarters across to Marin. As it turned out they had to pull him from the frothy cold water before he made the beach—but to give him credit, he was not a young man. In the *Chronicle* the next day there he was on an inside page, sputtering and shaking on the sand, steam rising off his body. Rachel, Myron's mother, is next to him in a sweater and baggy wool pants. Myron still has the newspaper clipping in one of his old butterfly display cases wrapped in tissue paper in a drawer in Boston.

On the day Myron called home from Albert Einstein to say that three years of studying and money, three years of his life, had been a waste, he could imagine the blood-rush in his father's head. But he knew what to expect. He kept firm, though he could feel the pulse in his own neck. Itzhak, his roommate at medical school, had stood behind him with his hand on Myron's shoulder, smoking a cigarette. But Abe simply did not believe it.

Myron didn't expect him to believe it: Abe, after all, didn't understand quitting. If his father had been a sea captain, Myron thought, he would have gone down with his ship—singing, boasting, denying the ocean that closed over his head—and this was not, in Myron's view, a glorious death. It just showed stubbornness. His father was stubborn about everything. When he was young, for example, when stickball was what you did in the Bronx, Abe played basketball. Almost nobody else played. In those days, Abe told Myron, you went to the Yankee games when Detroit was in town and rooted for Hank Greenberg to hit one out, and when he did you talked about it and said how the *goyishe* umpires would have ruled it foul if they could have, if it hadn't been to center field. In Abe's day, baseball was played by men named McCarthy, Murphy, and Burdock, and basketball wasn't really played at all, except by the very very tall, awkward kids. But not Abe Lufkin. He was built like a road-show wrestler and he kept a basketball under his bed. It was his love for the game, maybe, that many years later made him decide to have a kid. When Myron was born, Abe nailed a backboard to the garage. This is my boy, he said, my *mensch*. He began playing basketball with his son when Myron was nine. But really, what they did was not playing. By the time Myron was in the fifth grade Abe had visions in his already balding pharmacist's head. He sat in the aluminum lawn furniture before dinner and counted out the one hundred lay-ups Myron had to do from each side of the basket. One hundred from the left. One hundred from the right. No misses.

But it paid off. At Woodrow Wilson High, Myron was the star. Myron hitting a twenty-foot bank shot. Myron slipping a blind pass inside, stealing opponents' dribbles so their hands continued down, never realizing the ball was gone. Myron blocking the last-second shot. It was a show. Before the games he stood alone under the basket, holding his toes and stretching loose the muscles in his thighs. He knew Abe was sitting in the stands. His father always got there before the teams even came upstairs to the gym. He took the front-row seat at one corner and made Rachel take the one at the opposite corner. Then at halftime they switched. This way Abe could always see the basket his son was shooting at. After the games Abe waited in the car for Myron. Rachel sat in the back, and when Myron got in, Abe talked about the game until the windows steamed or Rachel finally said that it was unhealthy to sit like this in the cold. Then Abe wiped the windows and started the car, and they drove home with the heater blasting up warm air between the seats.

Abe had always believed the essence of the body was in the lungs, and sometimes, to keep Myron in shape for basketball, he challenged him to breath-holding contests. They sat facing each other across the kitchen table without breathing while an egg timer ran down between them. Myron could never beat his father, though; Abe held his breath like a blowfish at low tide. Myron's eyes teared, his heart pounded in his head, his lungs swelled to combustion, while all the time his father just stared at him, winking. He made Myron admit defeat out loud. "Do you give?" Abe whispered when half the sand had run down through the timer. Myron swallowed, pressed his lips together, stared at the sand falling through the narrow neck. A few seconds later, Abe said it again: "Do you give?" Myron squeezed his legs together, held his hands over his mouth, stood up, sat down, and finally let his breath explode out. "I give," he said, then sat there until the egg timer ran down and Abe exhaled.

There was always this obsession in the Lufkin family, this holiness about the affairs of the body. What were wars or political speeches next to the importance of body heat, expansive lungs, or leg muscles that could take you up the stairs instead of the elevator? Abe told hospital stories because to him there was no more basic truth than keeping your bronchial tubes cleared, or drying between your toes. Any questions of the body were settled quickly and finally when Abe showed Myron the smelly fungus between his own toes, or opened the *Encyclopaedia Britannica* to pictures of stomach worms, syphilis, or skin rash.

Any religious fervor in the family went instead into this worship of the body. Rachel did not light candles on Friday nights, and Myron was never *bar-mitzvahed*. Instead there was health to be zealous about. It was Abe's way. But at times he wavered, and these were nearly the only times Myron ever saw him unsure—in the evenings when he read the newspaper and talked about the state of Israel, or on Friday nights sometimes when he stood in the living room with the lights off, staring out at the sidewalk as the congregation filtered by in wool coats and *yarmulkes*. It put Abe into a mood. The spring after Myron's fifteenth birthday he told Myron he was sending him to a Judaism camp in the mountains for the month of July. They were outside on the porch when Abe told him.

"What? A Judaism camp? I don't believe it."

"What don't you believe?"

"I'm not going to a Judaism camp."

"What's this? Yes, you're going. You've got no more religion than *goyim*. I've already sent the money."

"How much money?"

"Fifty dollars."

Then Abe went in from the porch, and that was the end of the argument. Myron knew he would have to go off in the hot, bright month of July. That was how Abe argued. He wasn't wordy. If you wanted to change his mind you didn't argue, you fought him with your fists or your knees. This was what he expected from the world, and this was what he taught his son. Once, when Myron was fourteen, Abe had taken him to a bar, and when the bouncer hadn't wanted to let him in Abe said, "This is my *mensch*; he's not going to drink," and had pushed Myron in front of him through the door. Later, when they stood in line to pee away their drinks, Abe told him you can do what you want with strangers because they don't want to fight. "Remember that," he said.

But the day after he told Myron about the Judaism camp, Abe

came out on the porch and said, "Myron, you're a man now and we're going to decide about camp like men."

"What?"

"We're going to decide like men. We're going to have a race."

"We can't race."

"What do you mean, we can't race? We sure can. A footrace, from here to the end of the block. I win, you go to camp."

"I don't want to do it."

"What, do you want it longer? We can do what you want. We can make it two times to the corner."

Then Abe went into the house, and Myron sat on the porch. He didn't want to learn religion during the hottest month of the year, but also, he knew, there was something in beating his father that was like the toppling of an ancient king. What was it for him to race an old man? He walked down to the street, stretched the muscles in his legs, and sprinted up to the corner. He sprinted back down to the house, sat down on the steps, and decided it wasn't so bad to go to the mountains in July. That afternoon Abe came out of the house in long pants and black, rubber-soled shoes, and he and Myron lined up on one of the sidewalk lines and raced, and Abe won going away. The sound of Abe's fierce breathing and his hard shoes pounding the cement hid the calmness of Myron's own breath. That July Myron packed Abe's old black cloth traveling bag and got on the bus to the mountains.

But what Abe taught Myron was more than just competition; it was everything. It was the way he got to work every day for thirty-seven years without being late, the way he treated Rachel, his bride of uncountable years, who sewed, cooked, cleaned for him, in return for what? For Sunday night dinners out every single week, a ritual so ancient that Myron couldn't break it even after he moved out of the house. For Sunday dinners out, and a new diamond each year. It was a point of honor, an expectation. Obviously on a pharmacist's salary Abe couldn't afford it. He bought her rings, necklaces, bracelets, brooches, hairpins, earrings, lockets—one gift at the end of each year for, what is it, almost forty years? One year Rachel was sick with mild hepatitis and spent the holidays in the hospital. On the first evening of Chanukah Abe took Myron with him to visit her, and in the hospital room he pulled out a small bracelet strung with a diamond and gave it to her, his wife, as she lay in the bed. But what is the value of a diamond, he later asked Myron in the car, next to the health of the body?

It was two years later that Abe tried the swim across San Francisco Bay. But there were other things before that. At the age of fifty-four he fought in a bar over politics. Yes, fought. He came home with his knuckles wrapped in a handkerchief. On his cheek there was a purple bruise that even over the years never disappeared, only gradually settled down the side of his face and formed a black blotch underneath his jaw. That was when he told Myron never to let the other guy start the fight. Always get the first punch, he said. Myron was sixteen then, sitting in the kitchen watching his father rub iodine into the split skin behind his knuckles. The smell stayed in the kitchen for days, the smell of hospitals that later came to be the smell of all his father's clothes, and of his closet. Maybe Myron had just never noticed it before, but on that day his father began to smell old.

Myron was startled. Even then he had been concerned with life. He was a preserver, a collector of butterflies that he caught on the driving trips the family took in the summers. The shelves in his bedroom were lined with swallowtails and monarchs pressed against glass panes, the crystal dust still on their wings. Later, in college, he had studied biology, zoology, entomology, looking inside things, looking at life. Once, on a driving trip through Colorado when Myron was young, Abe had stopped the car near the lip of a deep gorge. Across from where they got out and stood, the cliffs extended down a quarter of a mile, colored with clinging green brush, wildflowers, shafts of red clay, and, at the bottom, a turquoise river. But there were no animals on the sheer faces, no movement anywhere in the gorge. Abe said that life could survive anywhere, even on cliffs like these, and that this was a miracle. But Myron said nothing. To him, anything that couldn't move, that couldn't fly or swim or run, was not really alive. Real life interested him. His father interested him, with his smells and exertions, with the shifting bruise on his jaw.

Years later, on his first day at Albert Einstein medical school, the thing Myron noticed was the smell, the pungency of the antiseptics, like the iodine Abe had once rubbed into his knuckles. On that first day when a whole class of new medical students listened to an address by the dean of the medical college, the only thing Myron noticed was that the room smelled like his father.

* * *

Medical school was a mountain of facts, a giant granite peak full of outcroppings and hidden crevices. Physiology. Anatomy. Histology. More facts than he could ever hope to remember. To know the twenty-eight bones of the hand seemed to Myron a rare and privileged knowledge, but then there were the arms and shoulders with their bones and tendons and opposing muscles, then the whole intricate, extravagant cavity of the chest, and then the head and the abdomen and the legs. Myron never really tried to learn it all. It wasn't the volume of knowledge so much as it was the place where he had to be in order to learn it. The anatomy labs reeked of formaldehyde, the hospitals of a mixture of cleanliness and death. All of it reminded Myron of men getting old, and that is why in three years of medical school he made the minuscule but conscious effort not to study enough. He let the knowledge collect around him, in notebooks, binders, pads, on napkins and checks, everywhere except in his brain. His room was strewn with notes he never studied. Once in a letter home he said learning medicine was like trying to drink water from a fire hose.

But that was something Abe would want to hear. Once on a driving trip through the Florida deltas, Abe came upon three men trying to lift an abandoned car from a sludge pit with a rope they had looped around it. Only the roof and the tops of the windows were showing above the mud, but Abe got out anyway and helped the men pull. His face turned red and the muscles in his belly shook so much Myron could see them through his shirt. Myron didn't understand the futility of his father's effort, or even know why he helped save a useless car for men he didn't know, until years later. Abe did things like that; he loved doing things like that.

Myron, on the other hand, just didn't want to study. His weren't the usual reasons for quitting medical school. It wasn't the hours, and really, it wasn't the studying and the studying. It was something smaller, harder, that in a vague way he knew had to do with Abe. Perhaps he saw his own father in the coughing middle-aged men whose hearts he watched flutter across oscilloscope screens. But it was not Abe's death that he feared. Heart stoppage or brain tumors or sudden clots of blood were reactions of the body, and thus, he had always believed, they were good. Death, when it was a fast action, didn't bother him. The fatty cadavers in anatomy labs were no more than objects to Myron, and it meant nothing to him that they were dead. The only time in his life that he had had to really think about death was in his childhood, when the phone rang in the middle of the night to tell Abe about his aunt in Miami Beach. The next morning Myron had found his father downstairs drinking coffee. "Life is for the living," Abe had said, and even then Myron could weigh the seriousness in his voice. It was plain that death meant only a little if you still had the good muscles in your own heart, and that people's bodies, once underground, were not to be mourned. And besides, there really was no blood in the medical school anatomy classes. The cadavers were gray, no different when you cut them than the cooked leg of a turkey. They had none of the pliable fleshiness, none of the pink, none of the smells and secretions that told you of life.

No, it wasn't death that bothered Myron; it was the downhill plunge of the living body—the muscles that stretched off the bones into folds, the powdery flesh odors of middle-aged men. He longed for some octogenarian to stand up suddenly from a wheelchair and run the length of a corridor. Once, a drugged coronary patient, a sixty-year-old man, had unhooked an IV cart and caromed on it through the corridor until Myron cornered him. When Myron looked at the blood spots that were in the old man's eyes, he wanted to take him in his own arms then and there, in his triumph. That was why Myron wanted to quit medical school. He hated the demise of the spirit.

So he let the work pile up around him. In his third year he felt the walls of the lecture halls and the sponged hospital floors to be somehow holding him against his will. Fifty-year-old men who could no longer walk, or whose intestines bled and collapsed, Myron felt, were betrayers of the human race. He was convinced of the mind's control over the flesh.

In the winter of his third year he started jogging. First two, three miles a day, then, later, long six-mile runs into the hills and neighborhoods around the medical school. He left in the early mornings and ran in the frozen air so that he could feel the chill in his lungs. He ran every morning through November and December, and then January after the holidays, until one morning in February, when the grass was still breaking like needles underneath his feet, he realized he could run forever. That morning he just kept running. He imagined

Itzhak sitting with two cups of coffee at the table, but he ran to the top of a hill and watched the streets below him fill with morning traffic. Then onward he went, amidst the distant bleating of car horns and the whistling wind. He thought of the hospital, of the arriving interns, sleepless, pale, and of the third-year students following doctors from room to room. He ran on the balls of his feet and never got tired.

When he returned to the apartment Itzhak was at the table eating lunch. Myron took a carton of milk from the refrigerator and drank standing up, without a glass.

"You ever think about passing infection that way?"

Myron put down the carton and looked at the muscles twitching in his thighs. Itzhak lit a cigarette.

"You're a real one," Itzhak said. "Where the hell were you?"

"Hypoxia. No oxygen to the brain. You know how easy it is to forget what time it is."

"Watch it," Itzhak said. "You'll get into trouble."

The next day Myron went to classes and to rounds, but that night he ran again, stumbling in the unlit paths, and after that, over the next weeks of frozen, windless days, he ran through his morning assignments and spent the afternoons in a park near his apartment. There was a basketball hoop there, a metal backboard with a chain net, and sometimes he shot with a group of kids or joined their half-court games. Afterward, he always ran again. He loved to sweat when the air was cold enough to turn the grass brittle, when a breath of air felt like a gulp of cold water. After a while, Itzhak began to ignore his disappearances. One day when Myron returned from running, Itzhak took his pulse. "Damn, Myron," he said, "you *are* running." His professors tried to take him aside, and Myron could see them looking into his pupils when they spoke. But he ignored them. One night he returned late from running, still dripping sweat, picked up the telephone and dialed, and heard his father's sleepy voice on the other end of the line. "Pa," he said, "it's *kaput* here."

So why the quitting now? Why the phone call at ten-thirty on a Thursday night when Abe and Rachel were just going into their dream sleep? Myron could hear the surprise, the speechlessness. He heard Rachel over the line telling Abe to calm himself, to give her the phone. He imagined the blood rushing to Abe's face, the breathing starting again the way he breathed the morning they pulled him from the frothy water in San Francisco Bay. Rachel took the phone and spoke, and Myron, because he had lived with his father for most of his life, knew Abe was taking black socks from the drawer and stretching them over his feet.

The next morning at seven Myron opened the apartment door and Abe was sitting there in a chair with the black cloth traveling bag on his lap. He was wide awake, blocking the passage out of the apartment.

"For crying out loud!"

"Who else did you expect? Am I supposed to let you throw away everything?"

"Pa, I didn't expect *anybody*."

"Well, I came, and I'm here, and I spent like a madman to get a flight. You think I don't have the lungs to argue with my son?"

"I was about to go running."

"I'll come along. We're going to settle this thing."

"Okay," Myron said, "come," and in his sweatsuit, hooded and wrapped against the cold, he led Abe down through the corridors of the building and out into the street. The ground outside was frozen from the night, the morning icy cold and without wind. Abe held the black traveling bag at his side as they stood under the entrance awning.

"I was planning to run."

"It won't hurt you to walk a few blocks."

It was cold, so they walked quickly. Abe was wearing what he always wore in the winter, a black hat, gloves, galoshes, an overcoat that smelled of rain. Myron watched him out of the side of his vision. He tried to look at his father without turning around—at the face, at the black bruise under the jaw, at the shoulders. He tried to see the body beneath the clothing. Abe's arm swung with the weight of the traveling bag, and for the first time, as he watched through the corner of his eye, Myron noticed the faint spherical outline inside the cloth.

They walked wordlessly, Myron watching Abe's breath come out in clouds. By now the streets had begun to move with traffic, and the ice patches, black and treacherous, crackled underneath their feet. The streetlamps had gone off and in the distance dogs barked. They came to the park where Myron played basketball in the afternoons.

"So you brought the ball," Myron said.

"Maybe you want some shooting to calm you."

"You're not thinking of any games, are you?"

"I just brought it in case you wanted to shoot."

Abe unzipped the bag and pulled out the basketball. They went into the court. He bounced the ball on the icy pavement, then handed it to Myron. Myron spun it on his finger, dribbled it off the ice. He was watching Abe. He couldn't see beneath the overcoat, but Abe's face seemed drawn down, the cheeks puffier, the dark bruise lax on his jaw.

"Pa, why don't you shoot some? It would make you warm."

"You think you have to keep me warm? Look at this." He took off the overcoat. "Give me the ball."

Myron threw it to him, and Abe dribbled it in his gloved hands. Abe was standing near the free-throw line, and he turned then, brought the ball to his hip, and shot it, and as his back was turned to watch the shot, Myron did an incredible thing—he crouched, took three lunging steps, and dove into the back of his father's thin, tendoned knees. Abe tumbled backward over him. What could have possessed Myron to do such a thing? A medical student, almost a doctor—what the hell was he doing? But Myron knew his father. Abe was a prizefighter, a carnival dog. Myron knew he would protect the exposed part of his skull, that he would roll and take the weight on his shoulders, that he would be up instantly, crouched and ready to go at it. But Myron had slid on the ice after the impact, and when he scrambled back up and turned around, his father was on his back on the icy pavement. He was flat out.

"Pa!"

Abe was as stiff and extended as Myron had ever seen a human being. He was like a man who had laid out his own body.

"What kind of crazy man are you?" Abe said hoarsely. "I think it's broken."

"What? What's broken?"

"My back. You broke your old man's back."

"Oh no, Pa, I couldn't have! Can you move your toes?"

But the old man couldn't. He lay on the ground staring up at Myron like a beached sea animal. Oh, Pa. Myron could see the unnatural stiffness in his body, in the squat legs and the hard, protruding belly.

"Look," Myron said, "don't move." Then he turned and started back to get his father's coat, and he had taken one step when Abe—Abe the carnival dog, the buyer of diamonds and the man of endurance—hooked his hand around Myron's ankles and sent him tumbling onto the ice. Bastard! Pretender! He scrambled up and pinned Myron's shoulders against the pavement. "Faker!" Myron cried. He grappled with the old man, butted him with his head and tried to topple his balance, but Abe clung viciously and set the weight of his chest against Myron's shoulders. "Fraud!" shouted Myron. "Cheat!" He shifted his weight and tried to roll Abe over, but his father's legs were spread wide and he had pinned Myron's hands. "Coward," Myron said. Abe's wrists pressed into Myron's arms. His knees dug into Myron's thighs. "Thief," Myron whispered. "Scoundrel." Cold water was spreading upward through Myron's clothes and Abe was panting hoarse clouds of steam into his face when Myron realized his father was leaning down and speaking into his ear.

"Do you give?"

"What?"

"Do you give?"

"You mean, will I go back to school?"

"That's what I mean."

"Look," Myron said, "you're crazy."

"Give me your answer."

Myron thought about this. While his father leaned down over him, pressed into him with his knees and elbows, breathed steam into his face, he thought about it. As he lay there he thought about other things too: This is my father, he thought. Then: This is my life. For a while, as the cold water spread through his clothes, he lay there and remembered things—the thousands and thousands of lay-ups, the smell of a cadaver, the footrace on a bright afternoon in April. Then he thought: What can you do? These are clouds above us, and below us there is ice and the earth. He said, "I give."

ALL LITTLE COLORED CHILDREN SHOULD PLAY THE HARMONICA

by Ann Patchett
(Sarah Lawrence College)

Sampson, Skipworth, Slonecker, Small, Smiley. Smiley, Grover T. There are still four people ahead of me on the list, I've got a while to wait. The s's, we're way the hell down there so we gotta hear everybody before our turn comes around. At first I thought I was miserable, but after the thirty-fourth audition (Claire Beth Fibral, who said God told her she could play the flute), I decided it was poor old Miss Neville who was having a rough go of it. She calls out a name on the list and hands over a piece of sheet music, asking if they can make any sense of it, most everybody says no. Then she asks them if there is anything in particular they think they could play. This is where she makes her big mistake, if you ask me; just cram something in their hands and talk about it later. Every kid says they's just sure they can play the so and so. The girls all say they can play the flute, the boys say the bass. They is all lying.

Some group of old white men decided all little colored children should play musical instruments, that it would keep their minds off breaking out store windows or sitting in front of the Five and Dime looking uppity. That's why we're all here now, Miss Neville says that's legislating. I think they must have legislated this one up in spring, when it was cool outside and music sounded real pretty. But this here's August and even the flies are looking for a house with the fan on. It's Miss Neville who's got to decide who's gonna play what. She's gotta listen to every kid in Central Valley Junior High blow or bang or strum on something before she can assign them a place in the school orchestra. Ain't no telling how long she's been the music teacher here, most everybody's got a story or a guess. Harvey Rachlin says his older sister was in Miss Neville's orchestra when she went here, and his sister is a grown-up woman now, with a baby and everything. Some people say that Miss Neville stays at school all the time, that they let her sleep under the piano or something. I can't figure her out; I crawled up on the bleachers to watch her for a while and she looked like she was listening to all of them. You can tell by her face that she thinks every kid that comes up might really be able to play. Then when she really hears them her face gets kinda sick, like they were all hitting her in the stomach. I would think that going through an audition once would be more than any regular person could suffer, I don't know what it would be like year after year.

They've got the whole school mashed into this one basketball gym. The ninth graders get folding chairs, which they make a very big deal of. The rest of us get bleachers or the floor. I got this nice little spot between the door and the risers where nobody can step on me. From where I'm sitting the whole world is knees and ankles, not one person in there who cares a rip about keeping his socks pulled up or his shoelaces tied. You never think about feet until you're down there with them. Miss Neville calls out a name and then I see a pair shuffle onto the stage and wait a minute, then shuffle back to their place, which has almost always been snatched up.

I don't want nothing to do with their spitty old instruments. No way am I gonna spend four years sucking on some piccolo that somebody sucked on before me. It had been my intention to keep Roy Luther out of school, sorta separating my class time from my free time, but this is an emergency.

Me and Roy Luther hooked up when I was six years old, so we've been together a little more than half of my natural lifetime. My daddy, Mr. Nigel T. Smiley, runs the numbers where he works in the bakery making fancy doughnuts. He used to let a couple of us kids sit in the back room with his business friends, we made the place look honest. One day I was hanging out on a cherry crate playing with this special aggie that had been my birthday present. This man comes over and says that it was a real fine marble, that he'd never seen a shooter quite like it. I say, Yessir. He says he'd like to have that marble for his little boy. I didn't look up, I was scared he was gonna take it. He says, wouldn't I like to bet him something for that aggie? He pulls out this silver bar, the size of three Havana cigars. Then I look up, it was the most beautiful thing I'd ever seen.

"We'll shoot us out some craps, boy." The man says to me, "I win, I take your marble home to my boy; you win, you get to keep this here harmonica."

Man, I'll tell you I wanted that thing. I didn't know what it was or how to use it, only that I'd die right then and there if I didn't get it. I nodded my head. The man dips one of his fingers into a tiny pocket on his vest. He must have just been eating Cracker Jacks or something cause when he pulled it out there were two dice hanging on it. The other guys, mostly soldiers that hung out during the day started coming around, checking out the action and laughing at me 'cause I'm the sucker. Just then, a big metal door smashes open and Papa walks in from the front room. Kids used to tease me about my father being white, 'cause he was always plastered with flour. Nobody ever said anything to him about it.

"What you doing with my boy?"

"Just a friendly game of craps, Nigel. Your little shark here's hot after my harmonica." He shook up the dice to show he meant business.

Papa looked down at me. "You gambling with this man?"

I was pretty little then, I just nodded my head yes. One giant, floury hand come swinging down through the air and clipped me right above the ear. I went sailing off my cherry crate and slammed back against some drums of cooking oil. What everybody says about seeing stars ain't true. I saw big, furry spiders.

"How many times I got to tell you kids? You never, ever gamble with a man without letting me check out the dice. Jesus you is a fool." Papa plucked the pair of spotted cubes out of the other fella's hand and rattled them around. "Loaded." He shook them in my face, "Loaded!" I thought he was gonna hit me again, but he walked into the other room and got a fresh pair. Everybody knew Papa used clean dice. He gave the new set to the man. "Now you talk about gambling with my son."

The man shook his head like a little black bunny rabbit. "Just joking with you, Nigel, just trying to teach the boy here a lesson, hee hee. He can keep his dirty old marble."

"You gamble with my boy, mister." Papa picked me up with one hand and shook me like a sneaker with a rock inside. "You let the man roll first, Grover."

His roll came up two specks, Papa says Snake Eyes. I gathered up the dice and threw them out again. A howl went up. A two and a five, sweet, sweet seven. Roy Luther must have been the man's name, because it was engraved on the side of my "Hohner Marine Band." I thought it had a good, solid sound to it. I knew right away this was going to be my special thing. All the other kids in my family got something special. There's the oldest and the youngest, and the twins that get all their clothes to look alike and get their picture taken a lot, and my brother Wilson who has his very own fish, and Delilah who twirls in the marching band, and Albert who skipped two whole grades just for being smart. Up till now I never had a thing that made me me. I'd walk into a room and Mama would call me two dozen names before she could place who I was. That first night I was sitting there staring at Roy Luther when the twins come up and try to take him away. Mama tells them to scat, "That's Grover's thing," she told them. "Leave it be." I slept with Roy Luther between my head and shoulder, so I'd be sure to wake up if someone tried to make off with him. Me and Albert share a bed, he thinks it's him I don't trust, but I couldn't let it go. Albert slept facing the wall after that.

There was a good three years I didn't have too many friends. My brothers and sisters told other kids they didn't know me, even Mama made me stay a good piece behind her when we went out. My thing wasn't so much being a harmonica player as it was being a bad harmonica player. I played all the time, grinding up and down that same old scale any place I could catch my breath, in the bathtub, under the dinner table. I was as bad as Original Sin. It was like learning to talk all over again, except this time there was no one to listen to. My hands didn't know anything about playing harmonicas, they knew about marbles and baseballs, and my mouth was a gum-chewing mouth. There wasn't no music in that mouth when things started out.

Back then, I took Roy Luther to school. Every five minutes or so a new sound would come into my head and I would raise my hand, asking if I could visit the washroom or get a drink of water. If the teacher said yes I would dart outside and try blocking up a different set of holes, blowing harder or softer than the day before to see how it sounded. Somebody'd always rat on me and Roy Luther would spend the rest of the day sitting in the principal's desk drawer.

I got used to the way it was always cold, tasting part like a tin can and part like the old Lifesavers and ticket stubs I kept in my pocket. As much as I loved the sound, I loved just putting it in my mouth, letting it hit against a filling in my tooth and running a shock clear through my eyes. It got to where I couldn't walk through a door without someone saying, "Grover, go way!" I'd shinny up into the sugar maple and stay there. First the birds all flew away, then after a while they got used to me, I even learned a few of their songs. One morning I was playing outside the kitchen window before breakfast, I heard Mama say, "Listen to the nightingale, will you? Glory but that ain't God's finest bird."

And that's when things started turning around.

I sat under the front porch and played a fire engine and my little brother ran outside, hooping and hollering for everybody to come watch the fire. Then he spent the whole day looking for one. I sat in the alley behind the white grocery store and played "What'll I Do?" so soft you could barely hear it, and just about everybody that walked out of the store was humming that song without knowing why.

It was like one day I was the stinkbug somebody stepped on and the next day I was a fistful of wisteria. Mama stopped sending me outside all the time. I could play the things she heard in church on Sunday. When the radio went out I was the chief source of entertainment in the family. I got to sit in the red leather chair and blow my brains out till I got dizzy or my tongue went thick; once I got going I could feel the vibrations go past my jaw and head for my stomach. The whole family spread out at my feet, except for Papa, who would listen from the other room. On those days it could rain ice or be a hundred and five in the shade and everybody was happy. I could play the popular stuff and make them dance till they fell down. I could play the blues and break them in half.

Suddenly nobody remembered that I'd ever been bad. Now folks say, "Grover! Hey, Grover T., that sounds real fine, come play in my store," or, "Hey son, come sit in my diner where it's cool." Like we was all best friends or something. Mr. Thompson used to say I wasn't even to think about walking down the street where his soda fountain was; now he calls me over all the time, tells me I'm good for business. I go, he gives me free lemon Cokes.

After school I went to the community library and tried to teach myself how to read music. The place had two or three books called *How To*. I'd sit there for hours looking at the henscratches, trying to make sense of it all. Finally I figured out that each line was two spaces on the harmonica, and that the black spots were where my fingers should go and how long I should leave them there. I'd run down to the bathroom with the book inside my sweater and give it all a try. The guy who stacked the books caught me a few times, said I was a real stupid kid, then he'd show me how to do it. He said he had a girl once who played the harmonica, said that's why he dumped her. You play a long time and your lips go funny on you he told me.

On Fridays, Papa had me come down to the business to play while the men waited to find out who won the races. It seemed to calm them down a whole lot. They all wanted to hear the new Benny Goodman stuff, everybody liked swing. A bunch of their sweeties waltzed in and said I was awfully good. One of them said I was cute as hell, and I was only ten back then. Everybody made a circle around me and started laughing and clapping their hands. Papa told me to get him a cigarette from the front room. One of the women held my arm, told me to stay put, that she had plenty of smokes. Papa looked down at me, way down, like I wasn't any bigger than a lizard. He said go get him a cigarette. I did. He told me to light it so I did that too. He said he was glad to see I could do something useful for a change. The one with the peach-colored dress that swung way down in the back, the one who said I was cute, asked couldn't they have another song, maybe "Coming in on a Wing and a Prayer"? I looked up at Papa, he liked that song a lot. But he said it was a fool's song, that it was a good one for me 'cause any fool could play the harmonica. Then he ripped Roy Luther out of my hands. I felt all dizzy, like I couldn't breathe. He might as well have ripped off my face. All of the sudden I remembered I wasn't nobody, just another little nobody colored kid at the bottom of the barrel.

Then I heard him blow, Lord, you'da thought they was killing a cow, *slowly*. His hands were so big and dry they couldn't move to change the scale. Nobody laughed, he wasn't the kind of person you'd laugh at. He didn't say a word, just gave Roy Luther back to me and left. After that, we didn't talk too much about music.

Miss Neville calls out my name. I am number sixty-nine and she looks like somebody's hit her in the stomach hard. She's this little bitty old white woman with her hair knotted to the back of her head in a vise.

"Grover T. Smiley?"

"Yessum."

She hands over a piece of sheet music, "Can you make any sense of this?"

I glance over it; it's something I already learned, a real easy piece. "Yessum."

She looks up a little bit, I'm only the third person to even say I knew what it was. "What would you like to play Grover? Do you know the bass?"

"No, ma'am, I brought my own."

The kids in the assembly hall aren't listening, most of them are asleep or whispering. Miss Neville sits down at the edge of the table and folds her arms across her chest. "Alright then."

"You want me to play this, ma'am?" I hold up the music. I was hoping she'd say no 'cause I know stuff that's a lot prettier than this.

"That will be fine."

I pull out Roy Luther from my pocket and put him in my mouth real quick. If you go too slow, somebody always says, "Oh no, not the harmonica. I thought you could play a real instrument." I jump right in, without even getting a good breath. Miss Neville looks up, first to stop me and then to listen. After the first few bars the kids that were asleep wake up and the kids that were talking get quiet and everybody sits up real straight, like it was gonna make them hear better. Roy Luther has that sort of effect on people. I finish, it was an okay job I guess. Everybody claps real politely, like they were at a picture show. Miss Neville takes my arm.

"Do your parents know about this?"

She let everybody else go on. Carl Smith through Herman Zweckler got to miss their audition altogether. Roy Luther and I were taken to the principal's office and asked to wait there.

Miss Neville comes in looking all pink and flustered. That's one thing you can say about white people, they're always changing color on you. She smacks this stack of sheet music in front of me and says, "Can you play this?" When I know she thinks I can't. I don't know what to do, if I should tell her no, that I can't read a note of the stuff and the other thing was just a freak of God, or that I can, which I could. Mama says to always tell the truth, Papa say to go with the flow. The piece on top is one of my favorites, Schumann's "Scenes from Childhood." I say yes.

Miss Neville tapped her foot real fast and looked at me like she thought I was crazy. Finally she threw her hands in my face and said, "Well then *play* for God's sake!"

I never heard a teacher take the name of God in vain before, it made me like her. I folded my lips into my mouth to get them ready and then pulled up Roy Luther. He tasted like my house keys. Harmonicas remind you that everything in your head is all hooked together, playing is a lot more than the mouth, it rolls into the back of your neck and through every tooth individually. My eyes don't read music anymore, it goes straight to my tongue and fingers, each pressing on the two different sides like they was trying to break through for company. My head likes this piece a lot. The notes sound real good in the little office and I start to forget all about Miss Neville and the school orchestra. I just keep my eyes on the paper and play. It's a real pretty song.

When I get through, Miss Neville is looking up at the ceiling real hard, like there's something important up there. I look up too. She turns around, all watery and pale again. She thinks I'm making fun of her by looking up, but she lets it go. "That was lovely, Grover."

I knock the spit out of Roy Luther and thank her kindly.

She swats at her eyes with the back of her hand. "Have you been playing the harmonica a long time?"

"Six, seven years."

"That's just fine."

"You want to hear something else? Some swing maybe?"

She looks like she's come back down now. "I'll have to contact your parents at once, your father has a phone where he works, doesn't he?"

Papa didn't like being bothered at work. "You gotta call my folks?"

"Certainly, yes."

She rang up Central and got connected. Papa didn't like being bothered at work.

"Mr. Smiley? Yes, hello, this is Miss Neville down at Central Valley. I'm calling about your son. No, Grover. No, there isn't anything wrong, quite to the contrary."

This was news to me.

"It seems we have stumbled upon a rather remarkable musical gift . . . yes, I do think this is important. Did you know about the situation? About his music?"

I motion for her to hold the line, she puts her little hand over the receiver. "Tell him it's about Roy Luther."

She looked confused so I nodded at her, the way Mama does us kids when we're not sure if we're doing something right. "Mr. Smiley? Grover says to tell you it's about Roy Luther . . . you know about that? Well, he demonstrates an amazing aptitude for the instrument. I would like to have a conference with you and your wife at once, to make arrangements to put Grover in a special program, perhaps even a special school. I've never seen a talent like this, Mr. Smiley. It is a force to be reckoned with."

I was sent home early with a "Gifted Child Form," and told that it should be completed and returned the next day so that plans could be made. The form was pretty easy stuff, name, age, place I was born. One space needed my middle name. I thought about it, I'd always just written Grover T., nothing more than that. I asked my folks about it, they said there were lots of kids, they couldn't remember no fool *middle* name. I wrote the *T* in the blank. It looked kinda stupid sitting there by itself. I wrote in Truman, because he's the vice president and seems like a real friendly white guy. On my form for gifted children my name was Grover Truman Smiley. It looked pretty good. Papa signed the form without reading it, said he didn't want no more *music* teachers calling him at work. I said I was sorry.

I found Miss Neville in the principal's office typing away. I gave her the form, which she clipped onto the thing she'd been working on.

"I've been doing a lot of planning for us, Grover." She didn't look at me, she just worked at her desk, shuffling and making notes in a little pad. Somehow it all looked real important, the way she was putting it together so carefully.

"I didn't mean to be a bother, ma'am."

This stopped her dead. She laid all the papers back down and took hold of my hand, you could tell she wanted to be real nice. "You won't ever be a bother, Grover. You are the most important person in this whole school to me."

I looked at the floor, there was a little red ant making his way toward the bookshelves.

"Do you know how long I've been a music teacher?"

"No, ma'am."

"A very long time, and I've had a few good students. Not very many, but enough to make it worth my while."

She let go of my hand, I was glad and stuffed it in my pocket. She went beneath her desk and brought a wallet out of her purse. "I've kept photographs of all of them. I felt like they were my children." She unfolded this strip of plastic and out stumbled about five little colored children, one of them's got a violin and the next is standing beside a piano. They all look like regular kids, they's *all* smiling. "Every one of these children had a chance to be very fine musicians, to do something important with their lives. And do you know what happened?"

"No."

"Well, Charles Hunt," she pointed to the kid with the piano, "he got a job in his uncle's filling station, and my prize pupil, Cynthia Rachlin, she married a checkout boy at the A&P and had a baby."

It was old Cindy Dobbs, Harvey Rachlin's big sister.

"And all the rest of them did about the same. They all had a chance and gave it away. I didn't become a music teacher to force children with no musical ability to join an orchestra, I simply wanted to find the ones who could make something of themselves. This," she held up the papers, "is my letter to the governor, it's all about you and . . . and . . ."

"Roy Luther."

"Yes, I've told them how talented you are and what I think we should do about it. They'll listen to me."

"You wrote the governor?" I rocked back on my heels a little. I remember seeing his picture in the post office. He was the only person besides famous criminals who got his picture there. "You think he's going to want to hear me play? You think he's got a favorite song or something?"

Miss Neville licked the envelope and pressed on a stamp with the heel of her hand. ''I'm positive you'll play for the governor someday, you might even play for the president of the United States.'' She smiled at me for a second and then her face got all busy again. ''Of course, you won't be playing the harmonica then, you'll have learned a real instrument.''

I thought I must have heard her wrong. ''Ma'am?''

''Grover, you certainly don't expect to become great while playing a bucolic instrument.''

I wasn't even sure what she said, but I knew what it meant. I could feel myself getting lightheaded, the same way I did the night Papa tried to play. I never talked back to a teacher, come to think about it, I'd never talked back to anybody. I wasn't looking to cause trouble. All I ever wanted to do was play, maybe someday get that job in the bakery that every kid in the world wanted. Miss Neville was going to mail the letter.

''If it's alright, I think I don't really want to play for the governor after all.'' It sounded pretty polite to me.

''I wouldn't worry about it too much.''

''Do you think I shouldn't be playing the harmonica?''

She let out this big breath and turned around, she didn't want to miss the postman. ''I think you've done a wonderful job with what you have. I think all little colored children should play the harmonica if it would help bring them to the point you're at now. But people get older and they move on to different things. That's where you are now, that's why I'm trying to help you.''

I drew in my breath, which is a lot. ''No. No thank you, ma'am.''

She was just as surprised as I was. ''I beg your pardon?''

''They're talking about giving me a job at the theater, playing before the Sunday matinee. I'd like that, playing my harmonica for people.'' I tried to look at her, but decided best that I go before I lose my nerve. I darted past her out the doors and down the front steps. I could feel her watching me run down the street with Roy Luther flat inside my hand, her holding onto the letter.

By the time I got to Mr. Thompson's soda fountain I was all out of breath. I stood there for a long time, just fogging up the glass. Every now and then I'd take my thumb and make a mark showing I was here. I wondered if she'd mail the letter, but I was pretty sure not. She'd find somebody else for her wallet quick enough.

Mr. Thompson caught sight of me standing on the sidewalk. Any other kid he would have run off, but he calls me inside and asks if I'd please play him a song. Old Cindy Dobbs was sitting at the counter with her baby and gives me a nice smile, asks how I'm doing. Mr. Thompson says, "What do you feel like humming up today, Grover?" Suddenly I knew that everything was good, so I tell him, anything he's wanting to hear. They decide on "Don't Sit Under the Apple Tree With Anyone Else But Me." Then he draws me up an extra large lemon Coke, but I ask him, wouldn't he please give it to Mrs. Dobbs, cause I'm not so thirsty. I slip in Roy Luther, he tastes like butterscotch Lifesavers and warm nickels. I play so loud that people come in off the street to listen. It's the best feeling in the world, when you're playing one the people really like, especially when it's a happy song. If you ask me, nobody gives the happy songs half enough credit.

THE DROWNED
by Brad Owens
(Stanford University)

Fardin's Mortuary was at the end of Rue de L'Enterrement, on one corner of the T where the street ran into Boulevard Dehoux. The building wasn't much: two stories of adobe stuck together, Lyle supposed, to fit the lot, its corners met as if by accident. Some iron grillwork on the second floor hung loose above a window, like a false eyelash come unglued.

Lyle tried to brush the fine white powder off the shoulder of his jacket with his hand. The air conditioner had gone out, so for a week he'd driven with the windows open, breathing in the dust and taxi fumes. He'd gone back to smoking. There didn't seem to be much point, just now, in quitting.

Before he rolled the window up he smoked the last one in the pack. Then he sat a moment, going over what he had to say. Half a block away an army transport exited the Cassernes Dessalines and turned in Lyle's direction. The Cassernes was a prison and an army barracks. Years before, he had been told, the enemies of Papa Doc were tortured there. Lyle watched the empty transport pass, listened to the sound of loose chains rattling against its sides. He waited to get out until the sound receded into traffic and the dust had cleared.

The office smelled of ink and sulfur matches. Already Lyle felt queasy from the odor and the heat; he hoped he wouldn't be kept waiting. A small electric fan buzzed in one corner, uselessly, and from the wall above the wooden desk a grinning Papa Doc surveyed the tiny room. The man had been dead ten years, but that photo hung on walls all over Port-au-Prince. Occasionally one also saw a picture of the Pope. Lyle sat on a folding chair and felt a drop of sweat run down his calf.

In a moment Monsieur Fardin came through the door—a short, stout man in a vest and tie who had the white sleeves of his shirt rolled back and was wiping his hands on a towel.

"Excuse the hands," he said, setting the towel on the desk and turning up his clean, pink palms for Lyle to see. "I've been changing oil."

Lyle had stood, and now, not knowing what to do with his own hands, held them out, palms up. Both men laughed.

"Sit down," Fardin said, and pulled his own chair to him. "You're from the embassy."

"The U.S. embassy," Lyle said.

"What other?" Fardin smiled. "How can I help you?"

"I've come about the drowning victims."

"Of course." Fardin brought his hands together on his desk. "They're upstairs. But I must apologize. The plane came only yesterday, and so not all of them have been prepared. There are twenty-three."

A week had passed now since the bodies had washed up in Florida. Their wooden fishing boat had capsized in the surf and all but two had drowned. Economic refugees, the State Department said. These, like all the rest, were fleeing poverty, not persecution. And these, like all the rest, would be returned to Haiti.

"It's not the bodies, actually, I came to see about," Lyle said.

"Oh?"

"We've had some calls. About the coffins."

"Yes."

"The bodies are in coffins."

"Of course."

Lyle touched his temple with a handkerchief. "We've heard that wooden coffins have been substituted for the ones the U.S. government provided."

Fardin did not appear to be offended.

"Not at all," he said. "They're in the coffins they were shipped in."

"There was some controversy, you know, in the States. Whether to return the bodies here for burial."

"A sad thing," Fardin said. "All those people, and so close to land."

"It is sad, yes. You see, we want to make sure everything goes well. And if the coffins were"—what was the neutral word?—"replaced. . . ." He pulled his shoulders slightly up, as if his sentence were completed by the gesture. But Fardin pretended not to understand.

"It wouldn't look good if the coffins were replaced," Lyle said. Fardin nodded.

"Have any families come?" Lyle asked. "To claim the remains?"

"Two or three have come. But all the victims were from the north, quite far from Port-au-Prince. It would be impractical to take a body such a distance on those roads. And, as you know, the President-for-Life has donated crypts in the municipal cemetery."

"Yes." Lyle waited, thinking Fardin might go on, but the man just sat there with a patient smile. Lyle looked around the room, uneasily, hoping to find something to admire, but his eye went once again to the photograph of Papa Doc. He stood and extended his hand. "I needn't go upstairs, I think. I'm sorry to have troubled you."

Fardin took his hand and bowed.

Lyle looked forward to his midday meal. The quiet hour that he spent at home, away from all the hurry and confusion of the embassy, was worth the trouble of the drive. In the dining room, alone, absurdly, at a table that sat twelve, he'd clear his mind of Art Freleng and the ambassador and all the nagging, petty details of his work.

It surprised him how his job seemed, more and more, a thing from which he had to have relief. He'd never felt used up like this at other posts. He'd mentioned it to Dr. Alvarez, but Alvarez had only said he needed leave.

Rose was in the kitchen, her radio turned to the news. The broadcast was in Creole, but the word *Miami* caught his ear at intervals. He knew that they were talking of the drownings. He set his wineglass down and bent his head, attempting to regain his ignorance. It was no use. He turned his head and yelled into the kitchen, "Rose!" Immediately the radio went silent and in its place he heard the sound of her approaching sandals.

"Messer Lyle?"

He regretted his impatience. She was so easily upset. "I've had enough, Rose, thank you. It was very good."

She moved around the table, silently, collecting dishes on a tray. Her thin arms might have been a child's, and he felt, once again, the pity he had felt for her that afternoon when Alvarez had brought him to her on the wharf. It was a kind of reassurance, to feel that for another person. She would never understand that he was grateful to her for it.

"Rose."

She looked at him, as if expecting to receive a reprimand, and the look undid his intention to explain that he had not been angry at her. He realized how skittish she had seemed the last few days and wondered, briefly, why. He made a helpless gesture with his hands. "I'm sorry," he said. "I've forgotten what I meant to say."

He went onto the terrace for a cigarette, but when he touched the pocket of his jacket he remembered he'd run out. He slipped his wristwatch off and put it in his pocket, to remind him later to buy more. It was past time for him to leave, but he could not deny himself ten minutes in the fresher, hillside air. Why did the distances appear so vast? The ships docked at the wharf were toys; to reach them might have taken days instead of minutes. He knew better than to trust appearances, but he was tired of knowing that. He couldn't see what good it did, always knowing there was less to everything than met the eye.

"Messer Lyle?"

He turned and saw Rose standing with her hands clutched to her apron.

"Yes, Rose?"

"In the morning, I am going to the doctor."

"Have you not been feeling well? You're taking all your pills, I hope."

"Yes. It's only an examination, to listen to the heart."

"What time is your appointment? I won't be free to take you in the morning, but I can send a driver."

"No. It's only that I want to tell you that I won't be here to serve the lunch. I'll put it in the cold box. The doctor says it's good for me to walk.''

"All right. But don't make lunch. I won't have time to come back here tomorrow.''

He worried over her appointment, driving to the embassy. Her heart was weakened from some childhood fever, and the strain of being in the boat had almost killed her. Dr. Alvarez had said she'd never be entirely well. "The heart could fail under the slightest strain,'' he'd said. Lyle remembered asking if the heart could be repaired through surgery, and Alvarez's curt reply: "Perhaps. At great expense.'' Apparently he considered that the matter ended there. Lyle feared to let himself think otherwise; it was better not to have illusions.

Art Freleng never looked entirely comfortable behind his desk. He was a nervous man who chewed a pipe but never smoked it, and whose wife, reportedly, had carried on affairs in every foreign post and Washington. This was the reason, people liked to say, that he had never made ambassador, but Lyle thought otherwise. Art fit the role of DCM too well: a worrier, obsessed with detail, more comfortable with paperwork than people. He preferred to stay a little in the shadows. He was the perfect second-in-command.

Five years earlier, perhaps, Lyle would have considered Art a failure—a man who'd passed the point in life where he could reasonably hope for more. Somewhere in those five years, Lyle realized, he'd passed that point himself. He had put in almost fifteen years. In five more, if he chose, he could retire. That was his ambition now: a pension, not to have to work. What Art had, in fact, was more than Lyle could hope for now. Lyle envied him.

"Do you think Fardin was lying?'' Art asked.

"He was evasive, but he might have thought I wanted to inspect the corpses—they're probably a mess. He struck me as a man who has a certain pride in his profession.''

"I wish you'd gone ahead and looked at them—the caskets, that is.''

"I thought I'd better not. If he's taken them already he has time to put them back. I didn't want to catch him lying. He could only go against us then, to save his pride.''

"Last thing we need is those caskets showing up for sale somewhere in town." Art tugged experimentally at a loose thread on his shirt cuff. "You weren't here, the last time something like that happened. It was a great embarrassment for us."

Lyle waited, with his hands locked in his lap, for Art to let him get back to his work. A moment passed in which Art seemed to be considering. "All right," he finally said. "All right. You're going to the funeral tomorrow."

"I'd planned to, yes."

"That's fine. Now, before you go, you'd better have a look at this."

Art pulled a sheet of paper from the combination file and handed it to Lyle. The paper was a different kind than what department cables came on, with blue ink, like a mimeo machine, instead of black, and single spaced, which made it difficult to read. It was the way the agency did everything—even cables were a kind of hostile action. In the middle of the page were three names. One was circled.

"Quite a shock," Art said when Lyle looked up at him. "I find it hard to believe myself."

Lyle read the cable through again. The circled name was Dr. Juan Emilio de Santillana Alvarez, and farther down he was described: a Cuban émigré who'd settled first in the Dominican Republic, then in Haiti, after Castro came to power; his patients in Port-au-Prince had, for years, included diplomats from Western embassies, including the United States. Alvarez, the cable said, was an agent of the Cuban government.

Lyle set the cable on the desk. "Don't believe it, then. I don't. What do they mean by 'agent' anyway? That's awfully vague."

"You know what agent means as well as I."

"And you know Alvarez."

Art sighed. "I thought I did." He pushed back from the desk and reached into a drawer. Lyle waited for him to hold up proof: an envelope of photographs, an intercept. He wouldn't need to look at it to know. He knew already. Despite himself he believed them, and he believed so easily because it didn't contradict who Alvarez was. It was something more to know, not something different: an inconvenient truth, but not a damning one. Cuba was an adversary nation, Haiti a friend. That was policy, and Lyle was obligated to support it by his words and actions. But his feelings were his own. If Alvarez was working for his native country, it was no more than what Lyle himself did. Art found what he was looking for and shut the drawer. He only held his pipe up, rubbed its bone-smooth bowl.

"I hope they're sure," Lyle said.

"I think they must be."

"Do the Haitians know?"

"They may suspect, although we haven't told them anything. The Europeans and Canadians will be informed this afternoon. I'll be sorry if he's caught—but of course it's none of our affair; we can't interfere either way."

"No, I suppose not."

"Well, I wanted you to be aware. You used Alvarez, I know. We all did. Now we'll have to use the embassy's man in the DR. Don't think I've ever seen that man without a razor cut. Doesn't put your mind at ease."

"Won't it look suspicious, if Alvarez's embassy patients drop him all at once?"

"Maybe. But we can't risk any further contact. Anyway, I'd be surprised if he's around much longer."

Lyle only looked at him.

"I only mean I wouldn't be surprised if he's tipped off by someone from the other embassies. He has a lot of friends."

Lyle stood up. He pulled the creases of his pant legs, absently, until he got them straight. "He has a lot of grateful patients, too. I wouldn't want to be the one to turn him over to this government."

"Nor I," said Art.

The rain came shortly after dinner. Lyle sat in the den, a novel in his lap, and waited to see whether the power would stay on. In the evening, if he had light, he liked to read. If the lights went out they'd stay out hours. There was no distraction then, except the shortwave, and the broadcasts drifted in a storm.

Tonight it didn't matter. The novel irritated him. It was a thriller, with betrayals and state secrets and the safety of the free world riding on a single man. It struck him now as ludicrous. How much could one man do? He was remembering Alvarez on the wharf, the afternoon the U.S. Coast Guard cutter brought the people in from Rose's boat. Alvarez had moved among them, joking, sympathizing, using his doctor's authority to shield them, for a while, from the Haitian military officers who stood waiting to record their names. Lyle had been surprised when Alvarez came over to him.

"You're looking still for someone to clean house and cook?" he'd asked, and Lyle, not knowing what he had in mind, had answered yes. Alvarez had brought him over to meet Rose. "This one speaks a little French," he said. "She says that she can cook. And that she has no family. There's nowhere for her to go back to."

Lyle put down his book and went into the dining room. He poured out half a glass of bourbon, then reconsidered, and poured until the glass was almost filled. Before he put the cap back on he took a shot directly from the bottle and swished it in his mouth, like Listerine. He shuddered when he swallowed.

Through the open door onto the terrace he could see the dark trees shaking in the wind. Lightning struck close by, and in its flash he saw the blooms of pink hibiscus. The lights dimmed, then went out.

He set his glass down and went to find a candle in the kitchen drawer. The twilight was enough to see by, but the room was filled with shadows, and he didn't see that Rose was there until she came between him and the window. He'd thought she had already gone downstairs, to her apartment.

"You'll need candles if you haven't got some," he said, feeling for the box. He found it, took a candle out, and held it to a burner of the stove. He turned the knob, and watched the ring of blue gas flower in the dark. He dripped some wax into an ashtray and set the candle in it. When he'd done the same thing with another, he turned to offer one to Rose.

She didn't take it, and when he held it up he saw her shiver. Never had she seemed to him so much a child; not even on the wharf that afternoon when she had looked at him in just this way, expecting nothing. He had never seen despair so closely. It had been his impulse, then, to save her, as it was his impulse now to take her to him. But he told himself, she's not a child. He held the candle down, between them, and the yellow light fell on her arms.

"What is it, Rose? The storm can't hurt you."

She stood where she was, not answering, and he began to fear that she was ill. The light had gone now, and he heard the rain pour down. He thought about the flooded roads; he wasn't sure that he could get her to the doctor if he had to. Then, he realized, he wouldn't know where else to take her, if he couldn't go to Alvarez. He put a hand against her arm and led her to the kitchen table.

He sat with her, wondering whether he should try the phone, when she spoke in a whisper.

"I'm afraid."

"The storm? It's only thunder."

"Not the storm."

"What, then?"

She ran her hand along her forearm, as if trying to keep warm, and looked away. "I am afraid to die," she said.

"You won't die, Rose."

They sat in silence, watching as the candles burned, listening to the gusts of rain against the house. Finally, she said that she was tired, and thought that she should sleep now, but she shivered once again and he got up to get a sweater for her from his bedroom. On his dresser, where he laid his wallet and his keys, there was a pad of paper and a pen. As if he'd planned to do exactly this, he wrote two words—They know—and put the paper in his pocket.

The house was built into a hill, and Rose's room was on the side, downstairs. Lyle had not been in here since the first day he had brought her to the house, and carried down the furniture for her to use. He shone his flashlight in the door and saw the neat, bare room exactly as it had been then, except for pictures on the wall that she had taken from a calendar he'd given her. A mountain range in Colorado. Autumn in New England. Surf off Monterey.

"You'll be all right," he said, waiting as she got the candle lighted on the table, and another on the stand beside her bed. She said yes, and thanked him. Still he stood there, seeing nothing for the time until he realized that she was watching him. Then he pulled the folded paper from his pocket and held it out to her.

"Give this to Dr. Alvarez tomorrow. Tell him it's from me."

She took the paper, and he said good night. He started out, then turned back.

"Rose, the paper has to go to Alvarez. You mustn't give it to his nurse or anybody else. Only Alvarez."

She nodded. Then he went outside again and ran along the sidewalk, through the chilling rain, to reach the house.

* * *

Across the street from the main entrance to the Cassernes Dessalines there was a small store where Lyle knew he could buy cigarettes. He'd thought too late, the day before, to get any and knew he'd need more to get by until the commissary opened in the afternoon.

While he waited for a girl to change his ten-gourde note he watched the gate across the street. Soldiers stood just inside, leaning lazily against their ancient Mausers. The soldiers looked so young. The oldest one of them, Lyle thought, is younger than his rifle. They seemed to have no interest in the crowd that moved along the street in the direction of the cemetery and Fardin's. A Jeep pulled up, and one of the soldiers swung the gate in so that it could enter. Before he closed the gate again someone shouted and he held it. A moment later a woman passed out of the courtyard into the street. She was thirty yards from where Lyle stood, and he couldn't see her face. But he recognized the fabric of her housedress, and the way she bent her head to one side as she walked. He was almost sure that it was Rose.

He went into the street and tried to follow, but last night's rain had turned the streets to mud, and he had trouble moving very quickly. The crowd was gathered at the corner, at the mortuary, and when he couldn't move through them, he gave up. There might have been five hundred people there. He couldn't hope to find her.

He took out a cigarette and lit it. He was worried. It might have been Rose that he'd seen—Alvarez's office was only blocks away. But why would Rose have been inside the Cassernes? If she had a friend or relative in prison, she'd have told him. As far as he knew she had no one. Were they trying to get information from her about him? She'd be vulnerable to pressure. They'd consider her an undesirable—disloyal because she'd tried to leave the island. She could be jailed, and there'd be nothing he could do to help her. There was no information she could give them about him. Nothing they could use. But there was something else, now, she could give them.

He dropped the cigarette, half-finished, in the mud, and turned back through the crowd. When he was free of them he took his jacket off and carried it. The sun had risen high into a cloudless sky, and the beginning of the day's heat lifted from the muck a faint, unpleasant odor of decay. Fifteen minutes later, his shirt soaked through, Lyle was at the door to Alvarez's office. It was locked. A note taped to the glass explained the office would be closed until the afternoon, in order that the doctor might attend a funeral.

By the time Lyle got back, people had begun to move across the street from Fardin's to the cemetery. Men were bringing down the caskets, one by one, and loading them in hearses. The caskets were identical: a soldier's silver-gray, official issue, government of the United States. Their polished metal gleamed. Lyle stood at the bottom of the stairs nearby and watched the mourners leave the chapel. Alvarez was not among them.

There were twice as many people in the cemetery as had been outside Fardin's. Here the ground was even softer, and the debris the storm had washed down from the hills had not been cleared away, so that Lyle had to step over or around the garbage on the paths. The sun reflecting off the whitewashed mausoleums was blinding. The place smelled foul.

It was impossible to walk around the muck. His shoes were covered with it, the bottoms of his trouser legs were spattered. People began to take their shoes and sandals off and carry them. Men were rolling up their pant cuffs. Lyle edged between the mausoleums, but he could not see the hearses, or the caskets, or the crypts where they were to be interred. He scanned the crowd for anyone with light skin, brown, like Alvarez's, caught up once to someone with the same build and said, "Alvarez," but the man who turned around considered Lyle through light green eyes. A mulatto.

He came to a place where everyone had stopped, and was trying to see above the heads of those in front of them, and Lyle stopped, too. He couldn't think. The crowd pushed in against him. Somewhere from in front of him he heard men shouting in exasperated voices; a woman wailed, and cries and sobs broke out around him. Then the crowd grew quiet suddenly. Lyle shaded his eyes with his hand and tried to get the attention of a young man standing on a crypt above him.

"Please," he said, "what's happening?"

The man did not look down.

"Please," Lyle said. "Can you see what's going on?"

The man replied in Creole. Lyle couldn't understand exactly what he'd said, although he thought he'd heard the man say "hammer."

The man took off his torn straw hat and held it at his side. There was a loud, dull thud, of metal hitting metal, then another, and the crowd began to wail again, louder than before.

"What is it?" Lyle said. "What about the hammer?"

"The coffins," said the man. "They are too high."

He understood. The sound was hammering. The coffins were too high. They wouldn't fit into the crypts designed to hold pine boxes. Men were pounding down the lids to make them fit.

Lyle pushed through the suffocating crowd, trying to escape the crush, the smell of human sweat. The sound of hammers echoed off the mausoleums like bullets. Ahead, he saw Monsieur Fardin emerging from between two crypts. He ran to catch him.

"Yes," Fardin said. "We have had to use the hammers." He smiled complacently at Lyle. "I would never, as a man of business, think to do it. But you, Monsieur, you are the diplomat. No doubt you understand, more perfectly than I, political considerations."

Lyle returned, as stiffly as he could, the stiff bow Monsieur Fardin made in his direction, and watched the back of the man's black suit proceed, unhurried, toward the cemetery gate. A hearse was going out, but stopped and backed up to allow a Jeep to come inside. The Jeep sped by Lyle without slowing. A soldier drove, and in the back another rode, his Mauser pointed at the sky. An officer was riding in the front.

Lyle made his way back to the same crypt, where the young man stood, still with his ragged hat, his rapt expression. Lyle reached up to pull himself onto the crypt. The man looked down and, seeing Lyle, he waved him off.

"No room," he said. "No room."

"Let me up there, please," Lyle said. He held the pack of cigarettes out to the man, who took them, then gave Lyle his hand to help him up.

Now Lyle saw the caskets lined up neatly on the ground. The men who were hammering down the lids had taken off their shirts, and worked with fury as the crowd behind them complained. And, there, Lyle spotted Alvarez. He had his glasses in one hand, and in the other was a clean, white handkerchief. Lyle watched him rub a lens as though it were a lover's task, and when he dropped the handkerchief and bent to find it, Lyle began to shout his name. Alvarez stood up and gave no sign that he had heard. Some little distance back, Lyle saw the barrel of the Mauser held above the crowd, moving through it, seeking Alvarez, divining him.

THE DOCTOR
OF THE MOON
by Harriet Doerr
(Stanford University)

In early November there was an emergency. Sara left Ibarra at midnight, arrived in Concepción at one, and for the rest of her life could recapture this hour whole and bright, polished as it had been with fear. Time failed to blur the images, and five years later, or even ten, glimpses of them would intervene between her and a gathering of people, a display in a shop window, her own reflection in the glass. She would never afterward stand under a full moon without seeing corn shocks and chaparral, ditches flooded yellow with wildflowers, the chandeliered lobby of the Hotel París, and the telephone on the reception desk. Without hearing the doctor's voice as he answered.

"*Bueno,*" he had begun. "*Bueno,* señora."

When Sara realized a few minutes before twelve that her husband might die unless she found a doctor, she left the house and stepped into moonlight so radiant that the pepper trees along the drive stood in separate pools of shadow. Fermín, the watchman, was asleep at the gate. But at her approach he rose so quickly it appeared that naps made no difference to a man seventy-five years old.

"Please go to the clinic and get the intern. Don Ricardo is ill."

The old man turned his long somber face toward Ibarra, toward the plaza, the church, the *presidencia,* and the clinic behind it, though all these things were a kilometer away and out of sight. "The *practicante,*" he said.

"Yes, the *practicante.*"

"It is Saturday. He has left Ibarra for the night." The watchman noticed the widening of Sara's eyes. "But there are doctors in the state capital and the taxi driver knows every one of them. Chuy Santos has delivered patients to them all."

"Then we must find him." And she brought the car.

The wide brim of the watchman's sombrero prevented him from entering. He stood at the door, turning his head one way and another until at last Sara said without patience, "Take off your hat."

Moonlight had narrowed the aimless streets of Ibarra. Sara drove past the cantina, the post office, down the single block of the ala-meda, and crossed the arroyo on the arched stone bridge. She was approaching the convent when the watchman said, "Here," opened his door while the car was still moving, and stumbled off into the shimmering dark.

Sara saw she had stopped on the basketball court in front of a row of houses that appeared abandoned, their windows boarded against burglars and night air. In one of these lived her cook, who now must be roused from sleep and asked to stay with Richard. He cannot be left alone, Sara told herself, though she could not imagine what the cook might do in the event of a worsening crisis.

Sara walked from one house to another, calling in front of each one, until at last a sliver of candlelight fell across a sill. Behind it stood the cook, blanketed and unsurprised, her hair hanging below her waist. As Sara explained the emergency each woman regarded the other. What thick braids she has, thought Sara; she is wondering why I'm not down on my knees to pray. But the cook was dressed and already sitting in the car when the watchman came back with Jesús Santos.

Chuy bowed to Sara and said, "At your orders," as if the hour were four in the afternoon and the destination a ladies' tea canasta. When he understood the purpose of the trip he said, "Well then, you need not go, señora. I will find Dr. de la Luna, the finest in Concepción, and deliver him to your door."

"I must go," said Sara, "to give him the details. So he will bring the right medicines." At this moment three words, "bag of tricks," entered her mind and lingered there. "And in case Dr. de la Luna cannot come . . ." She looked at the convent, the school, the row of eight houses, all freshly whitewashed by the moon. "In that case, we must find the next best."

Chuy Santos contemplated her. He saw before him a headstrong woman who believed she could bend providence to suit her. "*A sus órdenes,*" he said.

Ten minutes later the cook sat at the threshold of Richard's door, prepared to bring him water, bring him ice, bring him broth. But the patient remained unaware of her presence. He was an explorer in a hostile land, set on by savage tribes, pinned by lances to a burning wall.

As Sara turned to go, she saw the cook cross herself.

There was a wooden crate of pots and pans on the backseat of the red Volkswagen, also two baskets of green *chiles,* and a birdcage made of twigs. Chuy saw no need to explain this cargo which was to travel with them the eighty kilometers to Concepción and the eighty kilometers back. Sara got in beside the driver, who leaned over to slam the door, said "*Vámonos,*" and started off.

When they had skidded twice on the gravel surface to miss hobbled burros grazing by night, Sara said, "Why don't you blow your horn?"

"It is out of service," said Chuy, and flung the car down the mountain on a zigzag course.

At the bottom of the grade the taxi veered south on the paved road and traveled a line so direct that Concepción might have been a magnet and the Volkswagen an iron filing. The pavement rolled out ahead of them and rolled up behind them and in its unwinding cast out along its edges half a dozen hamlets of a few houses, a silo, and a soft-drink stand. Between these huddled clusters a patchwork of stripped fields and harvested orchards pressed up to the pavement as if passing traffic might renew them. But until the red taxi reached the outskirts of the capital, it was the only car on the road. As far as Sara could tell, it was the only car in Mexico, the only car on earth.

An overhead light which was never extinguished shone dimly on the tasseled green fringe that bordered Chuy's windshield and on the wax rose that hung from the mirror. It shed its faint glow on a plaster statue of the Virgin of Guadalupe that swayed on the dashboard. The beams of Chuy's headlights crossed at a point twenty feet ahead.

"Can you see where you're going?" Sara asked.

"I could find my way along this road drunk, blind, or crazy," said Chuy, and turned off the headlights to demonstrate his control. At this, the whole countryside was misted over with silver—the endless thoroughfare before them, the fields on either side, and all the wide desert beyond that swept to the hills. It was in this spectral light that a scavenger dog raced from a plot of land onto the road and was struck.

"Stop," said Sara.

"On what account?" The driver continued on.

"It may still be alive."

Chuy looked sidelong at her obstinate profile, the profile of a child afraid of the dark who will enter a crypt at night to prove he is not. If I tell her the dog is only hurt, thought Chuy, she may ask me to bind its wounds. If I say it is certainly dead, she may insist that I inter it.

"We must think of don Ricardo," he told her, "not of animals who have no souls."

From the birdcage behind came a twitter. He plans to sell these things at one o'clock in the morning, Sara supposed. Get rid of them all while I talk to Dr. de la Luna.

But Chuy was thinking, not of a sale, but of Big Braulia, a pomaded woman of forty, wide and generous of mouth, breast, and thigh, the wife of a locomotive engineer. During her husband's absences, Braulia observed an independent schedule of her own. As soon as Chuy had introduced the señora to Dr. de la Luna, he hoped to visit the engineer's wife in her rosy-pillowed room behind the fruit-and-vegetable market.

He switched on the headlights. In their sudden beam the ditches that would line the road on both sides from here to Concepción flamed all shades of yellow with marguerites, marigolds, and daisies.

Sara was startled into speech. "Look at those flowers!" And was shocked by her words, on this mission, at this time.

"There will be fewer tomorrow," said Chuy. "Tomorrow is All Souls' Day. These you see will be cut to lay on graves."

There was a silence while Sara watched the wildflowers spring into the light ahead. Then she asked Chuy the time and he glanced at the moon. "It is twelve-thirty," he told her. The taxi raced on, pulling to the left because of its alignment, knocking because of its cylinders, polluting the shining night because of its rings. The caged bird chirped twice and Chuy began to sing. "*Ay, ay, querida!*" sang Chuy.

Until this moment Sara had heard only scraps of song from Jesús Santos, torn phrases that trailed behind when the red taxi passed her in its rush up the road from Ibarra to the mine. But these scraps had been clues enough for her to guess that he could sing as he was singing now, in a voice to confuse rational discourse and stab the heart.

While her husband's fever mounted forty kilometers behind and Dr. de la Luna slept oblivious forty kilometers ahead, Sara listened to Chuy sing. He stopped at last and Sara, more affected by this voice, under these circumstances, than she could bear, failed to acknowledge the performance and simply asked, "Do you think it's dead?"

"What dead, señora?"

"The dog you hit."

Chuy sighed and struck the palms of his hands against the steering wheel for patience.

"By now that animal is in heaven with children who throw sticks for him to chase and old women who feed him bread."

On their left a solitary lantern hanging from a shed marked the town of Viudas. In the dark Sara recognized this place she had often seen by day. The streets of Viudas sloped and fell off into gullies, dragging with them crooked houses and the infants, cats, and grandmothers inside.

Chuy sang two more songs and had started a third when Sara spoke again.

"How do you know that Dr. de la Luna is the best in Concepción?"

"Because when Pepe Torres stumbled into the ore classifier, two doctors, first one and then the other, set his legs and at the end of a year he was still on crutches. Then Dr. de la Luna broke them again and lined up the bones as straight as a rifle barrel. Now Pepe can walk by himself."

"But my husband has no broken bones."

"Dr. de la Luna also specializes in don Ricardo's illness." And Chuy waited to hear what the illness was.

Sara said nothing, but against all reason began to believe this was true of the doctor. To the left of the road an expanse of chaparral and cactus made a horizon of its own and on the right the chapel dome of a derelict hacienda gleamed smoke-blue above stone rubble. But what if Richard dies before I can bring this expert to him? What if he dies before I get back, before I can tell him? Tell him what? she asked herself. Tell him about the dog, the moon, the flowers, the lost streets of Viudas. Tell him that Dr. de la Luna is a specialist in his disease. Tell him to wait. For the doctor. For me.

"Wait," she said to Chuy.

"What for?" he said, as he had the first time.

"The birdcage is about to fall."

Without decreasing his speed Chuy swept his arm into the backseat and set the cage straight, scattering seed and splashing water from a tiny cup. The bird beat its wings against the sticks that imprisoned it, ruffled its feathers, and clung to a dangling perch.

Chuy began to sing again in his resonant tenor about men whose women had left them for sailors, for bullfighters, for pimps.

If Richard dies tonight, Sara wondered, will I return to Concepción on this same road tomorrow to advise the coroner? Will I select a coffin at La Urna de Oro, drive back to Ibarra with it, and call Luis and Paco Acosta from the garden and the water carrier from his burros at the gate?

"Please help me with this coffin. Let me open the front door. Take it into the bedroom. Thank you."

When the taxi reached the plaza of Concepción the square was dark except for a single street lamp at each corner. Moonlight, filtered through the branches of jacarandas, illuminated the blue-tiled pond, the façades of the cathedral and the government palace, and the plate-glass windows of Woolworth's and the bank. Two dim bulbs burned at the Hotel París, one over the entrance and one at the far end of the lobby, over the reception desk, where the night clerk was opening a paper bag of food.

Sara stood with Chuy outside the hotel's etched-glass door and heard the cathedral clock strike one. "Please wait," she told him.

"I have a matter of business to attend to," said the taxi driver. "In the neighborhood of the market."

"You must be back in five minutes. Without fail." Sara, ignorant of Big Braulia, presumed that in this short time, in the early hours of the morning, Chuy expected to find customers for the pots and pans, the *chiles,* and the bird. "If Dr. de la Luna agrees to come, we must go immediately to his house."

"His house is behind his waiting room and I have been there a hundred times," said Chuy. "I could drive there one-handed and backward and not miss a turn." He looked in the direction of the market, four blocks away. This talk will have to stop, he thought, or it will be too late. Too late for Braulia and too late to deposit at don Ricardo's bedside the finest physician in this state of Mexico.

Chuy pushed open the door of the Hotel París. "There is the telephone, señora. And the night porter to help you." For he believed that it was unlikely the American woman and Dr. de la Luna would be able to communicate. Only in Ibarra was her Spanish understood, and the doctor spoke very quickly in the idiom of Yucatán where he was born.

"Not a second more than five minutes. We must drive back with the doctor at once."

"*A sus órdenes,*" said Chuy.

Sara entered the hotel and walked the length of the lobby, which was painted in panels of coral and white, and hung with the framed faces of French royalty. The night porter was eating rice and *chiles jalapeños* rolled in a tortilla. With his free hand he reached for the directory under the desk.

There was only one Dr. Alonso de la Luna. She dialed and began to count. At the sixth ring a man's voice answered "*Bueno,*" and when she remained silent said "*Bueno*" again. She uttered four words, "Dr. de la Luna," and paused. "*Bueno, señora,*" the doctor said. Sara spoke the phrases she had memorized somewhere between Ibarra and Concepción. "My husband is ill, eighty kilometers away. I have a taxi to take you and to bring you back." When the doctor answered she understood only four or five of his words.

This is a man I've never seen, she reminded herself as she listened. I am handing Richard's life over to a stranger on the recommendation of a taxi driver. I am taking the word of Chuy Santos, who owns an old Volkswagen, can drive by the moon, sing like an angel, and sell a caged sparrow in the dead of night.

Leaning against the marble-topped desk of the Hotel París with the receiver clasped to her ear, Sara struggled to interpret the slurred dialect of Dr. de la Luna. "Please speak more slowly. What did you say? *Cómo? Cómo?*" And while she said "How? How?" to the doctor, an interior voice addressed Richard. Don't die, it said. Then, perceiving this imperative to be unreasonable, changed its refrain to, Don't die now.

The doctor was growing impatient.

"*Cómo?*" said Sara. "*Cómo?*"

"Tomorrow is November second, All Souls' Day," Dr. de la Luna would remark when he roused from dozing in the Volkswagen and noticed the road spilled over on both sides by the flowering tide of yellow.

These were words Sara understood. She leaned forward from the narrow space Chuy had cleared on the backseat when he returned to the hotel twenty-five minutes late. Her face was close to the doctor's. "Have you ever seen such flowers, such a moon, such a night?"

Dr. de la Luna turned his head and regarded her through heavy-rimmed lenses that magnified his eyes. This American woman with the pale flying hair and the gray eyes as big as a child's at the zoo is temporarily deranged. From what she has told me, her husband may or may not survive this fever. She is disoriented, Dr. de la Luna told himself. But the gray eyes were still on his.

"You are right, señora," he said at last. "There is splendor all around us." He unbuttoned his suede jacket, then buttoned it again.

She continued to lean over his shoulder. "How fortunate it is for my husband and me, for our peace of mind, that you are a specialist in his particular disease."

The doctor stared at her. "But I am not," he said. "I am an orthopedic surgeon."

Fear drained the light from the fields, the desert, and the hills. The horizon gathered and the landscape drew in. She felt the world shrink until it fit between her ribs.

* * *

As it turned out, Richard would not die that night in the house of his ancestors, in the bed with an altar screen for a headboard. He would die more than a year later in a San Francisco hospital on a winter day with air so clear and a sky so clean that Sara, standing at the window of his room, said, "If this were Ibarra and summer, today would be the first day after the first rain." The capped nurse who was on her rounds heard this and made no response. Richard made no response. As it turned out, he would die on a holiday, Washington's Birthday, so that the tray of juice and gelatin he would not touch was trimmed with plastic cherries and a paper flag. Richard, lying with closed eyes, looking inward, never saw the decoration appropriate to the day of his death. Sara would notice it and drink a cup of tepid consommé as she sat with her hand on his and listened for his breathing. When it stopped she felt nothing, unconvinced by anything as slight as this, the almost imperceptible difference between breath and silence, that he was dead.

And afterward, on her return to Ibarra, would be startled when miners approached her, took off their hats, expressed their sorrow. When a memorial mass was arranged on the first anniversary of Richard's death she sat bewildered at the front of the church. The people of Ibarra watched her enter and leave the nave dry-eyed, and said, "She is North American and not a Catholic." Outside the church Sara shook hands with the men who had sponsored the service—the mechanic, the carpenter, the welder, the foremen of the underground shifts.

"My thanks to all of you." But she was still not persuaded he was dead.

When the drive back to Ibarra proved after all to have an end, and they approached the house, the taxi's headlights revealed the watchman in his sombrero and two sarapes, standing at the open gate exactly as Sara had seen him last, at midnight. Beyond the *sala* the cook still sat in her chair at the bedroom door. Richard lay dying on his side of the bed just as he had lain there dying before.

When she saw this, Sara would believe that time had stopped. The watchman would never leave the gate, the cook her chair, Richard this bed.

Dr. de la Luna performed his examination. "I will treat him now and leave instructions for the *practicante*."

"Shall I send the taxi for you tomorrow?" Sara would ask.

"Send the taxi day after tomorrow at noon." The doctor turned from the bed and moved toward the door. "Unless . . . But then, in any case . . . In that event . . ."

He buttoned his coat and left.

Later on, she remembered of all that night only what mattered least. The midnight ride from Ibarra to Concepción, Chuy's reckless haste, the struck mongrel, the countryside washed of its meagerness by the moon, the ditches streaming gold with wildflowers. And through widening time, as she slept, as she woke, as she lived her day, came unsummoned glimpses of herself crossing the long lobby of the Hotel París to pick up the telephone.

In the end she had managed to make the arrangements after all. She finally understood Dr. de la Luna to say he would drive back with her to Ibarra.

"As you have described it to me, señora, we have nothing to fear. It is a simple case of pneumonia."

Sara realized the time had come to explain the situation. She waited a moment to practice the words before she spoke. "And there is the leukemia," she said, pronouncing it le-u-ke-mi-a, dividing the vowels, turning the *e*'s to long *a*'s. She only forgot that there is no *k* in the Spanish alphabet.

The doctor corrected her. "*Le-u-ce-mi-a*," he said, stressing the third syllable.

"*Leucemia*," repeated Sara, as though he had instructed her, "Repeat after me. *Leucemia*." As though he taught first-year Spanish and said, "Please repeat these words. *Los ojos*, the eyes. *La mano*, the hand. *El día*, the day."

OPEN HOUSE
by Walter Mosley
(City College of New York)

His name was Raymond but we called him Mouse because he was small and had sharp features. We could have called him Rat because Ray really weren't like a mouse at all; that is to say he wasn't a shy man. But we were fond of old Raymond so Mouse stuck on him.

I liked Mouse because he always got what he wanted. He never worked but his girlfriends kept him in nice clothes and he was always pleased with himself. Mouse lived in a different house every month but he was more at home in a chair in the street than I was in the apartment I lived in for three years.

He had a girlfriend down in Galveston named Etta Mae Harris. Every Saturday night she'd come up to Houston and spend from that time until Sunday noon with Mouse—and with the rest of us too because we were a crowd.

Etta was a beautiful woman with green eyes, light skin, and big brown freckles. She loved to dance and laugh and it seemed like everybody got happy when she walked into the room. When Etta was happy she didn't giggle; she laughed loud and hard and tears came to her eyes. And if you heard her laugh you just had to go along with it.

One of those Saturday nights I had an open house in my apartment. What that means is I opened up my doors for to party and anyone who could make it was welcome in. The only thing you had to have was a quarter if you was a man or a dime if you was a girl; and anyone carrying a weapon, gun or knife, was expected to check it at the door. I had music, liquor, and dancing from sundown to sunup and everyone there slaved harder that one night than they had all week long.

That particular Saturday we had everyone there and ready. There was Jelly Head Johnson with his greased back and concked hairdo and hot-tempered Ruby Nickerson—who we called Little Red because of her angry nature and her wavy red hair. Of course Etta Mae and Mouse breezed in. He was very natty in his white gabardine suit with lavender patent leather shoes and a cluster of violets over his heart. Etta had on an electric blue dress suit with pink carnations on her lapel and a white-silk box hat (they were the rage right then).

"Etta, you lookin' too good fo' Mouse t'nite," I said.

"Don't you know it Easy."

Ezekiel's my real name but only my dead momma called me that.

"The hen ain't bad but it's the rooster gonna crow Ease," Mouse put his arm around Etta's big waist. Etta was a healthy girl with some meat to her. She did hand laundry twelve hours a day, five days a week and was stronger than most men I knew.

"Git yo' hands offa me Raymond you might as well be huggin' ona mirrah." Etta laid a hefty hand against Mouse's shoulder and pushed. A less vain man would have gone down but Mouse just hopped once and took two skips into the next room.

"Lips here Easy?"

"Him an' horn Etta. He got Willie an' Flat Top wit' 'im so we gonna dance t'nite."

"That sounds right." Etta was looking in the direction that Mouse skipped off to. She really loved that man. I found out how much when I was down in Galveston once, looking for work. I made my pitch and was somewhat successful but in the morning all Etta could talk about was how sweet a man Mouse was and how lucky I was to have him for a friend.

" 'Scuse me Easy," Etta said, and she was off to corner her man.

The party was right. Lips was a kite on his alto sax tied down to Wille and his stand-up bass. In between them was Flat Top, probably the best drummer we had in south Texas. Flat Top didn't bother to bring his drums unless it was a paying job. He just brought some sticks and two cardboard boxes, then he'd pound down some rhythm until he wore them soft and sent down for more.

I shuffled in and grabbed Little Red.

There were people there from all over Fifth Ward and beyond. There was no'counts, churchgoers, day laborers, and there was gangsters too. A party wasn't right unless you had some bad men in their broad-rimmed fedoras with the slinky yellow women in the fox furs and the slit skirts. Man they were hot. The pimp, portly Joe Withers, came with three womens—and one of them was white! I had a hit on my doorstep and scotch on the table.

There was dancing in the parlour, must've been forty of us there, and blackjack on the bed. The men told lies in the kitchen and the only place for romance was down on the porch.

I was still dancing with Red when Lips turned the heat down. She leaned into me kind of heavy and said, "I got me a thirst Easy."

I could hear that. I sat Red down in a corner and shimmied my way through to the kitchen. That's where it started.

"Etta ain't what you gonna call timid." It was Mouse talking. "She take what she want, and I be ready t'let her have it—if you know what I mean." He was leaned back in a fold-up wood chair with a big black cigar in his teeth and his purple shoes up on my table; Mouse had big feet for such a small man.

"Yeah that girl ride you home—the long way." Mouse gave us a big wink and rolled that cigar around with his tongue. He liked to brag on Etta's charms but I didn't like it too much so I got Red's drink and moved back to the dancing. But before I left I noticed portly Joe watching Mouse real close. Joe was a light-skinned fat man, he always had a few beads of sweat in the middle of his forehead. The girls said he had hands like steel traps and, like most pimps, that he was good with a knife.

When I got back Red was standing in the corner dancing slow-alone with her eyes closed.

"You lookin' satisfied Red," I said.

"It's the music Easy. Like that preacher say, 'The choir is the spark but the holy fire is in my soul.' " She took her drink and danced me into the crowd.

"Easy," Red said as she pressed her nose into my chest.

"Yeah Red?"

"It's too bad you know." She put the flat of her hand on the back of my neck and I could feel it all the way down my spine.

"Whas that honey." I hunched over like I was trying to hear what she had to say.

"It's too bad you know 'bout how you got yo' nose open behind Etta Mae an' you cain't see how no other girl might be feeling." She looked up into my face then and I got scared. I don't know what it was but that fear and the look in her eye got me excited. I said, "Etta Mouse's girl Red. I git my own."

She didn't take her eyes off of mine. She looked at me for a long time and finally she said, "Wanna go outside fo' a walk?"

I said I would.

Then she laid her cheek against my chest and whispered, "I'ma jus go my wrap then."

She kissed me and squeezed my hand almost shy when she asked me to wait a while before I went down the stairs to meet her.

When she left I casted around for a while, looking for Etta Mae. I knew I wouldn't be seeing her for a week and I thought I'd just say a little something. But she was nowhere to be seen. I looked everywhere. Mouse was still in the kitchen; asleep on my sofa chair with his leg thrown over the arm and that cigar dangling from his fingers.

He looked so peaceful lying there; I got the thought that, if I left with Red, Mouse would take Etta in my bed if he didn't have any place else to go. That got me mad and I went out looking for Etta again.

I was still searching when someone grabbed me from behind and pulled me back.

"Easy! Fat Joe Withers down on the porch whippin' on Etta Mae!" Red's eyes were wild and that wildness seemed to jump from her right into me. By the time she dragged me downstairs to the porch I had my Texas jackknife out and I was ready to use it.

First thing we saw was Etta doubled over with Joe twisting her arms from behind. He was yelling, ". . . I'ma be the last thing you evah spit on!"

"Get offa me niggah! Lemme go an' I tear you up!"

I never heard Etta foulmouthed before and it made me kind of frantic. "You let her up Joe!"

"Stan' 'way from Easy. This bitch done talk dirt t'me, done spit on me too. She gonna have t'answer on that!"

"Let me go! Let me go!" Etta was hollering.

When I moved up with my knife Joe must've loosened his grip because Etta twisted around and hit him solid in the gut; he had to go down but he was reaching for his pocket too. I knew that if he had a pistol someone was dead so I was moving fast. But Red screamed like a crazy woman and grabbed the knife out of my hand with a strength I didn't know she had.

"I kill 'im Easy!" She was screaming and jumping so crazy that Joe froze on his knee with a scared look in his face. "A woman cut his fat ass an' the judge let her loose by mo'nin'!"

Red swung wide and missed that whole fat man.

She came full around and got me in the thigh. It was like she just cut me down. But she might've saved my life though because when Joe saw all that blood he turned to run.

I was lying there trying to hold back the blood while Red screamed and jumped up and down, she was that upset. Etta was at the front gate, yelling down the street after Joe, who was running fast.

With the both of them making all that noise and my leg like it was I started to despair. I crawled up to a chair on the porch with Red jumping all around me, still screaming.

Just then Mouse came strolling out the front.

"Etta! Etta! Whas happenin' baby?"

"What you mean whas happenin'? Where you been?"

"Calm down honey." He walked down the stair to meet her. He had his hands in his pockets. "Where's yo' hat baby?"

"My hat! I nearly get my arms broke an' Easy bleedin' like a pig an' you askin' 'bout my hat!"

"What happened t'Easy?" Mouse looked around to my corner. He never got upset unless you played with his money or caught him in a lie.

"What happened? That pimp come talkin' filth t'me, an' then he stick Easy. . . ."

"What?" Mouse almost sounded upset. "What he say?"

She told him in words louder than I needed to hear outside my house.

Mouse took his hands out of his pockets and said, "What?"

The blood was thick between my fingers so maybe I was light-headed; maybe that's why Mouse sounded like he was mad. He bent down to get the knife from where Red had dropped it.

"Why I cut that mothah down!"

He was really shouting and headed for that gate. Etta was in front of him though and I noticed Mouse wasn't in a hurry to get around her.

"Hold on Raymond. . . . He gone now. . . . Hold on. . . ."

"I'ma getta hold a his fat ass! That's what I'ma do. Mothah fuckah mess wit' my woman. The woman I love too. . . ."

"It's okay now baby. You stay here with me." She grabbed Mouse by the arm and he stopped.

"Lemme go now Etta! You gonna get hurt tryin' hold a man wit' a knife in his hand!"

I started to fade then. I was thinking about sunshine and palm trees far away from there.

"Baby stay here with me now," Etta said so softly I don't even know how I heard it. It was like she was whispering in my ear, but she was talking to Mouse.

Mouse looked in Etta's face. "I love you baby. Don' you know that? Man come up an' mess wichyou then he playin' with me. An' I don' like that."

I didn't hear much else of what they said but for a minute I saw that look in Etta's eye. She looked at Mouse like he was a plate of dirty rice at the end of a long day.

I fell back into the chair, weak from bleeding.

Red was doing something to my leg and lots of other people had come down from the party. But all I could hear was the ocean washing up on the beach; I couldn't quite see it because it was so bright (I know now that my head was back and the electric light on the porch was shining in my eyes but then I was sure it was the California sun).

"Where's Etta?" I heard somebody say.

"She gone Easy," Red answered. "Her an' Mouse took off, ain't even seen if you gotta bandage."

I was thinking about how Mouse once told me that you could eat the fruit right off the trees in San Diego or LA and how you could sleep right outside the weather was so nice. He said the green in the trees was more like gold. I was talking to Mouse, lyin' up on the beach and eating fruit off Etta's big beautiful chest when I passed out.

I didn't go back to my house. Red took me home that night and changed my bandages every couple of hours and sponged my face. She took care of everything. I could see that she felt more for me than just one night at a party. And maybe I would've stayed but something happened when I was on the porch. I knew right then that I had to go find something for me; something that was going to be mine. I thought it was California.

So on Monday morning, while Red was out working, I took some money from her basket and hobbled down to the train station.

I felt crazy. Inside I was laughing out loud but outside I was sober like a judge. I got my ticket and limped right up to the first car when someone called to me.

"Hey, hey brother!" The porter had on a white jacket with brass buttons and red trim. "That ain't our car up there man. You go git in that one down next to the las'." My eyes followed his white glove down to the back of the train.

"Wha'?" I must've sounded a fool but I just couldn't get his meaning.

He smiled a big gold-toothed grin and said, "Thas alright man, colored car only one got seats."

"You got it wrong man. I'm goin to California an' I'm sittin up front where I can see it comin'."

He was a head taller than me with wide shoulders. He was still smiling too. "Then you gonna have t'jump."

"Huh?"

"You gonna have t'jump right outta yo' skin you wanna sit anywheres but where I tell ya."

When he said that the dizziness came back and I had to lean up against the train. Sometimes the truth hit you so hard it's like that. What that porter said meant one thing but I saw something else.

I saw the pink naked bodies of five rabbits hanging on my grandmother's porch and their skins, heads and all, thrown across the bannister. My grandma was toothless but she laughed anyway saying to herself, "Lil babies done jump outta they skin right into the soup." She laughed for a long time.

The porter was all tensed up ready to strongarm me but I didn't need to fight him. I just stood there with my hand on the train, looking at him.

He said, "You sick man?"

"I don't know," I said and I meant it.

"You better get on back to yo fam'ly man. Sumpin' wrong." He turned up his nose like I smelled. I left the station for my house.

I limped down the street dizzy and sick to my stomach. And while I was walking I was thinking about something Mouse had said once. We were drunk in my house after an all-night poker game. He won as usual so he was full of advice.

"Easy," he said. "You gots to know how to play the game if you wanna win it. You see if you gamble you cain't have nuthin' t'lose. Cuz if you worried 'bout losin' then you be too busy watchin' yo' ass to see what's goin' on right there in yo' face." He leaned back in the chair and looked me directly in the eye. "Thas right Easy, here I got all you'all boys' money an' you think you los' it. But thas like if yo' girl gimme some time an' it break yo' heart. . . . You see, I cain't afford t'be like that; man you know Etta could take you home t'nite an' give you breakfast in the mo'nin' too. But that ain't nuthin' t'me cuz I'ma poor man." Mouse shook his head like he felt sorry for me. "And a poor man ain't got nuthin' t'lose. Soon as you see that you gonna have it right. . . ."

THE EARS OF DENNIS AND PETER
by Mark Dewey
(University of Virginia)

It was nearly dark and snow was beginning to flake off the gray sky and fall, white in the air. A drop of water waited on the point of the new brass nail in the boy's earlobe, and fell on Ken's hand when he squeezed the boy's shoulder. Ken breathed clouds, and these rose between him and the boy's father, floated through the door to the screened porch. The two men had always been friends, a friendship stretching over years, and growing thin. Roger, the boy's father, pinched the head of the brass nail. It was round, like a ladybug, but harder, and cold. He turned it slowly, crumbling its collar of dried blood, and the boy closed his eyes. The wind came over the fields and turned the boy's hair, and snow fell on the boy's neck, where it melted. He opened his eyes and his father said, "Go in."

Ken had quit, but Roger offered him a cigarette anyway, slowly taking the pack from his shirt and slowly shaking out a brown tip. Ken turned away. He wasn't wearing any coat. His shoulders were damp, and his hands were wet and red. Roger lit the cigarette he'd offered and looked across the river. Through the bare branches he could see Ken's house, the yellow-lighted windows, and the chim-

ney, letting go the smoke of hard wood. He could see Ken's footprints on the bridge, and on the road, and in the yard.

"I'm sorry," Ken said.

Roger ran a finger down the stair rail, knocking off the hill of
snow, and considered inviting Ken onto the porch. It didn't seem
time for that yet. He wondered whether Dennis had cried out, if
Dennis's cry had brought Ken down to check the boys. He hoped so.

Ken said, "I guess they still need watching every minute."

"They shouldn't."

Ed, Roger's springer spaniel, came around the corner of the house
and stood beside the stoop. He looked up at Ken and twitched his
nose. "Ed, sit!" Ken said. Ed came up the steps and rubbed his ear
against Ken's knee. Ken shook his head and said, "You wrecked
him, Roger."

Roger sent the dog onto the porch and closed the door. "He's a
dog," Roger said.

Ken grunted. Then he shoved his hands in his pockets and said,
"Well, I'm sorry."

"Hey. You can't tell what these kids are going to do. You and I
cut our hands and pressed the cuts together when we were kids. They
pierce each other's ears with nails. You didn't do it."

"Maybe I should have let your boy go ahead and do Pete's. Serve
him right."

Roger flicked his cigarette into the yard. It made a dark hole in
the snow. Stopping the boys had been a mistake, it put Roger ahead,
and Ken seemed to realize that. He said, "Well," and held his thick
hand out to shake with Roger.

The wind made Roger glad Ken wasn't wearing any coat, and
glad he hadn't asked Ken in yet. Surely Ken would not forget that
he'd been kept on Roger's stoop, without a jacket, in the cold.

"Coffee?" Roger asked, with half a smile. It was too late an
invitation for Ken to accept.

"No."

They shook hands and Ken crossed the yard and Roger watched
him make new footprints in the snow, watched him fold his arms
and hug himself, watched him lean against the wind. He wanted to
see if the big man would run. He didn't run, but at his door he looked
back. Roger supposed that if Ken could have seen his glad eyes and

round grin, their long, cold friendship might have finally reached an end.

The house smelled of chicken and green pine. Roger put another sticky log in the stove and held his hands in the heat, waiting for pitch to bubble from the log and make a smokey mess. He could hear his wife making gravy in the roaster with a metal whisk. When there was trouble with Dennis, Tina cooked harder, fixing the usual foods with additional noise, as if she wanted him to hear how much she loved him, her only child, her only mouth to feed. Roger went into the kitchen and said to make more.

"It's chicken and rice," said Tina, watery-eyed.

"Whatever it is, make more."

She laid one hand on her forehead, but the other kept the whisk splashing in the roaster. Roger tugged her apron strings. "Hey," he said. "It's no big deal. He'd been talking about it for months."

Tina stopped whipping the gravy. She turned off the stove and waited for the gravy to stop bubbling. Then she said, "It seems so brutal."

"What?"

"To do it with a nail."

Roger tried to turn her by the waist, but she wouldn't face him. He said again that it was no big deal, but if she could have seen his grin she would have known how big a deal it was.

Dennis was called down. At meals the boy was pleasing to his parents. To see him eat her cooking made his mother feel that there would always be at least a cord of nourishment between them, and it made Roger feel he still had something for the boy, something the boy needed and wanted and liked, and he felt grateful to the boy for eating.

Their meal was soft, almost silent. Nothing crunched. The bones slid easily out of the drumsticks, and the gravy was smooth, and the rice was as quiet as cotton. They drank milk. The clatter of plates and glasses was muffled by the fuzzy cloth on the table and the steam that boiling rice had put in the air. They ate in the kitchen. The boy's ear was inflamed, but it looked clean, and the nail looked as clean as a needle. Roger let the boy keep quiet. He didn't want the boy to explain, he wanted him to eat.

Long after he'd finished his own meal, Roger stayed at the table serving his son more rice, more chicken, more gravy. The boy kept his eyes on his plate and his fork in his hand, chewing slowly and swallowing hard. Roger let him clean his plate completely, then filled it again. When Roger scooped out a third helping, banging the rice spoon against the boy's plate, Tina said, "Dennis," but Roger held up his hand. When she left the table, neither he nor his son looked after her.

The boy ate on, and Roger watched him. He wondered if the boy felt he was being punished with food, if he understood that he was being forced to make a family of them by consuming what his father bought and his mother cooked. He wondered if, in fact, this was a form of punishment, or just a way to gratify himself. He couldn't tell. He couldn't tell if Dennis was actually hungry or just pigheaded, but he shovelled it in, he ate like an athlete, he ate like a star, and when all the food was gone his father felt obliged to him, indebted, a way he wouldn't have felt if the boy had said he was full, or let the child of someone other than Ken Johnson drive a brass nail through his ear.

He let the boy go to his room and did the dishes by himself. There was nothing left over to give to the dog, or to save for the following day. That, too, thanks to the boy. As Roger rinsed the serving dishes, he imagined the scene at Johnson's house. Somehow he was certain that the stage was in the basement, beside the big wood bench where Johnson kept his nails and screws and tools. He saw Dennis volunteer to be the first, maybe even bribing Peter with the promise of a record or a tape. He felt the boy's thrill when Peter agreed, saw his eyelids droop, the corners of his mouth turn up as Peter chose a hammer, and saw the shock on Peter's face when Dennis screamed and Ken came running down to find the drop of blood on Dennis's shoulder and the hammer in Peter's hand. It was better than anything Roger could have figured out himself. He thought of taking up a dish of ice cream to the boy, but decided to wait, to let him get hungry again, to show some respect.

Roger went into the living room to smoke beside the fire and the dog. He opened the stove and listened to the hum of heat that turned the black logs red, and dried his lips. It was a snowy night in March; Roger was delighted by the thick flakes, by the burying of spring a little deeper, by the chips of wood on the floor, the smell of the dog's fur warming, the fire busy stopping cold and darkness at the windows and the doors.

So Roger was already full of the goodness of life when Peter Johnson called. The ring was no surprise, nor was the haste that Dennis made to answer. At night kids called for Dennis. Roger was glad for the boy. Let him talk to whoever it was. He'd done something bold, let him tell. Roger listened for the troubling of papers in the letter rack and the squeak of the basement door, for Dennis stretching the cord around the corner to sit on the basement steps and talk. Instead he heard Tina clear her throat and say, "Dennis?" Then he heard the boy come up behind him with the phone.

"Dad," he said. "It's for you."

That was a surprise.

"It's Peter Johnson."

"Why does he want to talk to me?"

The boy didn't answer. He just handed his father the phone and stepped backward toward his mother. Tina put her hands on his shoulders and he leaned into her.

Peter Johnson was crying. He said that his parents were fighting and his dad had a gun.

"Did you call the police?" Roger asked. "Don't then. Just stay in your room with your sisters and I'll be right there."

Roger pulled on his coat and said he'd be right back.

"What's wrong?" Tina asked. "Where are you going?"

"I'm just going over to Johnson's. I'll be right back."

He paused to lay his hand on Dennis's head, but Dennis drew his head away. Rightly so, Roger thought. Roger ought to keep his blessing to himself and wield the club his son had given him, albeit inadvertently, like a man.

The sky was still gray but the snow had stopped, and the sheet of clouds was beginning to ripple. Roger could hear Johnson's dogs, the whole kennel it sounded like, barking, not wildly but steadily. He put his hand, still warm from the fire, into the snow on his truck and felt for the door handle. The engine turned over slowly. For a moment he was afraid he'd have to walk. He didn't know what he was going to do when he got there, but he knew it wasn't right to go on foot.

All the lights were on, the lights at the end of the driveway and the lights on the porch and in the house. Roger sat in the truck and looked at dark shapes moving past the windows. Johnson looked even bigger when you couldn't see his face or his hands or his clothes, and poor Lois looked no bigger than a child. It occurred to Roger that maybe the small shape was a child, maybe Peter, maybe even Angela, and he knew he should rush in, but he waited, gloating. Johnson had gone off his nut again, and nobody knew it but Roger, and Johnson's wife and kids, and Johnson's dogs.

The dogs were a bad sign, and that was good. Johnson never let them go on barking. They often set each other off; one smelled a pheasant or rabbit and the rest tried to bark it to death, but Johnson always came right out to calm them down. They were his livelihood, and they were his pride. At the corner of the house Roger put his fingers in his mouth and whistled three short blasts, the way Johnson had taught him to do, and the dogs fell quiet. Then he stood beneath the light on the front porch and took a deep breath before trying the knob. He heard Johnson's wild voice. He heard booms, either the floor or the wall being struck like a drum. Then he heard nothing.

Johnson was a big, strong man. He'd hit Roger once while they were fishing, knocked him cold and left him lying with his legs in the creek. He wasn't dumb, he was just impatient, and force was usually the fastest way. His arms and his shoulders put him in charge, and that was fine if he knew what he wanted, if he knew how he felt, but it got ugly if he didn't know. Roger rang the bell, and opened the door, and went in.

"It's Roger," he called, walking down the front hall toward the living room.

Ken and Lois were sitting on the sofa, still as ice. Her eyes were red and swollen, but probably only from crying. Ken's eyes were blank, unfocused. He looked as if he was preparing a tremendous effort, like flexing every muscle he had. On the coffee table lay a pistol, pointed at the space between them.

A door opened and Roger looked down the hall. Peter stepped out of the farthest bedroom. For a moment he was still, like his parents, staring, and Roger wasn't sure that Peter saw him, so he waved. Peter took a long-handled comb from his pocket and went back into the bedroom, combing his hair. Roger glanced at Ken and Lois. Neither of them blinked.

"How's it going?" Roger asked. He risked a smile.

A vein in Ken's neck filled. It got as thick as a finger before he allowed it to drain. Lois squinted at the window that reflected her and Ken. Roger went to the bedroom.

The girls were together on one of the canopy beds, hugging their knees, wrapped in a blanket. They, too, were still, but keenly alert. Their eyes latched onto Roger when he came in, and didn't let him go. On the other bed sat Peter, combing back his dull long hair, wearing boots and jeans and a T-shirt with the sleeves and neck cut out. He had a toothpick in his mouth.

Roger asked the girls if they were frightened and they nodded carefully. "Want to come over to my house? Sit by the fire with Ed?"

They nodded again.

Roger helped Amy with her slippers. Angela got her own slippers and tried to take the blanket off the other bed, but Peter wouldn't get up. He kept combing his hair while she tugged and tugged, and kept on combing after she began to cry and pound his leg. He rolled the toothpick across his mouth.

Roger picked up Angela and said, "You coming, Peter?"

Peter shrugged. Then he stood and put the comb back into his pocket. Roger led them all down the hall and out the front door. He put them into his truck and went back inside.

Ken and Lois hadn't moved a hair. Roger said he'd take the kids to his house so Ken and Lois could work things out. Neither of them seemed to notice him. He picked up the pistol.

"I'll take this, too," he said.

Ken grunted, once.

Roger put the pistol in the pocket of his coat. The pistol was heavy; it had the weight of evidence, of proof that Ken had made a mess. It wouldn't be an easy item to retrieve.

Tina was waiting at the kitchen door when Roger carried the bundled girls up the back steps. Her face was milky and her dark eyes glittered and flickered. Her hand fluttered between her lips and the girls' heads while she spoke their names, over and over, in a pitch that reached up to cheer them. Roger had to push her aside to get into the house. Dennis stood by the phone, looking past his father out the door. Peter was still on the back steps, in his broken T-shirt, the wind restyling his hair. He had to be invited in.

"Peter! Come in, come in!" Tina said.

Peter said hi, and he and Dennis made for the stairs, already half whispering to each other. Tina called them but Roger said to let them go. The girls sat at the kitchen table, still wrapped in their bedspreads, still quietly alert, examining the kitchen and the faces of their parents' friends. Roger thought they wouldn't look much different if they'd driven all night and been brought sleeping from the car into the kitchen of a distant relative, to whom they had nothing to say.

Tina acted the aunt. She heated milk and brought cookies. She talked about how big they were and how small they used to be. She stroked their golden hair. She asked Angela if she was seven yet and managed to look awestruck by the news that Angela was eight. She asked how Angela liked second grade.

"I'm in third," said Angela.

Tina plopped down in a chair. She dropped her chin and leaned toward Angela. "You've got to be kidding!" she said. Angela smiled. Tina turned to Amy. "She's just kidding, right?" Little Amy smiled, too.

Fresh pink came forth on Tina's cheeks as she mixed big mugs of hot chocolate. Her ears began to glow like half-hearts. She questioned them tirelessly: did they like sharing a room, what did they do that weekend, did they ever get to play with the dogs, what was their favorite dinner; and she responded to their one-word answers by folding her arms beneath her breasts, and nodding, and saying, "Uh-huh, uh-huh, uh-huh." She told them secrets about herself: "You know, I like to eat cold beans for breakfast." Grins and faces of disgust. "I used to wear a wig!" She wrapped the dishtowel around her head and struck a flirty pose. "My husband"—she pointed to Roger—"thinks I'm skinny, but I weigh one-twenty-five." Angela rolled her eyes up, as if to check a list of figures in her forehead, and then looked back at Tina in shock.

They took their hot chocolate in to sit by the fire. Tina went up to get blankets for the floor. Alone with Roger, the girls were quiet again. They wouldn't meet his eye. He wanted to know what had happened, what they'd seen or heard, but he didn't need to know, it was enough to have them in his house, and they probably couldn't have told him even if he'd asked. They sat down on either side of Ed, and Roger turned down the lights and opened the stove so they could see the fire.

Ed had the noblest blood in Dane county. He was descended from a dog owned by the Duke of Sussex. Ken Johnson had borrowed money from a bank to buy Ed, and Ed had sired champions that brought four figures. Ed had made the reputation of Ken's kennel. Rich men from Chicago and Milwaukee left their dogs at Johnson's year-round; when they came to get their dogs for a hunt, they brought other rich men up to look at Ed. Then one day Ken went off his nut and clobbered Roger by the creek. It was a matter of frustration, a thousand petty losses over nearly thirty years, losses on both sides, losses that lived on in baffling emotions, not in memory or mind, and brought a big, impatient man like Ken to blows when he was hurt and didn't understand. Your old friend makes a crack about your hat, your truck, your fishing vest, and Boom! you take him out. It was something that happened with Ken; men suffer these things the way plants suffer weather, except men know. Later Ken came down with Ed and all Ed's papers to make peace.

Tina brought a book of bedtime stories that she kept with others on the dresser between bookends shaped like hands. She settled herself on the floor and started reading *Winnie-the-Pooh* to Johnson's girls. They stretched out, Amy with her head on Tina's lap, and Angela beside the dog. Tina read well, with a voice for every animal. It was dark in the room, and Roger thought of turning on a light, but then he noticed Tina wasn't looking at the page.

They laid the limp girls on the big bed in the extra room. Angela opened her eyes and fixed them on Roger, then she fit herself along her little sister's back, her arm draped over Amy's ribs, her hand curled under Amy's chin. Roger couldn't tell if she was protecting or seeking comfort. Tina sat on the edge of the bed, freed strands of yellow hair from the corner of Amy's mouth, and hooked them over her ear. She stroked the two smooth heads and whispered a prayer. "Now I lay me down to sleep; I pray the Lord my soul to keep. If I should die before I wake, I pray the Lord my soul to take." She took away her hands and sat quietly in the dark.

Roger got the gun from his coat and laid it on the kitchen table. It was a .44 Magnum, heavy and oily blue. It smelled more like a piece of machinery than a weapon. On the blue tablecloth, in the light of the hanging lamp, beneath the hanging basket of onions and potatoes, beside the white sugar bowl and the white grains of spilled sugar, the gun looked strangely domestic, like a special tool for a difficult job. Roger laid a napkin over it.

Tina came down and leaned against the stove. She'd put on her bathrobe and unpinned her hair.

"They're lovely little girls," Roger said. He pulled the chair beside his out from the table. Tina sighed, and then sat down. She crossed her legs, and Roger laid his cold hand on the leg that parted Tina's robe. He wanted her to make a perfect evening for him. Her leg was warm, and she let his hand grow warm upon it, but when he started inching up she uncrossed her legs and closed her robe. She crossed her arms and hugged herself.

"He doesn't deserve them," Roger said.

"They could do worse."

Roger glared at her. The waxy look was back on her face, the color he wanted was gone, and he felt cold for having wanted any pinkness, anything at all, from her. He pulled the napkin off the gun. "This was lying on their coffee table," he said, "pointing at them."

Tina looked at the gun for a moment. Then she reached out and spun it, like a bottle. When it stopped it was aiming at Roger. He told her the gun wasn't loaded, but he knew that it was.

Tina went up to bed. She was tired, she had to work in the morning, and all of this had taken something out of her. Roger stepped out to the back porch for a breath of the night. Johnson's lights were still on, but that meant nothing. Ken and Lois would probably sleep that way, fully lit, with plenty to hide but no kids in the house to see. They'd wake with sore, bleached eyes, feel embarrassed that they'd left on all the lights, and feel embarrassed and relieved that Roger had taken their kids for the night. He imagined Lois coming down to get them in the morning, tight from being rattled, whispering to Tina in the kitchen, thanking Tina, Tina saying Oh, you'd do the same for me, though both knew that she'd never have to.

He went into the living room and fed logs to the fire. On the stove door sill he laid a cigarette and watched it light. Ed lay on the blankets Tina had spread for the girls. Roger smoked and combed the bangs along Ed's belly, freeing loose fur and making balls and flicking them into the stove. The dog moaned. Ken was right, Roger had wrecked him. Roger kept Ed in so much that he shed out of season. He wouldn't go out in the cold of February unless Roger put a sweatshirt on him. He never ran anymore, but he still dreamed of running, moving his legs in his sleep. He still had that.

Tina was asleep when Roger lay down beside her, still dressed. It troubled him to sleep in his clothes, and some nights he liked to feel troubled. Some mornings he liked to wake fully dressed with a sense that a troubling darkness had passed in the night, and he had been ready to face it. He lay on his back and looked at Tina's ear. He wanted something to say, something soft to bring her near him, something sharp to poke into her ear, but he was mute inside and she was sleeping anyway. He sat up and looked at Tina's face. The mouth he had wanted was open. In the darkness he could see her teeth, two small flagstone paths, go down the hill into her throat.

He heard the floorboards aching in the hall. He heard water in the bathroom, and Dennis's door. He heard the boys' voices through the walls and the rugs and the bedding, indistinct, but coming, gaining confidence without getting any clearer or louder, as if the boys believed that no one was awake to listen. Roger listened. He heard them thinking they had got away with something, so he got out of bed.

Dennis's door was ajar. Roger poked it. Tina had made a pallet for Peter on the floor, but it was still smooth, so was Dennis's bed; they hadn't been used. The boys were bent over Dennis's desk, examining something under the light. They snapped to when the door opened, and when Roger stepped in Peter Johnson reached for the desktop.

"Leave it!" Roger said.

The boys closed ranks in front of the desk, so Roger had to separate them by the shoulders. Gleaming on the oak was a row of small brass nails, a line neatly laid. They were all of a type, but they weren't all alike. Some had slightly larger heads, some points were longer, more triangular, some shafts were scored. Dennis stepped away from his father and looked at the floor, but Peter Johnson didn't move. He looked at Roger with that same blank stare he'd used in his sisters' bedroom. He took out the long-handled comb and went to work on his hair.

Roger didn't like him, never had. He was a tough kid, he'd probably wreck some cars and cost his dad some money, drink and smoke and screw himself some girls, maybe spend some nights in jail before admitting to himself that there was anything to be afraid of in this world, and Roger was willing to give him all that, he deserved it, but Roger wasn't going to let him stand there in Dennis's room, in the middle of the night, and comb his hair.

Roger reached for his son's jaw and turned the pierced ear into the light. "Where the hell do you kids come up with this stuff?"

Roger turned to Peter, who still worked on his hair. When Peter raised the comb to put the teeth in at his forehead, Roger snatched it from his hand. Peter fought a smile.

"It's in the Bible," he said.

"Oh yeah? How does it work?"

Dennis looked up.

"Do you just press the nail through with your thumb?"

The boys didn't answer.

Roger closed the bedroom door and said, "Show me."

"Show you what?" Dennis asked.

"Show me how it's done. I want to see it."

Peter and Dennis looked at each other. Peter smirked and sat down on the desk. Roger grasped his arm and eased him off. "Pick one, Peter," he said. "Which one do you like? Which one would you put in your ear?"

Peter looked at Dennis, then looked down. He didn't choose, so Roger picked one for him. "Here," he said, giving Peter the nail. "What's next?" He still had Peter's arm.

The boys were quiet.

"Dennis!" Roger said. "What's next?"

Dennis stared at his father a moment. Then he said, "Open the closet door."

Roger led Peter to the closet and opened the door. "Now what?"

Dennis came over and positioned Peter on the threshold, the side of his head, from the ear back, against the doorjamb and the ear itself pressed out at right angles to the head by the molding around the doorway.

"Then," Dennis said, "you put the nail where you want it and drive it through."

Roger took Peter's nail and put its point on Peter's earlobe. "How? With a bat, with the heel of a shoe?"

"No, Dad, with a hammer."

Roger imagined Peter's pupils wedged into the corners of his eyes as sixteen ounces of clawed iron rushed at his face and then out of his field of vision along the side of his head, maybe close enough to scratch, iron and brass and cartilage and wood making a four-part thud.

"Then what?"

Dennis shrugged. "That's it."

Roger smiled: Peter Johnson, nailed to a doorpost, trying to comb his hair.

"Hold him here," Roger said. "I'll be right back."

He gave Dennis Peter's arm and went to the basement for a hammer. Ken would understand. He wouldn't understand why his son would do such a thing, but he'd understand why Roger would let him. That would make more sense to Ken than wrecking a good dog.

Both the boys were sitting on the bed. Peter's hair was hooked behind his ear and the nail lay on his hand. They looked up at Roger. He held the hammer out to Dennis.

"Here," he said. "Go ahead."

The boys looked at each other a moment. Then Dennis reached a bottle of rubbing alcohol on the floor between the desk and the bed. That was why he'd gone to the bathroom. He filled the cap and Peter dropped the nail in. The odor rallied through the room.

Peter went to the closet and Roger offered the hammer again but Dennis took a small ball-peen from his desk. "I'll use this one," Dennis said.

That seemed wrong to Roger, and he didn't know why. He caught Dennis's arm, and searched the boy's eyes, but they didn't tell him. He held his hammer up again, but that changed nothing. He let it fall to his side, and let go Dennis's arm, and stepped back.

Peter laid his ear against the edge of the molding. Dennis wet his fingers in the alcohol, and then pinched Peter's lobe. "You ready?" Dennis asked. Peter nodded slightly. Dennis put the nail in place and tapped it through. Peter winced, and then reached up behind his ear to free the nail from the wood.

And that was it. Dennis examined his work, then he and Peter smiled at one another. They shook hands. Dennis looked at Roger and said, "After while I'll bend it down with a couple pair of pliers."

Roger took his hammer back down to the basement and hung it

on the rack. He looked at his tools, all hanging in their places, neatly filling the black lines he'd traced around them. Then he put on his coat and went out.

He walked to the end of the driveway, then he turned to face his house, though he had no idea what he hoped to see. He saw that it was snowing again, flakes as full and round as dandelion heads, glowing flakes that caught whatever light the world sent up into the heavens and carried it back down. No one else was out to see the snowflakes do this, only him. He watched the snowflakes brighten his yard and house. Beyond his house the woods went dark over the ridge, and he could hear them breathe, hard and long and only when the wind blew. Without the wind the woods were still and silent.

WHY WOULD A MAN
by Emily Hammond
(University of Arizona)

The week his divorce from Gail became final, Alex witnessed a fight between two Korean women; one bit off the tip of the other's little finger and swallowed it. Aside from the timing, there was no connection between the two events. He didn't even know the Koreans, had never met them before that night, that dinner party. But there he'd been with Maureen, an old friend from college. She knew the Koreans.

That day he'd been in Santa Cruz on business, and had brought along Maureen's number in case he decided to look her up. Actually there were two numbers, which he'd copied from the address book at home, written in Gail's hand; she'd been the one to keep up with Maureen in the eight years since college.

Alex called the first number from a pay phone. No answer. He dialed the second and got an acupuncture clinic. This time he asked for Maureen and heard, "Just a minute, please."

"Hello?" she said. "Alex!" While they talked he pictured her as he'd last seen her two years ago, the same as in college, the same flyaway hair and mismatched clothes—stripes with plaids, dots with stripes—clothes bought at rummage sales that somehow looked great on Maureen.

Her only really big news, she said, was that she had shortened her name to Maura and was studying to be an acupuncturist. Alex wondered if she knew about his big news, the divorce. Since she didn't mention Gail, he assumed she did, probably through Gail herself. In any case, he wasn't about to bring it up. Instead he told Maureen—Maura—about the business, his business, this business trip: he was down from Marin to drum up more customers, more restaurants. "I wholesale vegetables to restaurants . . . remember?"

"Oh, the weird vegetables, bok choy, baby this, baby that. Baby crookneck squash?"

"Right," he said, and when the conversation slowed, he asked her out to dinner.

"I'm supposed to have dinner at Dr. Kim's," she said. "Wait a second . . ."

Alex was put on hold. Who was Dr. Kim? He deposited another quarter, wishing he had phrased the invitation differently. It wasn't meant as a date; he just wanted to have dinner with an old friend. Ever since the divorce he'd been feeling nostalgic, lonesome, cut off. Divorced. The word was like cold steel, and he envisioned himself with a bad shave, ill-fitting clothes, frayed collars. But there was nothing wrong with his shave or his clothes. They weren't falling apart, certainly not his shirts, and Gail had never been the type to see after his clothes anyway. *He* felt frayed, that was it, as though his neck, his skin, could unravel like fabric.

"Alex?" He pressed the receiver to his ear more tightly. "You're invited too. Dinner at Dr. Kim's, how does that sound? I can give you directions here."

"Who is Dr. Kim?"

"What? Oh. This is her clinic." As though he ought to know. "Didn't I tell you? I'm studying here, under her supervision." Maura then gave him directions to the clinic, which he jotted down on the back of his motel receipt. Following an afternoon at restaurants—two French, one seafood, one health food place—Alex headed over to the clinic. Maura's directions were needlessly complicated; he finally threw them aside and consulted a map.

The clinic was in a medical building. He gave his name to the receptionist and almost didn't recognize Maura when she passed by: white coat, rubber gloves, her flyaway hair cut short, smooth, parted on the side. She was carrying a tray of needles which, she explained, had just come out of the sterilizer. "Be right back," she said, and when she returned, minus the gloves and needles, they hugged each other. She offered to show him around the clinic.

"I can even give you a treatment," she said.

"For what?"

"Anything. Allergies, headaches, back trouble, nerves. Anything."

He passed on the treatment—he didn't like needles—but accepted the tour. While explaining the basics of acupuncture Maura showed him the sterilizer, the needles sorted by size. They peered into several examination rooms which didn't seem much different from any doctor's. Then she opened another door. Inside was a fat man lying on a table, needles sticking out of him like a pin cushion. The needles were attached to wires, hooked up to a machine.

"What's he being treated for?" Alex whispered.

"Various things, obesity mostly." She closed the door.

"What about the machine? What's that do?"

She was about to answer when a tall Oriental woman approached them in the hallway. "Dr. Kim," Maura said, touching her sleeve. "This is Alex."

Dr. Kim held out her hand and shook it. "You're having dinner at my house," she said, and let his hand drop. Deliberately. Her eyes were dark and unreceptive. "Excuse me," she said, and went into the fat man's room, closing the door.

Alex stared after her, insulted. Why had she acted that way? He turned to Maura—hadn't she noticed? She was describing how the machine warmed the needles, sent gentle waves of electricity throughout the body. "In the old days," she said, "they vibrated the needles by hand." Alex barely listened. The last thing he wanted was to have dinner at Dr. Kim's. But when he tried to figure a way out, some last-minute excuse, he felt exhausted, physically weak. In the past year he'd come to associate this feeling with Gail, to blame her for it. Before their separation he'd been cheerful and energetic enough, despite Gail's continual depressions, or maybe because of them. Then she'd moved out, leaving him with nothing but the furniture and a damp spirit. He couldn't help hating her for it even though he still, unfortunately, loved her.

Alex trailed after Maura without really seeing her, down the hallway, following only the heels of her shoes, the sound of her voice. She talked about Dr. Kim, how she was not only an acupuncturist but a medical doctor as well, how her parents had emigrated from Korea shortly after Dr. Kim was born.

"She was a genius as a child," Maura said, "a prodigy." Alex imagined Dr. Kim emerging from the womb, a fully developed adult, complete with medical degrees.

Exchanging her white coat for a sweater, Maura said that Dr. Kim had taught her so much, *so much* about the workings of the body, the workings of the mind. "She's given me a sense of direction," she said, leading Alex out to the parking lot. He felt momentarily comforted by her baggy green sweater with its design of footballs across the back; this was the Maura, the Maureen he knew. She turned to face him. "Do you know what I mean?"

"Sort of."

Maura wanted to stop by her place to change, so Alex followed her there in his car. They parked in an alley and walked through a small courtyard littered with potted plants in various stages of decay.

"Those are my herbs, and that"—Maura pointed to a tiny, weed-infested plot—"that's my vegetable garden."

Alex glanced at the sliding glass doors of her apartment. A huge, hairy animal stood on its hind legs, licking the glass. "Is that a dog?"

"Dog? Oh, the dog. That's Rex. Do you grow vegetables?"

People always asked him that, assuming that since he sold vegetables, he grew them too. "No," he said, "no time or interest." He was working ten, twelve hours a day and besides, why grow vegetables when he could have his pick from the warehouse? He wished Maura would hurry up and unlock the door. Her bug-eyed dog made him nervous; barking and howling, it pounded its paws on the glass as though any minute it might come crashing through. When finally she did open the door, the dog jumped up on Alex, paws on his shoulders, wagging, drooling, licking.

"Down!" Maura pulled the dog off. "He's been cooped up all day, I'd better walk him. You go on in."

Except for the futon mat on the floor, there was no place to sit, so Alex wandered around noticing the clothes in the bookcase and the books in the boxes. Typical Maureen. In college she had owned so many secondhand clothes she'd kept them in plastic bags under her bed, and she would be forever digging out some choice item to give you—a gold lamé scarf, black clumpy shoes from the fifties, a man's shirt with five species of birds all over it. "Here, take it," she'd say. Once, when she heard that he and Gail were thinking of getting married, she rummaged around and pulled out a gaudy satin wedding gown with a six-foot-long train. Both of them winced. As it turned out, they didn't get married for another six years. They lived together all that time, and when they did finally marry, it was only to separate a year later. In fact, the wedding dress incident had marked the beginning of Gail's indecision about their marriage, about him. She was the most indecisive person he had ever known. Deciding what to do on any given day was almost more than she could handle, and he sometimes thought the first and only decision of her life had been to leave him.

Alex opened the refrigerator, hoping for a beer or soda or juice, and was confronted by a multitude of small paper bags. Looking inside one, he saw a white hunk of something. Old cheese? He wasn't about to smell it. The only drinkable item in the refrigerator was a yellow viscous liquid in an unmarked jar. He drank water instead, rinsing out the glass first.

Maura was still a lousy housekeeper, that much hadn't changed. There were dog hairs on the futon, dustballs in the corners. In that way, she and Gail were alike, although Gail wasn't filthy, just disorganized. Wherever she went, clutter followed. She would announce she was going to clean out a closet, and hours later he'd find her lost in a pile of clothes, books, papers, and boxes, vaguely reading letters, on the verge of tears. "I feel so overwhelmed," she'd say, her small white face tense and frightened, the face of a misplaced child; he'd always loved that face. It was true that once Gail left, there was a lot less clutter—Alex had been the superior housekeeper—but now the house was falling apart in ways he'd never anticipated. The roof leaked, the floors had warped, and recently there'd been an invasion of mice. He could find the droppings but not the mice. Although he'd set traps everywhere, he had yet to catch a single mouse.

On Maura's wall were two posters: the human body, front and back, speckled with red dots. Examining the dots more closely, Alex saw they were connected by lines, like a map of a subway system.

"Pressure points," said Maura when she returned. That's where the body stored toxins, she explained. If not released through acupuncture or massage, they would build to unhealthy levels. "Toxins contaminate the body," she said, "and that's what makes us sick." To Alex the theory seemed absurd, as though the body were a kind of toxic waste dump.

Then, without warning, Maura said, "I'm sorry to hear about your divorce."

So she did know. Alex braced himself for yet another discussion of his personal life. What happened? How's Gail taking it? Do you still see each other? Any chance you'll get back together? Are you seeing anybody else? All the stupid, useless questions people asked. Relatives, friends, people he hardly knew. Sometimes they even said, "Don't feel you have to talk about it." But that was exactly what they wanted, for him to talk about it.

Before Maura could ask any questions, he asked her a few. Impersonal questions. How did she like living in Santa Cruz? Had she met a lot of people? How did she like her apartment? Would she stay here or move?

"Move," she said. "It's the dog, he needs more room. He's not a puppy anymore."

While Maura changed in the bathroom, Alex watched the dog as it roamed the courtyard, knocking over pots left and right, urinating on the vegetables. When she came out, he barely recognized her. Again. Except for the sweater with the footballs, she must have thrown away her wild, rummage-sale clothes. What she had on now was disappointing, almost depressing: some drab green outfit, matching blouse and pants, and those black, rubber-soled Chinese shoes that everyone wore these days.

Maura locked the dog inside and they left. She drove too fast—up, down, around hills, along cracked paved roads with soft shoulders and muddy potholes. Although it hadn't rained, everything was dripping, green, soggy, wet. "They don't get a lot of sun back here," Maura said at the base of the steepest hill yet. She floored it, wheels spinning, mud flying: up a dirt road not much wider than a path, barely enough room for a car, so overgrown with trees it was like driving through a beaver's nest, the branches so low they scraped the roof of the car.

"Wait'll you see Dr. Kim's house," she said as they passed an apple orchard, then a clearing. "There's a view of the ocean, the hills, the valleys. . . ."

Alex didn't see the house at first. It was sunk into the side of a hill, and they had to walk down some stairs to get there. Maura went in without knocking and Alex followed, into the kitchen, where Dr. Kim stood between two other Orientals, a man and a woman. The woman was much shorter than Dr. Kim, with shiny clipped hair, and the man was somewhere between their heights. He had on a dark suit, white socks, and sandals. Introductions were made by Dr. Kim, who then led them into the living room. Alex didn't quite catch the names of the man and woman, and when he asked Maura to repeat the names she whispered instead, "He's Dr. Kim's ex-husband and that's his wife. They're all good friends."

In the living room were two couches at a right angle, a coffee table, a large picture window, bare walls. On the table were five glasses of white wine and another bottle, newly opened. Alex sat next to Maura on one couch, while Dr. Kim and her ex-husband and his wife—whatever their names were—sat on the other. Alex considered asking Maura for their names again, but she seemed so engrossed in the conversation, some of which was in a foreign language, that he decided not to bother. Since nobody included him in the conversation and he didn't speak Korean, assuming the language *was* Korean, Alex gazed out the window. The view was spectacular: dark hills rolling out to the distant ocean, a pink sky, the sunset. It almost hurt to look at the horizon, it was so red, like something inflamed.

Already the wine had gone to his head. He was tired, hungry, and he couldn't get situated on the couch. It was the type with a low back and too many pillows—you either slumped back among them or sat up like a board. Straightening up, Alex turned his attention back to the conversation, the English part at least, only to find himself staring at the little woman. Compared to Dr. Kim she was tiny, a toy woman, yet not delicate or sweet. She was perched on the edge of the couch like a brittle doll, her wineglass poised on a kneecap the size of a silver dollar. From what Alex could gather, she was some kind of teacher, while *Mr.* Kim—he couldn't help thinking of him as Mr. Kim—was apparently a lawyer. The two of them, along with Dr. Kim, seemed to be discussing their respective students, clients, and patients, though clearly Dr. Kim dominated the conversation. For some reason Alex was surprised to hear Dr. Kim talk in Korean, and surprised whenever the little woman or Mr.

Kim spoke in English. Maura didn't say a word, only listened with a rapt expression. As if *she* could understand Korean. Alex was annoyed: since they could all speak English, why didn't they?

And the invitation had been for dinner, hadn't it? Or were they going to sit here all night drinking wine? He poured himself another glass, finishing off the bottle. Instantly Mr. Kim hopped up and went into the kitchen, returning with a new bottle which, strangely, he placed next to Alex. What was this, some kind of hint? Alex put his glass down and looked at Mr. Kim, who smiled back politely and stationed himself by the other couch.

All conversation had stopped, all faces turned to Dr. Kim. What were they waiting for? Alex noticed her charcoal gray suit, her long yet coarse fingers. At last she spoke to him, her dark eyes somehow deliberate, as deliberate as when she had dropped his hand earlier that day. "What is it that you do, Alex?"

"I'm a wholesaler," he said. "I sell vegetables to restaurants."

"Exotic vegetables," Maura added, as if that detail would make a difference. Surprisingly, it did. Everyone smiled, even Dr. Kim.

"Tell them," said Maura.

He started by listing the vegetables he sold. Bok choy, baby okra and artichokes, baby crookneck squash, Italian tomatoes, certain varieties of mushrooms: oyster, shiitake, chanterelles. . . . He had always liked talking about his vegetables. He felt an affection for their names, their odd shapes and sizes, their tastes. And, he considered them superior to what most people thought of as vegetables—green beans, corn, carrots, iceberg lettuce, dull and ordinary. Next he described the mechanics of wholesaling: the delivery trucks, the early morning phone calls, the farmers, the chefs. Before he knew it, he was explaining how he'd gotten into wholesaling vegetables in the first place. The summers in his father's markets, the double major in business and botany, the MBA, the stint at the L.A. Produce Market, the start-up funds and business loans. A distinct wave of drunkenness passed through him. Though he didn't slur his words, he felt dizzy, boozy, as if his organs had come unmoored. *Floating kidney*. The phrase dipped and swayed in his mind. *Floating kidney*. Wasn't that a disease? He paused, more than ready for someone to interrupt, ask a question, change the subject. But they all looked at him, waiting, expectant. He realized he was in the middle of a sentence, only he couldn't remember which sentence.

"Go on," Dr. Kim said.

"I forgot what I was—"

"You were talking about a loan."

"Oh." Reluctantly he picked up where he had left off: once he'd secured a loan, he moved the business out of his garage and into a dilapidated warehouse. He brought the subject back around to the present, his current warehouse, the long hours, the risks involved, his plans to expand into supermarkets. Never had he talked so much about this one subject, his business. He wondered why he kept *on* talking, why couldn't he stop? He tried to read the faces of the others; weren't they bored yet? But their faces were blank. He noticed the hair of all three women, cut in exactly the same style—parted on the left, the hair no longer than their chins. The effect made him stop talking. He simply stopped.

"In short," said Dr. Kim, "you're a middleman. That's all you're really trying to say."

Alex leaned back against the pillows. Everything the woman said came out like an insult. "If you want to be simplistic about it, yes. I'm a middleman."

There was a long silence.

"Why?" Dr. Kim said.

"Why what?"

"Why do you do what you do?"

"I like it," he said. "I like to think of people—" He shifted on the couch. "I like to think of people sitting in restaurants, eating my vegetables."

"How humble," she said.

Alex glanced around at the others for a clue. What was going on here? Maura was absolutely no help. There she sat, head in hand, elbow on knee, gazing into space. And over by the couch stood Mr. Kim; in all this time he hadn't moved. As for his wife, the little woman, she merely tapped her tiny high-heeled shoe and sipped at her wine.

"Why would a man sell vegetables he doesn't grow?" said Dr. Kim. "You don't grow them, do you?"

"No. Am I supposed to?"

"Why would a man sell vegetables he doesn't grow?"

"I don't want to *grow* the vegetables, I want to sell them—"

"Exactly," she said.

"Exactly?" Alex looked again at the others. No one defended him, certainly not Maura, who acted as if Dr. Kim's question were wise indeed, one they would all do well to consider. "How do you think restaurants get their vegetables? Do you think the chefs go out and pick them by hand? I sell vegetables to restaurants, I provide a service. Do you have a problem with that?"

"I'm only asking a question," Dr. Kim said. "Why would a man sell vegetables he doesn't grow?"

"Why would a doctor, a woman, stick needles into people?"

Dr. Kim laughed, a laugh that indicated she thought it a clever, if irrelevant, question, one that needed no reply. "Really, you take my questions too seriously." And with that, Dr. Kim stood up.

Maura whispered to Alex, "She likes to invent questions."

"I don't think she likes to hear the answers," he said, as Dr. Kim left the room, followed by Mr. Kim, who in turn was followed by the little woman.

"That means it's time to eat," Maura explained.

"What is this, a religious cult?"

He apologized immediately; Maura looked so hurt. And as they went into the kitchen, Alex thought about the way Dr. Kim's ex-husband had followed her out of the room. Soundless in his Hush Puppy sandals, like a goddamn houseboy. He pitied the man for ever having been married to Dr. Kim. He could just imagine it, being put on trial for various minor offenses, day in, day out. "Yes," she would say, "but why would a man leave wet towels on a door when he could hang them on a towel rack?"

"Vegetables," Dr. Kim announced, pulling the lid from the steaming pot on the stove.

"She grows them herself," Maura told Alex.

"I figured." He could just picture the vegetables from her garden, like most homegrown vegetables: small, pale, bug-eaten, pathetic.

Serving up plates of brown rice and vegetables smothered in sauce, Dr. Kim passed them around as though to recipients in a soup line. Then they all marched out to the dining room. Dr. Kim presided over the meal while the others, aside from nipping at their wine now and then, huddled down into their plates, eating quickly, furtively. Not Alex. He sat across from Dr. Kim and deliberately picked at his food. The vegetables were ordinary, overcooked, and overwhelmed by Dr. Kim's phlegmlike cheese sauce. Then he tasted something delicious, unexpected: an oyster mushroom. He found another and held it up on his fork. "I suppose you grow these too?" he asked Dr. Kim.

"Here in this house, as a matter of fact," she said. "Most people think they're grown only outside, under trees. But you, of course, know better."

As she described in detail how she had converted one bathroom into a small mushroom farm, Alex wondered about the others. Surely they had heard all this before, though you'd never guess from the way Maura leaned forward in her chair, as if receiving divine knowledge. Mr. Kim was as passive as always. But when he caught Alex's eye, he smiled. It was like a reflex; whenever he looked at Alex, he smiled. Only the little woman appeared bored, dinging the side of her wineglass with her tiny, sharp, manicured nails. Then she shifted her eyes without moving her head, back and forth, between Dr. Kim and Alex, back and forth, like a cat.

"You claim to sell mushrooms," Dr. Kim was saying now. "But the mushroom is not a vegetable, it's a fungus of the class Basidiomycetes."

"I'm well aware of that," said Alex, though he hadn't known the exact name of the class. Did the woman have to be an expert on everything? Fortunately, she didn't make an issue of it. Instead she rose from the table and invited Alex to see her mushrooms.

Leaving the others to clean up, Dr. Kim led him into another part of the house, past bedrooms and studies lined with books, to a dimly lit bathroom. In the tub and along the walls were shelves of mushrooms, growing in trays of dirt or blocks of compressed sawdust. Alex waited for the lecture to begin, for Dr. Kim to tell him that mushrooms were a source of protein or prevented cancer, something along that line. But she hardly said a word, other than to point out the two types she grew: the common mushroom found in any market and the oyster.

While she busied herself in the room, Alex examined her oyster mushrooms, admiring their curved stalks and creamy pearl gray caps, soft as eyelids. Of all the mushrooms he sold, the oyster was his favorite. It wasn't tough and meaty like the shiitake but tender, almost helplessly delicate. Alex was enjoying himself for the first time that night. He even felt a certain affinity with Dr. Kim, a feeling that she too liked this room with its moist, clammy odor, the smell that only mushrooms have, of things growing fast, faster than nature intended. He watched as she went from shelf to shelf, misting the mushrooms with water. Then she examined them individually, touching a cap or stalk here and there, as though checking cribs in a nursery.

"Look." She held out a block of tiny oyster mushrooms, their heads like pins. They had just begun to fruit but were shriveling up around the edges. "Look," she said.

Alex saw the dark rot forming on the crust of the block and all at once felt an ache, pity for these mushrooms that couldn't take care of themselves but depended on Dr. Kim for survival. Sensing her eyes on him, he felt compelled to ask, "How long have you been growing mushrooms?"

"A long time," she said, "a very long time."

The answer had a strange effect on him. It was all that an answer should be: sad and human, elegant and true. Also, the answer made him feel that Dr. Kim understood him and that up until now, he had misunderstood her. And in still another sense, the answer made him want to seek protection, though he couldn't say why.

In any case, when Dr. Kim suggested they join the others in the living room, Alex followed, docile and trusting. But when he actually saw the others—Mr. Kim and the little woman on one couch, Maura on the floor in front of them—he didn't know whether to trust Dr. Kim or not. Why should he? After the way she had acted all night?

Alex sat down beside her. Exactly where she *told* him to sit, he noticed. She poured him a glass of wine and he drank it. She poured him another glass and he drank that too. He began to think he was in love with her. What was the matter with him anyway? He thought of *The Wizard of Oz:* "Are you a good witch or a bad witch?" That's what he wanted to know, was she good or bad?

He could certainly understand why Maura had fallen under her spell. The woman was charismatic, larger than life. He looked at her now, the way she monopolized the conversation with her voice, her hands, and how the others appeared to sway beneath the movements of her long, ringless fingers. He too was swaying. You're drunk, he told himself. There was something he wanted to tell Dr.

Kim, he didn't know what. As if able to sense this, she turned to
him, the pillows molding themselves around her like obedient pets.
"Tell me about your wife," she said.

"Ex-wife." Not this, he didn't want to talk about this.

"Maura told me," she said.

"Told you what?"

"About your divorce."

He couldn't believe the woman's audacity, but what he really
couldn't believe was that he was going to tell her all about it. And
that in the end, he would be grateful to her for getting this information
out of him. He told her about the two incidents that bothered him
most. The first had occurred the night before the wedding, at the
rehearsal dinner. Getting to the dinner was bad enough. He'd come
home from work to find Gail standing at the door naked, a mascara
wand in her hand. "All afternoon I've been trying to put on
makeup," she said. She was beautiful like that, naked, but a wreck.
"I have to wear makeup, how can I not wear makeup? How can we
get married? I don't even know how to put on makeup." Once he
supervised the putting on of makeup and got her into her dress—she
almost left the house without her slip, and her dress was see-
through—they'd driven to the rehearsal dinner, fighting all the way.

"About nothing," he told Dr. Kim. At the dinner Gail had been
so nervous that she went around telling everyone she might not show
up the next day. They thought she was kidding but no, she insisted
she was perfectly serious. He would never forget the faces of his
family, his friends. Confused, embarrassed. He felt they would never
forgive him for being such a fool.

Here Alex paused, though Dr. Kim didn't ask questions. She
listened. He mentioned, because he thought he should, that the
wedding had gone fine, although both he and Gail looked like ghosts
in the pictures. The other incident had happened six months ago,
around the time the divorce papers were being drawn up. Gail had
come over to discuss *something,* as she put it. Secretly he hoped for
a reconciliation but no, she had a list of things she wanted from the
house, a couch in particular. He refused to give her the couch. She
could have everything else, but not that. He loved that couch; it was
covered in a peach-rose fabric. She threw a tantrum until finally he
gave in. And when she got her way, instead of being pleased, she
broke a bottle of wine on the floor—

Dr. Kim interrupted. "Did you tell her you loved her?"

"That night?"

"Any night."

"Of course," he said, and went on with his story. What bothered him most, he told Dr. Kim, was the look of hatred on her face, especially when she broke the bottle. He had tried to give her everything before and during their marriage, and when she wanted a divorce, he gave her that too. The more he did for her, the more he tried to make her happy, the more she hated him. "People like me," he said, "can't make people like Gail happy."

"Did you tell her you loved her?"

"Why do you keep asking me that? Of course I told her I loved her; I did everything I knew how to do—"

"But did you tell her?"

"*Yes,* I told her. I told her and told her."

"Why would a man—"

"Don't ask me that—"

"Why would a man divorce a woman he loves?"

"Because she wanted it that way, all right?"

"But why would a—"

"Stop asking me questions! What are you, my analyst? First you want to know why I sell vegetables instead of grow them, or some stupid thing, *now* you want to know—" He stood up. The others watched him, interested. "What *I* want to know is why do you want to know?"

Dr. Kim got up and started to leave the room. "Wait a minute," Alex said, "I want to ask you a question."

"Yes?"

"When I met you at the clinic today, why did you let go of my hand like that?"

"Because it was cold and white."

Alex sat down on the couch, his body heavy, sinking into the pillows. "Maura," said Dr. Kim, "why not give your friend a back rub?"

Maura hopped to her feet as if glad to be of service. To Dr. Kim, not Alex. Still, he allowed her to lead him over to a rug not far from the couches. She asked him to remove his shirt and lie down on his stomach, and he complied, thinking of all the things he could say to her about Dr. Kim. The woman was a tyrant who enjoyed dissecting people's brains, it was as simple as that. And you're just her dumb little handmaiden, he wanted to tell Maura. But he was too worn out to say anything. Never had a back rub felt so soothing.

Then he heard tense, angry, foreign voices, the voices of Dr. Kim and the little woman. From where he lay, Alex could see them arguing on the couch with Mr. Kim between them. They leaned across him, almost growling, while Mr. Kim sat placidly as though listening to nothing more taxing than a difficult passage of music. And judging from the feel of Maura's hands on his back, she too was undisturbed. The voices settled into a low rumble for a while, then rose to a screeching.

"What are they fighting about?" said Alex, trying to get up despite Maura's sitting on his back.

"We're discussing vegetables," said Dr. Kim, to which the little woman added, "None of your business!"

"Shouldn't we leave?" Alex asked Maura.

"Dr. Kim likes me to stay."

"What's that supposed to mean? Is it always like this around here?"

She eased his shoulders back down onto the rug, saying only, "I have the greatest faith in Dr. Kim." She started the back rub all over again, going from his neck to his tailbone, concentrating on his shoulder blades. "Please try to relax," she said. That was the crazy thing. Despite the racket, he did relax—his muscles simply gave up fighting. In time he even got used to the voices, the volume rising and falling; there was a certain music to it all. He began to doze, only to be awakened by Maura jabbing her fingers into his backbone, as if she were trying to disconnect the vertebrae.

"What are you doing!"

"Pressure point massage," she said. "It hurts because of the toxins."

It hurt like hell. What was in there that could cause so much pain? What were toxins anyway? He imagined the line of pressure points up and down his back, little bulbs filled to bursting, pus and words and bitterness. He heard a voice inside his head, a singsong voice he dreaded. Why would a man divorce a woman he loves? Because he doesn't really love her. No, no, too simple. It was more complicated than that. Too complicated. He listened to Dr. Kim and the little woman, their unintelligible words rising, falling, rising, the perfect background for his thoughts. Sometimes shrill, sometimes plaintive, their voices became figures in his mind, nasty Oriental nymphs, bleached white, bodies naked, yelping, screeching, howling, keening, all the sounds of love.

Dazed, he opened his eyes. The little woman was hurling a vase; it hit the wall and shattered. She screamed in the face of Dr. Kim, who yowled back in Korean, while the odd Mr. Kim remained on the couch, peering about like a bird. The little woman picked up something else to throw, a dish. Mr. Kim rose to his feet and gently removed it from her hands. He spoke soothing words to both women, then returned to the couch. The women embraced, and the little woman brought Dr. Kim's hand to her cheek, kissing the fingers.

The next thing Alex knew he was on his knees, searching for the tip of Dr. Kim's little finger. Everyone had rushed at the little woman, but she held fast with her teeth. And nobody knew that the little woman had actually swallowed the tip of Dr. Kim's little finger, until she made a point of telling Alex, who continued to grope around on the floor, thinking perhaps she'd been mistaken.

Then Alex was speeding to the hospital in a car, holding on to Dr. Kim in the backseat while Maura drove. Dr. Kim's face was chalk white, and she had a kitchen towel wrapped around her finger, but she was talking, conjugating verbs in German, French, and Spanish. She said it felt better to talk. Actually she was in better shape than Alex. He couldn't stop thinking about the tip of Dr. Kim's little finger. You'd think it was *his* finger. Dr. Kim herself said it would be fine, all she needed were a few stitches. Alex had to keep reminding himself—it wasn't the whole finger, it wasn't half, or even a third, one-fourth, or one-eighth of Dr. Kim's little finger. It was probably less than one-sixteenth: a tiny bit of the nail, no bone loss, only the very, very tip. Still, he could not stop thinking about the tip of Dr. Kim's little finger. He felt attached to it somehow, even now as it lay in the pit of the little woman's stomach. He considered: if I'm attached to the tip of Dr. Kim's little finger and the tip of Dr. Kim's finger is inside the little woman's stomach, then I'm attached to the lining of that stomach. Circular logic, but he felt better, more connected to all living things.

LOOKING FOR JOHNNY
by A. M. Homes
(University of Iowa)

I disappeared a few years ago; I disappeared and then I came back. It wasn't a big secret. It wasn't one of those beam-me-up-Scotty deals where I was here and then all of the sudden I was there. I didn't get to go to another planet or anything. I was gone for a few days and then I came home and the police wanted to know everything. They wanted to know about the car, who was in the car, where I went, what happened. They said I could draw pictures, show them with dolls, but I didn't know what to say. I disappeared when I was a child. I disappeared when I was nine.

I came home from school, had cookies and Kool-Aid, and went into the living room to watch TV. My retarded sister Rayanne was in there and she kept imitating the people on TV. She was older than me and really was retarded. She kept talking to the television and didn't stop when I told her to. Finally, I couldn't stand it anymore so I left. I said, " 'Bye, Mom, be back in a while,'' and I picked up my basketball and went to the playground. There were other kids there and almost everyone had their own ball. There were about ten balls going and sometimes they would hit each other in midair and go off in completely the wrong direction. Sometimes I'd trip over another guy going in for a shot and he might kick me in the butt and say "Asshole," or something.

It got late and it got dark and the other kids left one by one or sometimes in twos and threes. I was alone on the court shooting baskets, and I couldn't miss. The ball kept dropping through the net and I felt like I had magic in me. I was making all my shots, counting them to myself. When I got to fifteen in a row, I heard someone clap. I stopped playing and noticed a guy standing at the far edge of the court.

"That's fifteen straight up," he said. I shrugged. I shot again and the ball sailed through the hoop.

"Nice going, Johnny."

I caught the ball coming through the hoop and put up a hook shot. It went wide. The guy ran in, caught the ball, and held it pressed into his hip, like a teacher confiscating it.

"My name's not Johnny."

"Johnny's not a name. It's like 'hey you,' only nicer."

He bounced the ball a couple of times and then held it. "You ready to go? Your mother said I should pick you up. She had somewhere to go."

I remember being mad at my mother because she was like that. She was the kind of person who would take Rayanne somewhere and send someone I didn't know to pick me up. She knew lots of people I didn't know, mostly on account of Rayanne. She knew all the people who had retarded kids and I never wanted to meet them.

"I was looking for you, Johnny," the guy said.

I shrugged. "My name's Erol. Okay? Erol," I said.

He kept my basketball and walked towards his car. It was an old white station wagon, a Rambler with a red interior.

"Did she have to take my sister somewhere?"

"It's okay, Johnny. We'll stop at McDonald's."

He talked like he didn't hear anything I said. He talked like it was something he had to practice in order to get it right.

"Are you hungry?"

I'm not retarded. If something had been really strange, like if the guy had a wooden leg, I would have noticed. I would have gotten up from the table and walked away. I would have walked when he got up and said he was going to call my mom. He said he was calling to ask if she wanted us to bring home food for them. He left me at the table with burgers and fries and I thought more about how many of his fries I could steal than whether or not I was ever going home again. I had no reason to leave; I was at McDonald's with two burgers, large fries, and a shake. I didn't know what crazy was. I didn't know that sometimes you can't tell the difference between a real crazy and a regular person and that's what makes them crazy in the first place.

The guy came back, said my mother wasn't home, and that he was going to take me to his house until she got back. "Hey, hey, Johnny," the guy said. In the car I played with my basketball. I turned it around and around on my lap.

"I have to pick up something. Is that okay, Johnny? Do you want anything?" I shook my head. "Is there anything you want?"

"No," I said.

I waited while he went into the drugstore. It was one of those times when the sun goes down but it isn't dark yet. There was a weird blue light pressing down on everything, outlining it. I stood next to the station wagon and bounced the basketball.

"Hello, Erol," Mrs. Perkins said. She was pushing a grocery cart across the parking lot even though you weren't supposed to. She was pushing the cart and it sounded louder than a train. The wheels kept going all over the place. Her two kids were there, squished into the little seat up front that barely holds one.

"Hi," I said as she passed me.

"Are you with your mother?" she asked. Mrs. Perkins lived three doors down and thought that everything that had anything to do with anyone on our street was her own personal business.

"I'm waiting for a friend of hers."

Mrs. Perkins shook her head and started pushing the cart again. My mother always said that Mrs. P. didn't like us because there wasn't a man in our house. She didn't think that it was right and my mother agreed with her. My mother thought there should be a man in the house, but after my father left she couldn't find one. I think it was because of Rayanne. No good guy would want to live in a house with a retarded kid.

"Who was that?" the guy asked when he got back into the car. "Don't you know not to talk to strangers?" He slammed the door.

"It was Mrs. Perkins. She lives on my street. She has two little kids. She's not a stranger.'' The guy didn't answer and we drove away real fast.

"I've got a little something for you, Johnny," he said. He pulled a bottle out of a paper bag. "Preventive medicine. You look like you might be coming down with something."

"I feel okay," I said.

"We don't have a spoon, so you'll just have to take it from the bottle cap."

"I'm not sick."

"Look," the guy said. He took his eyes off the road to look at me and the car swerved into the other lane, the wrong-direction lane. "If I tell you to take your medicine, you take it. I'm not used to children talking back to me. Your parents might stand for it, but I won't. Got it?"

I wanted to tell him that I didn't have parents, that my dad didn't even live with us, and didn't he know that, but I couldn't. It seemed like he was already annoyed with me. I figured it was because my mother wasn't home, he couldn't just drop me off, and now he was stuck taking me everywhere with him.

He put the bottle between his legs and twisted the top until it opened. "Four capfuls," he said, handing the bottle to me. Even though I felt fine, I did it. It was hard as hell to pour it in the car and I was scared I'd spill, but I did it. I swallowed the stuff. Cough medicine, grape only worse. It tasted like the smell of the stuff my mother used to polish the furniture. "Good," the guy said. He pulled a Kit-Kat bar out of his shirt pocket and handed it to me. "To clear the taste."

We were quiet and he kept driving. It was dark. I watched the cars coming towards us, two white eyes, staring me down.

"Is my mom home yet?" I asked. I was getting tired.

"I called her from the drugstore and she said not to bring you home tonight. I think she wanted to be alone."

"What about Rayanne?"

"Alone with Rayanne. She needed you out of her hair for a while, no big deal."

I shrugged and thought about how much I hated retards, and how they stole the whole show for nothing.

"Where do you live?" I asked.

"We'll be there in a while."

"I'm tired," I said. "And I'm supposed to color maps for Geography."

"Don't worry, Johnny."

"What's your name?"

"Randy," he said.

And then I don't know what happened. I had my head out the window and felt sick from burgers, fries, shakes, and candy. I was throwing up out the car window while Randy was driving and he didn't even pull over. He didn't put his hand on my forehead like my mother did. He just kept driving and calling me Johnny.

"Wake up, Johnny," Randy said, shaking my shoulder.

It took me a few minutes to get my eyes to stay open, to remember where I was. "Here you go," he said, pushing a spoon of the same grape medicine into my mouth.

"It makes me sick," I said, after I'd swallowed the stuff. I told myself that I'd never swallow it again. I told myself to hold it in my mouth, in my cheek like a hamster, but not to swallow.

"I said you were sick. You didn't listen, did you?" He brought me a glass of water. "Do you want some tea, some toast, some ginger ale?"

I shrugged and felt dizzy.

"You have to eat," he said, and then left the room.

I lay in the bed and felt like I would pass out just lying there. I realized that I was almost naked. I wasn't wearing any clothes—except my underwear—and I thought about how my mother told us, especially Rayanne, to be careful of people who might want to mess with you. She said that anyone could be a person who would do a thing like that. She said it might even be someone I knew. She told me this a million times, but never said anything about what if someone took off your clothes while you were asleep. She never mentioned that and still I knew I didn't like it. I sat up and saw my clothes all folded up at the end of the bed. I saw them and thought everything was okay because someone who folds your clothes up and puts them on the end of the bed doesn't seem like the kind of person who would mess with a kid. I reached down, grabbed my clothes, and put them on under the covers.

"Hey, Johnny," Randy said when he came back into the room.

He was carrying a tray made out of cardboard. On the tray was a plate of eggs and toast and a glass of juice.

"I'm sick, I can't eat."

"Oh, but you have to eat, you're a growing boy."

"I want to go home."

"Your mother won't want you back if you're sick."

"She'll take care of me."

"Don't be a baby, Johnny."

"Today's my day to collect lunch money," I said.

"You said you were sick. Do you go to school when you're sick? Don't play games with me. Eat your breakfast."

I shook my head.

"What did I tell you to do?" he yelled. The veins in his neck popped out and he went white like sugar. "You do what I tell you and never say no to me, you hear. Never say no to me."

I looked at Randy and thought about how some people were jerks. I thought about how I couldn't wait to be grown up, to have my own private TV, to be alone always. "Now, what did I tell you?"

"Eat the breakfast," I said.

"So do it."

"I'm allergic to eggs." I took small bites of the toast.

"Are you really allergic?" he asked. "Do you want cereal? There are some Rice Krispies in the kitchen. Do you want Krispies?"

"No." I paused. "I want to call my mother and tell her I'm sick. She'll come get me."

"I don't have a phone, Johnny. There isn't a phone."

Randy stood there watching me. He watched everything I did like I was something under a microscope. "Do you like to read?" I shrugged. He pulled a stack of old magazines out from under the bed. "I saved these for you. I have to do some work outside. Is there anything you need?"

"Where's the TV?"

"Don't say television to me. It'll kill you. It makes you so you can't think. Can you think, Johnny?"

I shrugged and he walked out. Randy's magazines were the slippery kind that parents read. They were the kind that Rayanne would spread out all over the floor of the dentist's office and then go skiing on until my mother stopped her. I got out of bed and walked down the hall. The first room was Randy's. It was small and filled with light. There were two windows and a breeze was leaking in from somewhere. The air seemed to spin around, picking up dirt from the floor, making it dance and glow like gold. There was a mattress with green striped sheets, and rows of empty soda bottles, alternating Yoo-hoo, RC, and Mountain Dew, were lined up around the edges of the room, across the windowsill, everywhere. I was in the room, looking, and Randy's hands sank down on my shoulders as if they were taking a bite out of me. He gripped me by the muscle across the top of my back, across my shoulders.

"I was just looking," I said.

"Whose room is this?" he said.

I shrugged.

"Whose?" he asked.

"Yours."

"Did I say you could look? Did I say you could come in here? Did you ask? No!" he yelled into my face. "Some things belong to a person himself. They're private and you can't take them away."

I could smell his breath. It was hot like a dog's. I tried to turn my head away, but he held it straight. He held it with his thumb pressed under my chin.

"You can't have everything. I don't go into your room, looking at your things, do I?"

I wanted to tell him that my room was at home and the room down the hall didn't have anything in it except a bed with blue flowered sheets and a Pepto Bismol–colored blanket. I wanted to tell him that he was starting to remind me of Rayanne because she always asked me to tell her things and then would explain them back to me all wrong.

"You really are a case," he said, and then walked out of the room. I followed him down the hall. "Are you a lost dog?" he asked.

"No," I said.

He put his hand on my shoulder and I thought he was going to push me away and say get lost or something. I thought he might crack my head against the wall.

"Are you feeling better, Johnny? Are you ready to go fishing? Do you have a fever?" He pressed his hand up to my forehead, held his palm there for a minute, and then flipped his hand over so that the back side was against my head. I felt his knuckles digging into the thin crevice in the middle of my forehead. "It's gone," he said, taking his hand away and walking farther down the hall.

When his hand was off my head I could still feel the knuckles in that small crack in my skull. I thought about how I'd always figured that gap was a sort of structural deformity. I didn't know it was normal. I thought it was something that could start moving, an earthquake of the mind. I thought the two halves might separate and split my head open. I thought the gap could close and force my brain out through my ears. It always seemed that if anything happened to that place, I'd end up the same as Rayanne. It was like a warning that something could go wrong and I'd be just like my sister. I rubbed my forehead, letting my fingers dip into that place. I rubbed and wished Randy hadn't touched me there.

"Hey, Johnny, is it time for medicine?"

"I'm fine," I said.

"It's good for you, come on." Randy held out the bottle. His fingers were wrapped around the label. He unscrewed the top and took a small swig, swished it around in his mouth, and swallowed. I shook my head. "I'm not about to force you. That's not what I'm about." He recapped the bottle and put it down on the ledge above the sink. "My mother used to dose us sometimes. Sometimes at night, she'd want us asleep and we'd still be going full speed and she'd come into the bedroom, hold my nose until my mouth opened, and pour stuff down me; sometimes it was brandy, sometimes I didn't know what it was. She always did it to me and not to my brother because he had asthma real bad and she didn't want to mess him up." He paused. "Are you hungry?" I shrugged. Randy opened the refrigerator. "A Fig Newton might work. I'm not a cookie person, but Fig Newtons aren't really cookies, they're more of a medical food, you know? There's milk in here too. There you go, Johnny." He handed me the cartons.

"I still want to call my mom."

"No phone."

"She's probably wondering where I am."

"No she's not, Johnny. She knows you're with me. I told you that yesterday."

"But aren't I supposed to go home soon? And why don't you have a phone? Everyone has a phone. It's probably illegal not to have one."

"Don't talk law and order to me. Everyone has a phone and a

television, and every other one has a video recorder and a washing machine. And then they have microwave ovens. It doesn't mean they're smart. Start collecting things and you get in trouble. You start thinking that you care about the stuff and you forget that it's things, man-made things. It gets like it's a part of you and then it's gone and you feel like you're gone also. When you have stuff and then you don't it's like you've disappeared."

"You have empty bottles in rows all around your room," I said.

"Empties aren't stuff. What are you, stupid?"

"I'm not stupid."

"Keep it that way," Randy said, and then he walked away and I heard the slap of the screen door.

I walked from room to room eating Fig Newtons and drinking milk straight from the carton. I remember thinking it was great that no one was making me pour it into a glass. The rest of the house wasn't much, just a living room with a busted-up sofa and a green chair made out of the same stuff as car seats, the stuff your legs stick to on summer days. I sat down on the sofa and then had to move over to save myself from one of those springs that you can't see but all of the sudden pops through and stabs you in the butt.

I sat there eating cookies and sort of daydreaming. I thought that this was the kind of life I'd live if it was just me and my dad, no mother, no Rayanne. I thought about how everything in our house got all weird when my dad came to visit. My mother would run around putting everything into piles on top of the TV or the coffee table. Then she'd go to the grocery store and buy things like broccoli and veal chops. We'd have to put clean clothes on and sit with her in the living room until she heard his truck coming down the street, the gears shifting down. My father would come into the house and we'd be standing there like we were in the army and you could tell from his face that he wished he hadn't come. It was like he wanted to sneak in and have us find him sitting there watching TV like he'd never been gone. It was like he made himself think that he didn't matter, that his leaving didn't matter. Sometimes he'd try and fake us out. He'd drop by without warning. Rayanne, my mom, and I might be out in the front yard and we'd hear the truck as soon as it turned the corner at the end of the street. Rayanne would look up and see him sitting twenty feet up in the cab and she'd take off, galloping towards the truck in her retarded way, legs getting tangled in each other, never sure which foot should go next.

The screen door slapped shut and somewhere in my head I heard it, but didn't really know where I was. I was still thinking about my father, his truck, and the view from up in the cab.

"Hey, hey, Johnny," Randy said. "Are you sleeping?"

"Not exactly," I mumbled.

"What exactly?"

I shrugged.

"You don't have to spend all day in the house. When I saw you out there playing ball, I figured you were an outdoor type."

I shook my head.

"I like to watch TV. I watch TV and my sister comes in. I can't stand her, so sometimes I have to get out of the house. My sister is retarded, did you know that?"

Randy nodded.

"No matter how old she gets, she'll never be better than a seven-year-old. She calls my father Uncle because she says that daddies live at home and uncles just come and visit."

"Yeah, well, get up. We're going fishing. What we catch is what we eat for dinner."

"I don't know how to fish."

"I'll teach you, Johnny."

I shrugged.

"Do you care about anything?"

I shrugged again.

"Don't shrug. Either talk or don't, but don't goddamn shrug at me. It's like saying go to hell, only worse. You're saying it's not even worth the energy it takes to say the words."

I walked through the woods behind Randy.

"The trick," he said, "is just like life. Don't let them know you want them. Play dumb and they'll act dumb."

He pushed the boat into the water and we waded in. My jeans got wet up to my thighs and felt like weights wrapped around my legs. Randy rowed out into the lake. He handed me a coffee can. "Take one out and put it right there on the end."

I looked into the can and saw about a thousand worms. "I can't," I said.

"You can and you will," Randy said, holding out the hook to me. He talked in the same tone my mother used with Rayanne when she wanted her to do something. "We can sit here until the moon is blue."

I turned my head away and put my hand into the can. The thin rolls of worm were soft and a little silky. They were stuck together, piled on top of one another. I had to look directly into the can in order to pick one up. I handed it to Randy.

"On the hook," he said. "Put it on the hook." I jammed it down on the hook, ripping its body, squirting worm juice into the air.

Randy cast the fishing line out over the lake, explaining how it was all in the flick of the wrist. He handed me the pole and I looked out at the thin plastic line. I looked across the lake and saw a man on the other side. I got up on my knees, nearly dropped the fishing pole, and waved. I kept doing it until Randy slapped my hand down. But the man across the lake had seen me. He waved back and then Randy had to wave to get him to stop waving.

"People here like to be left alone," Randy said. "You shouldn't have bothered him."

I started crying, not out loud, but to myself. I was crying and thinking about how I wanted to go home, put on dry clothes, talk to my mom, and watch TV.

"What's with you, Johnny? It's a beautiful day, you're out fishing, you've never fished before, but you're doing it, and you're acting worse than an old hat."

There was a yank on my line and I sat up.

"Pull back slowly, just a little bit."

I did what he said.

"Don't let him think he's caught. If he thinks he can get away he'll try and wait you out. But if you let him know he's caught, he'll fight like hell."

We pulled him in and then the fish was there, hanging from the hook, staring at me. Randy dropped him onto the floor of the boat. The fish flopped around.

"Say hello to dinner," Randy said.

"I'm not eating."

"You'll eat."

I shook my head.

"Bait another hook."

I watched the fish until its gills stopped flapping, until I was sure it was dead. I watched for about ten minutes and then jammed another worm onto the hook. Randy got a bite on his line and pulled in a small fish. He took it off the hook and threw it back into the water. "I'm not a murderer, Johnny," he said.

When we had three fish Randy put away the poles and we ate sandwiches right there in the boat with the fish at our feet. "This is the life," Randy said.

I could feel the sun on the place on my shoulder where Randy had grabbed me when I was in his room. I could feel the sun through my shirt and it was like hands rubbing a sore place. I leaned back in the boat and used one of the floating cushions as a pillow.

"Hey, hey, Johnny, wake up." Randy had rowed us back to shore. "You sleep a lot for a kid your age."

"It's because of being sick."

"You were out all afternoon and you didn't seem sick. It's all in your head. You're sick in the head."

I got out of the boat and helped pull it back into the woods. "Last night you said I was sick. I threw up."

"I didn't know you like I do today." He paused. "Pregnant ladies throw up—are they sick? It's your head, Johnny."

Randy cooked the fish for dinner. We ate and then I helped him clean up.

"My father's coming to visit soon and I have to be there," I said. "It's the law. My mother lines us up by the piano and I have to be there."

"Johnny, she knows where you are. If she wanted you, she'd come get you."

The morning after that Randy woke me up, told me to hurry, handed me a cream cheese sandwich, and said I'd have to eat it in the car.

"Where are we going?"

"Did you ever split wood?" he asked.

"I've peeled the bark off branches."

"Ever hold an axe?"

"No."

Randy drove to a small shopping center and pulled in near the hardware store. There was a 7-Eleven right next to the hardware store with a pay phone in front. I followed Randy into the hardware store, but put my hand in my pocket and felt around for a quarter. While Randy was talking to the guy about axes and wedges I pretended to get lost looking for some fishing stuff. I went outside to the pay phone, put the quarter in, and dialed. I dialed my mother and waited. I thought Randy was going to come outside and kill me. I thought he'd come out with an axe and take off my head. I didn't care. The phone clicked a couple of times and then beeped busy. A couple of people came out of the 7-Eleven and I thought of asking them for help, but I wasn't sure what I'd say. I put the quarter in again and dialed. Busy. I hung up, got the quarter back, and put it in again. It started to ring, but then I thought I'd dialed the wrong number. I only had one quarter and I thought I might have hit an eight and not a five. I hung up, put the quarter in, and dialed again. Still busy. I thought of calling the operator or the police. I hung up, dialed again. Randy came out of the store and saw me at the phone. He was carrying the axe in one hand and a package in the other.

"What are you doing?" he asked.

"Trying to call my mom."

"Any luck?"

"Line's busy."

He came over to the telephone and just stood there. He didn't get mad. He didn't kill me. He just stood there, listening to the phone beep. "Try again," he said.

I hung up, put the quarter back in, and dialed again. Busy. "Why is she on the phone?"

"Talking to someone," Randy said. He leaned against the wall of the 7-Eleven like he was going to stay there all day. He leaned back like he didn't care that I was calling home.

I felt like an idiot with him standing there, not trying to stop me. I felt mentally ill. Randy was telling the truth; my mother wasn't worried. She was sitting home, talking on the telephone.

"Let's go," I finally said.

"Go on, give it another try." I almost put the quarter in again, but then I wondered what I would say. What could I say with Randy right there, telling me to go ahead and call? I put the quarter into my pocket.

We went home and Randy showed me how to split logs; how to swing the axe with both arms straight, to swing up over my shoulder and then go straight down into the log. He explained about putting in the metal wedges so that with a few whacks the whole piece split open like an English muffin.

When we were done, Randy showed me how to cook; we made sandwiches and Rice Krispie squares. Then we went into the living room, ate, played poker, and passed a carton of milk back and forth between us. Sometimes when I drank, I'd tilt the carton a little too high and milk spilled out onto my face, ran back behind my ear and down my neck.

"A kid like you should have more to say," Randy said. "You should be nonstop, filled with ideas, things you're going to do, all that stuff."

I didn't look at him.

"It's like you're not all there," he said.

I was looking at the dirt in the cracks on the floor. Randy said it was like I wasn't all there and I thought about Rayanne and wondered if she had lots of things trapped in her head. I thought about how she didn't really understand how retarded she was and how she thought I was a genius or something. I thought maybe I was like her, not enough for everyone to notice but enough for a guy like Randy to catch on. I thought it was probably my parents' fault for not telling me. Maybe that's why my father left. Maybe my mother, Rayanne, and me were all the same; maybe we were all retarded.

"Are you sleeping, Johnny?" Randy asked.

I shook my head.

"What's wrong with you?"

I shrugged and waited for him to hit me. The Krispie pan was on the coffee table with a couple of pieces left in it. The milk carton was right there too. I reached my foot out and with the tip of my sneaker tipped the pan over. I knocked the pan over right in front of Randy.

He just sat there and looked at me. His face didn't change. "Feel better now?" he finally asked, sweeping the cards into a pile and then making them into a stack. I shrugged. He stood and I shriveled up. I didn't mean to, but he was standing over me and that's just what happened. "Don't be scared of me, Johnny," he said. "Be scared of yourself." He picked up the milk carton and took it into the kitchen. I heard the refrigerator door open and close. I heard Randy pull out a chair and sit down. I got up off the sofa and onto my hands and knees. I picked up the pan, took it into the kitchen, and put it down on the counter.

" 'Night, Johnny," Randy said. He was playing solitaire.

" 'Night." I walked down the hall to my room.

The next morning Randy was gone. I sat on the living room sofa and waited. I went outside and sat on the concrete front step. Across the dirt that was the front yard there were still pieces of wood that needed to be split and stacked. I picked up the axe. It felt heavier than I remembered. I raised it and went to work. About a half hour later Randy drove up.

"Where'd you go?" I asked.

He shrugged. "Put shoes on," he said. "Never work outside without shoes."

I followed him into the house. "I'm sorry for what I did last night," I said. I'd been rehearsing it in my head all morning.

He nodded.

I went down the hall to get my shoes. Randy was in the kitchen making eggs for himself. "I said I was sorry."

"I hear you." He scrapped the eggs out of the pan and onto a plate. I kept looking at him and he looked back at me. "Did you finish all the wood?" I shook my head. Randy started to eat and I went outside and kept splitting and stacking.

When the wood was chopped I went into my room and fell asleep. The slap-slapping sound of a basketball woke me up. Randy was dribbling down the hall. He stood in the doorway bouncing the ball. "Get up, Johnny," he said. "We're going."

"Where?"

He shrugged and threw the ball at me, hard.

I caught it. It was my ball. I hadn't seen it since the night Randy picked me up. I held the ball for a minute and then put it down on the bed.

"Take it with you," he said.

I followed him out to the car. "Do you know how to drive?"

"I'm way too young."

"Never too young." He moved the car seat as far forward as it would go. If I sat so I could see, my legs were nowhere near the pedals. "You're too short," Randy said. I slid over so he could drive. He pulled the seat release and the whole front seat slid backwards.

"Let's go fishing again," I said.

"I don't think so, Johnny," he said, and I was quiet for a long time. The road turned into highway and I could feel him making the car go faster. It was afternoon. The sun was starting to go down.

"Where are we going?" I asked.

He didn't say anything for a while. "You're not the kid I thought you'd be."

"What does that mean?"

He turned off the highway and we were someplace I'd been before. I turned the basketball around on my lap.

"I'm taking you back," he said. He made a few turns and I knew where he was.

"What's wrong with me?"

"You're not the right kid. You're not Johnny." Randy pulled up to the curb right at the bottom of the hill below the basketball courts. This was the exact same place he'd parked when he came up to the courts and called me Johnny. "Get out," he said, I sat there looking at the dashboard. "You've spent three days whining about calling your mother and going home. Now you're home. Go on, get out."

"Why?"

He leaned across me and opened the door on my side of the car. "Out," he said, shoving my shoulder.

I got out.

Randy pulled away from the curb, turned the car around, and went back down the hill.

I walked home, cutting through the same backyards as always. I walked the same way but everything felt different. All the things I'd always liked, knowing who lived where and what their dog's name was, only made me feel worse. I went past clotheslines and instead of thinking it was funny to see Mrs. Perkins' flowered underwear hanging out, I wanted to rip it down. I wanted to take everything down and tear it into a million pieces. I crossed through the Simons' yard and into our backyard.

Rayanne was there by herself, playing in my sandbox. She was thirteen years old, bigger than my mother, and she was playing in the sandbox. I stood there until she saw me. She looked at me and tried to jump up. She wanted to get up but she did it too fast and didn't know what she was doing. She fell down and had to get up again. "Erol, Erol," she said, galloping across the backyard. "Erol," she said, but it came out sounding like "Error, Error." She came towards me and I dropped my basketball. I turned and ran back through the yards. I ran until I didn't know the names of the people in the houses around me. I ran through backyards until I stopped hearing Rayanne's voice calling Error.

I WANTED
TO KNOW WHY
by Jonathan Ames
(Princeton University)

I've been thinking about suicide
ever since Roy Laudner killed himself. He was a handsome boy
whom everyone knew and said good things about. He was president
of the ecology club. And what stood out about him to me was that
the handlebars on his bike were the old-fashioned type, and I didn't
know why he didn't have the ten-speed handlebars like everyone
else. His bike even had mud guards and an old, fat leather seat. He
had curly brown hair which my sister wrote about in the poem. She
said it was like a "wreath of olive leaves wrapped around your
head." Her poem about Roy is still one of the most beautiful things
I've ever read, it was written like a letter to him. I remember the
last time I saw him he stopped with that black bike of his at my
friend Ethan's driveway. We had been playing basketball. And it
was a cool fall day and we talked a little while, Roy knew me
because of my sister, and I pretended I didn't notice his old-fashioned
handlebars. I was pretty happy after he rode away thinking what a
nice guy. And I felt cool in front of my best friend Ethan that a guy
in high school would talk to me. I also remember he had a catch
with me once down at the rec field and didn't make me feel like a
little kid. He was kind to me and I never really knew why.

And then it spread all over town that he hanged himself. My sister ran around our house screaming and crying, I stayed out of her way, and she ran into her room and slammed the door, shrieking. I wasn't sure who it was at first, and then I realized it was the guy with the bike. Slowly the facts started coming out and we all found out that he had hanged himself nude in the basement and was found by his sister. Supposedly she touched him once or twice and said, "Roy, quit fooling around," and then realized he was dead and ran out of the house. What struck me was thinking about him hanging there nude. I always have thought that must've been the first shock, seeing her brother all nude. I bet she even laughed, she was only fourteen, and I bet she's got some secret shame about seeing her brother's penis and feeling excited with him being dead. Over the years I would ask my sister to tell me all she knew about the suicide, I wanted to know every detail.

When my sister wrote the poem it was about how Roy might've loved her and she had loved someone else, but now that he was dead she knew she loved him, only it was too late to say "I love you." So she felt, like everybody did in their own way, that it was her fault, but it wasn't. The rumor was that he wanted to go to college, but his parents couldn't afford it. And that seemed to explain why he had the old-fashioned handlebars. So one day Roy stayed home sick from school.

I tried to imagine him walking around his house naked, carrying that rope. What was he thinking, was he crying, when he threw it over the beam and went swinging down, oh Roy, why? I asked my sister if he left a note and she didn't think he did. My parents said things like, "See? Parents should never hesitate to give to their children." Somehow when things like that happen my parents start feeling all high and mighty because my sister and I haven't killed ourselves. I hate it when they act like that.

At the end of the school year the yearbook came out. And we all skimmed through it looking for pictures of Roy. And sure enough, there he was sitting in the stands of a football game and it seemed to me his face stood out above all the rest. He was in a large crowd and everyone was shouting and smiling, except for Roy who looked so quiet and erect. And I thought, was he thinking about killing himself at that very moment? There was another one of him in the stands and it had the same eerie feeling, you knew he was dead now.

The yearbook was dedicated to him, he was the only one who had died, and it was at this time that I began to fantasize about my own suicide. Usually at night I'd put myself to sleep wondering if (and hoping) the whole town would cry for me the way they did for him. I even experimented in front of the mirror with a towel around my neck, but I didn't know how to tie it right (my father has always told me I'm no good with my hands), and I have never learned. I had only talked to Roy Laudner twice in my life, but I started mourning for him. My mother and sister didn't know it, but I'd take out the yearbook and look at him in those stands so alone, and I'd look at his senior picture in his tie, and I'd read my sister's beautiful poem, and I'd cry for him. It was my secret that I missed him.

In eighth grade a few years after it happened, my teacher started talking about suicide and she brought up Roy. She said, "You never know why someone might kill himself, but most likely it is when he has a problem that he can't talk about. When Roy Laudner killed himself a few years ago," and then my ears pricked up, she was talking about my Roy Laudner, how dare she say his name out loud, I was hating her, "they found in his dresser drawer that he had tied all his socks in knots." I wanted to scream, how did you know that? how can you tell everyone Roy's secrets? By this time I had thought so much about Roy Laudner's suicide, had played it over so many times in my head, that I almost felt I had walked down his basement stairs with him, looked at his naked body, watched him tie the rope (he was an Eagle Scout), and stared at him swaying and swinging, just like his sister. I just didn't want to think of Roy tying his socks in knots and the teacher had spoken about him as if he were nobody, and like everybody she blamed the parents for not seeing their son's problem.

The following year my sister started going out with Roy's younger brother, Paul, who looked just like Roy, the same tight curly hair, handsome face, and that smile that made you feel like you were friends. And so one day I went over to the Laudner house with my sister and I met the whole family. Roy's sister, the one who found him, was pretty and I had a lot of questions I wanted to ask her, but I couldn't. And you could see Roy in her face and I liked her, but she was older than me. I guess I liked her the same way my sister liked Paul. The two girls went to talk and Paul took me to the basement down the old dirty wooden stairs to show me a model he was working on. And I tried to look at the rafters without him noticing and figure out which one, and how did Roy do it (with a ladder maybe?), and then I saw his black bike old and lost in the corner with tools and broken furniture. I remembered Roy riding it, his arms bent to the handles, and then I wondered who had cut him down, who had held his dead naked body? And my mind would not stop and I never wanted to leave there, I wanted to figure it all out. I felt somehow that if I stayed there forever, I could watch it all happen again and I would know. But then Mrs. Laudner called us upstairs for dinner and I looked back at the basement to remember exactly how it was and to imagine Roy hanging above all the clutter.

When everyone was at the table I looked at the parents trying to see their pain and loss which I thought must be so evident (my parents had said they would not go on living if it was them), but I could see nothing in their faces. Yet I knew it was there surrounding all of us. I excused myself to go to the bathroom, but instead went to Roy's room which was also down the hall. My sister had pointed it out earlier and had whispered that it had been left untouched since he died. The door was open a crack and I went in. The whole room was neat and the bed was perfectly made. I saw a pair of sneakers by the closet and his jeans hanging over his desk chair. And a science book was open, he must have been studying before he died. I wished that I would find a note that no one else had seen and then I would know why, but it wasn't there of course, and I stepped out growing too scared to continue and made sure to shut the door the same amount it had been open. I went to the bathroom to flush the toilet and returned to the dining room. I was thirsty from my adventure and I asked Paul, "Roy, could you pass the milk?" Everyone stopped talking, I had evoked his name. I stared down at my plate unable to move and I was saying to myself over and over again so that God would hear, "I'm sorry, I'm sorry," and I wished that I were dead.

PHYSICS

by Suzanne Juergensen
(San Francisco State University)

You're feeling old as you deliver your talk to the college physics class. Old and jaded. As you look out over the rows of eager young faces, you think of how much you remind yourself of all the other women you know in their mid-thirties. You pretend to be more cheerful than you actually are. You talk about aerobics more than you ever do it and dress a lot younger than you ought to. You drive a Japanese car, spend more money than you make, and insist that you're not a yuppie, just like all of the others do. You're someone these students would never understand.

The talk you're giving is part of a career seminar—really, a sales pitch for cheap labor for the research and development department of the company you work for. "Business Isn't Bad" is the title of the talk. It is nothing you believe in, but you've been paid and you figure a lot of these kids are going to get into it anyway, regardless of what you tell them.

You don't even know anything about research and development. You work in the public relations department. What you do know is how to talk as though you know what you're talking about. You know how to placate, how to convince people that what you want them to do is something they've thought of on their own.

Afterward, one of the boys in the class approaches you—David. He says hello with the self-assured grin of someone who is testing himself. His perfect adolescent body towers over yours. He plants his long arms on either side of the podium and leans down to your level. You watch the arteries pulse in his neck. Eloquent, he says of your talk. As he talks, he blushes. He is impressed with your maturity, with your wit and your intelligence. Would you like to go out for pizza.

You have to get back to work, approve some press releases, check up on the receptionist, answer your phone messages. "Sure," you say. "I'd love to." He's got you hypnotized; you absolutely can't say no. This bothers you; ordinarily you're a person who has few problems in this regard.

Your relationships with men are friendly and resigned. You've had a lot of them, and it's hard to maintain any romantic illusions about how things might have turned out for you, because they didn't turn out that way. Romance is something you no longer trust.

David seems so genuine, so unblemished, and you like the idea of just sitting and talking for a while with someone who isn't suspicious of you. You want to comfort yourself in believing that all men started out this way.

At the pizza parlor, you watch him eat, cramming piece after piece into his mouth as fast as his hands can get it there. It is awesome to you that a person can become so immersed in eating. You have the feeling that he is not only hungry but driven, as though he would eat anything, relishing all of it equally.

You sip on your Coke as he continues his attack. It is an extra large with everything on it. He orders another shake.

Occasionally, his eyes move up from the plate, in deference to your presence there. "You bored?" he says.

"No," you say. You tell him you're having a fine time.

He shrugs his shoulders, smiling as he finishes the last piece, wipes his mouth and his hands with several small paper napkins, and adds them to the pile on the empty metal tray that he pushes toward the edge of the table. "There," he says, folding his hands in front of him. He looks at you with a new interest, as though you have just arrived. He looks at you like you are food.

It's then that you invite him over for dinner. This seems innocent enough. You just want to watch him eat again, marvel at the passion of it, at how much he can ingest.

It's innocent until after dinner when you find yourself on his lap and he's kissing you like you're the next course, which is suddenly just what you want to be.

So you invite him to sleep over. Your relationship with guilt is of the all or nothing variety, so if you're going to feel guilty anyway, as you know you are, then you might as well get something out of it.

In the morning you ask him how old he is. Eighteen, he says. Eighteen, to your thirty-six. You were hoping for twenty-one. Not that this would make much of a difference, except that now you're wondering if you could actually go to jail.

In an effort to encourage him to see this as a one-night stand, you make some comment about those lucky college girls he goes to school with. You sound more awkward than you'd hoped, so you keep talking, trusting yourself to end on a smoother note.

"Listen," he interrupts, "I know what you're getting at, but I'm just not that kind of a guy. I mean, I fall in love with someone and that's it. No more college girls for me."

You understand that he is confused, that it is sex he's in love with, not you. But the more you think about this, the more confused you become. You do want to see him again—though just one more time, you tell yourself—and you begin to feel the overwhelming need to confess.

You choose the receptionist at work—Lisa, another eighteen-year-old. She too is sweet and pure, and she owes you—you're keeping her from getting fired.

You whisper the story of your escapade to her in a corner of the coffee room, watch her tiny features assume a grave and grown-up expression.

"Maybe this will be good for you, Cynthia," she says. "Maybe this will mellow you out."

She's missed your point entirely, how you've so shamelessly acted out a fantasy that can't possibly continue. You begin to wonder if she isn't really as incompetent as everyone else seems to think, but you can't think of any appropriate response, so you thank her and smile in an awkward sort of way, feeling very much like an adolescent yourself.

Before you know it, you've got David's dirty socks and underwear in your laundry hamper. He apologizes but keeps forgetting to take them with him. The Pop-Tarts he eats for breakfast are out on your kitchen counter. It's surprising how many more flavors there are now than eighteen years ago when you were eighteen and used to eat them. There's a flavor now called mixed berry, which strikes you as kind of ridiculous for a product containing nothing real.

You're always buying the wine for dinner because David's not old enough yet to buy it himself. He's not used to drinking it yet either, so when he does, his face flushes and he says things like "True love never dies."

This embarrasses you and you tell him to stop, that he's just deluding himself, but of course he doesn't believe you. You decide not to push it, though, because you don't really want to be the one who's going to prove it to him, or at least not now, when things seem to be in a place where you want them.

At work Lisa asks you daily about the progress of your relationship with David, while Sorensen, your boss, asks you about Lisa's progress. You much prefer the talks with Lisa. She has become something of a therapist to you. You voice your concerns, she tells you there's no need to worry. Not that you believe her, but there's something endearing about her efforts, about the way she tells you "Love conquers all," the way her young cherry-colored lips mouth the words in such a serious way.

Your talks with Sorensen are more disturbing. "She's such a stupid girl," he says.

"Undereducated," you say, in your attempt to agree yet defend simultaneously.

"Cynthia," he says, "she's a baby. She doesn't sound *old* enough to answer a phone. You really ought to get rid of her."

Sorensen, you realize, needs a scapegoat, but he has no real ammunition yet against Lisa. This is her first office job, and there is much she doesn't yet know about office survival. But she's trying hard, and you hope you can get her education well under way before Sorensen discovers some more valid reason for you to fire her.

* * *

Do you love me? David's been asking you. Love? Well, maybe you do. Or could. You do, after all, have a lot in common. You both read, and so what if he's reading *Ulysses* while you're on Jackie Collins. An easy read, you say—just how you like it.

He is smarter than you. You can't even remember all the names of his scholarships and awards. He's accomplished more than you have in half your lifetime. You aren't sure how much more; it all depends on how you multiply two times zero.

So it flatters you that he wants you anyway, that he wants you all the time. Once, before dinner, he said you were the first truly passionate woman he'd ever known, and then he looked at you in a way that made you feel like hot pie filling, oozing out the seams of the crust. No one else has thought of you as passionate at all in at least ten years. The hell with dinner, you thought. What could food possibly mean in the face of such passion as yours? So you led him into the bedroom, both of you groping at clothes in the dark.

It intrigues you that someone can be so interested, make you feel so much younger than you are. It is the way you always wished you could have felt when you really were as young as you feel now.

You realize that you're becoming exactly what you used to complain about most in men. They had one-track minds, they used you, their interest stopped where your neck began.

You don't care about David's mind, at least not in comparison to the rest of him, and find your own attention wandering as he talks. You feel as though you're using him to satisfy something insatiable. You wonder if you'll start thinking about him in the same way you look at your job. You're overpaid, so it keeps you there, in a place you'd rather not be.

One afternoon David says he wants to have a serious talk. Great, you say, they're your favorite kind. He looks at you with an expression of longing that makes you want to roll your eyes and laugh. You really don't know what he's going to say to you yet, but already you're trivializing it in a way, you realize, that other men have so often trivialized you and your serious talks.

He's making you dinner, at your apartment, before the talk. He says it's going to be gourmet.

It's spaghetti, with some kind of clear garlic sauce, and broccoli, pineapple, and raisins on top. For dessert, there's lime Jell-O with Chinese pea pods and artichoke hearts. "I've always wanted to try something different with Jell-O," he says, scooping out a large lump of it onto your plate. He watches you as you eat it.

You can't believe how many bowls and pans he's gone through, the dirty spoons sticking to the counters, the stove top freckled with grease. The kitchen never looks this way when you cook. You're a wiper, a cleaner-as-you-go, an everything-in-its-place kind of a person.

David folds his hands in front of him on the table. He says he wants to talk about the future.

You envision a time machine, some Einsteinian device that travels faster than the speed of light and gets you there. Or keeps you where you are—you can't remember which. When you mention this, David looks a little hurt.

Maybe you're not being fair, you think, but you can't really think of much to say about the future. It seems amorphous to you now, something you used to fantasize about though never plan for.

He tells you he's not like any of those men you've known before who you're always complaining about. He doesn't need to be in control or to argue with you. He can talk about his feelings. Ask him anything, he says, anything at all about his feelings and he'll tell you.

But you already know what his feelings are. It's yours that nobody's talking about. Right now you have only one feeling—fear—which you're going to keep to yourself and hope that it goes away.

And he's not one of those men who expects to be taken care of, he continues. When he moves in with you, he'll cook and he'll clean and you'll have a lot less work on your hands than you do right now.

Fear is not the word for what you're feeling anymore. You tell him he's not moving in, that he's too young to know what he really wants yet.

Don't underestimate him, he says—he's probably the only man you've ever known who really appreciates you.

Maybe he's right, you think, but you don't say that. His momentum seems large enough on its own.

He says he's going back to sleep in his dorm room. "An early day tomorrow," he says, but you know that's not it. When you kiss him good-bye, his neck smells like soap. His skin is smooth, unblemished. He kisses your eyes. You're aware of the webbing of lines around them, and that he must see it too, and you're wondering if he is trying to kiss it away, to somehow wish you younger.

You turn off the lights and get into bed, but the streetlight leaks in. You can see a pair of David's socks balled up on the floor from last night and there's one of his physics demonstrations on your bookshelf—a spoon and a fork clamped together, suspended on a matchstick from the rim of a glass. As you see it now, it looks impossible, as though there is some kind of magic involved. But he's explained it to you. It's just physics, he's said, a demonstration of the center of gravity. He's explained to you why the sky is blue, why gravity makes you shrink. The room seems filled with him, even though he's gone. You're afraid of closing your eyes, afraid of losing him if you do.

Sorensen is on your case about Lisa again. She's put domestic postage on a batch of international mail. All of it was returned, and Sorensen witnessed the event.

"Cynthia, the girl is an idiot!" Sorensen shrieks at you. "Get her out of here!"

"Don't jump to conclusions," you say, as though you're the one in charge.

In talking with Lisa, you discover she can follow the postal charts but knows nothing about geography, so she can't select the proper chart. You tell Sorensen this was just a simple mistake—everyone makes them—and that it won't happen again. You tell Lisa to be in early the following morning for a geography lesson.

At home that evening David asks if you'd like to meet his parents.

Of course not. You wouldn't dream of it. In your opinion this kind of thing is best kept hidden.

Well, his parents are already on their way, somewhere in the air now between Idaho and Oakland. It's him they're coming to visit, he insists. Do you want to deprive him of seeing his parents?

No, no, of course not. See them all you want to, you say. You'll stay home for a few weeks and read. Jackie Collins has a new one out, you've heard, or you can reread an old one. There's a lot on TV that you've been missing.

"Just dinner," he says. "Just one dinner."

You're not hungry, you say, and probably won't be for a while. At least for two weeks, maybe forever.

"Coffee, then," he says.

"No."

"A drink?"

His parents, Rick and Adelle, are pleasant midwestern people. Rick is wearing jeans with Birkenstocks and a short-sleeved shirt with parrots on it. He is balding; the hair that's left is stringy and disheveled, as though he lets it grow until it falls out.

Adelle looks crisp in white wash-and-wear. Her auburn hair is parted in the middle, blunt cut at chin length. You keep staring at the hair, inspecting it for gray, hoping she is older than you.

No one is saying much. "Highball?" Rick says, unmistakably to you.

"No. Thanks." You're afraid of drinking anything at all because you want so much just to get drunk.

"Oh come on, have one. It's on me."

"Maybe a little later," you tell him, conscious of trying to smile sweetly, like someone much younger than yourself might smile.

You're not sure how much later it is that the room is swimming before your eyes. You've been talking with David's father about the good old days, back in the sixties, when there was so much peace and love and freedom, that "anything goes" kind of feeling. He's been talking about it, anyway—you would have agreed with anything either of them had chosen to say—but you suppose that he's trying to tell you, in his between-the-lines kind of way, that he accepts you, that it's all right with him that you've deflowered his son.

You wonder why—if it's because you keep agreeing with him or because he's had a lot to drink, or both, but you want to know what the variable is because you want to keep it constant. Parents, to you, are godlike, and a child molester like yourself craves the ultimate in forgiveness, for as long as it can possibly last.

Adelle suddenly interrupts. She is starting to look rumpled. There's a tuft of hair falling the wrong way across her part. Her lipstick has smudged and bled into the tiny lines above her upper lip. "Everyone talked a good line about peace and love then," she says, "but there were riots going on, violence everywhere. And free love was just a euphemism for a lot of sexual manipulation."

The table falls silent. "Well," Rick says, in an artificially cheery way, "is anyone ready for another?"

"You bet," Adelle says, glaring at you.

Rick turns, looking for the waiter.

"I have an announcement to make," David says. "Cynthia and I are getting married."

His parents look at him, then at you, in a manner that echoes your own horror and confusion.

You open your mouth to speak, but the waiter is suddenly standing there. "We'll all have another round," Rick says, as Adelle's eyes begin to fill with tears. When the waiter leaves, she begins to weep, choking out phrases that you can't quite make out. *Ridiculous* is one of the words that keeps coming up.

"Well," Rick says, clearing his throat, "this is certainly a surprise."

"Yes," you say, "to me too. I mean, David has these fantasies, but that's exactly what they are. We're not getting married." And then suddenly you find yourself crying too. It's like you're somebody else crying, playing along in someone else's melodrama.

Adelle just stares at you and stops crying herself, as though you've given her a reason to. "David's always been headstrong," she says. "Once he makes up his mind he wants something, it's hard to persuade him otherwise."

"We're not getting married. I don't know why he said that, but it's not true. Absolutely no chance of it. None at all. Ever."

"Maybe it's not the best match ever," Adelle says, "but it's all right. You don't have to cover up for him. At least things are out in the open now. It's better that way."

"Yes," Rick says, patting your shoulder, "now we can go on from here."

"David, say something. Tell them," you say.

"I think we're going to be very happy," he says, sliding an arm around your limp shoulders.

* * *

You're not driving, and not watching either, so you're never aware of where they're taking you until you get there. It's your apartment. They follow you inside.

"Nice place," Adelle says, as though she is genuinely surprised.

"Is that a lava lamp?" Rick asks, pointing to your table clock.

"It's a clock," you tell him.

"Far out," he says.

You close your eyes and shake your head no, as though that's going to make him disappear.

"Either somebody slipped something into that last drink of mine or that clock hasn't got any numbers on it."

He sits down on the sofabed and stares at it. There's an orange triangle for the hour hand, a blue square for the minutes, a green circle for the seconds. His eyes follow the circle. "I feel like I'm on mushrooms," he says. "Dave? Did you put anything in that last drink of mine?"

"Dad," David says, "come on." He is with his mother in the kitchen, going through hotel listings in the yellow pages. He's made a reservation for them at the Ramada Inn, which now claims not to have it, and there are no other rooms available. They keep calling other hotels; all of them are booked solid. David's parents can't, of course, stay with him because he's living in a dorm.

In the morning Adelle complains about the sofabed. David eats peanut butter and jelly–flavored Pop-Tarts with milk; his parents both want whole-wheat toast buttered on both sides, three-minute eggs, and herbal tea. They spread themselves out around your kitchen table.

You've always kept your apartment spare, uncluttered—the part of it that can be seen, anyway—and these people all seem very large. You picture the walls around you stretching, cracking, falling away, as you try very hard not to.

They ask you about showers. You have to tell them you don't have any clean towels, that you were just about to do your wash. Adelle frowns.

"Well, I wasn't exactly *prepared* for this," you say.

"No, of course not," Rick says.

"No need to apologize," David says.

"You've been such a dear," Adelle says.

* * *

On your way to work you remember Lisa's geography lesson. You're not as early as you said you'd be, but there's still time. She has to know just a little bit about it in order to select postal rates from their proper charts—there's one for North America, one for Central America, another for the rest of the world.

When you get in, she's waiting for you, sitting up very straight at her desk with her hands folded in front of her, an efficient smile on her face. She's imitating you; it's the way you try to look, sitting at your desk, when someone is late.

You sigh, and ask her to stand with you in front of the large world map on the wall above the copier. You point with a yardstick.

"So here's where you're from," you say, touching Ohio. "Can you tell me where you are now?"

"California," she says. "San Francisco."

"Point to it," you say. She gets it right.

"Very good," you say. "Do you know what continent we're on?" She hesitates.

"North America," you say, not wanting to risk a wrong answer. You outline the entire continent with the yardstick. "And this is South America," you say, outlining that. "Now, where do you suppose Central America might be?"

She looks at the map, takes the yardstick, and points to Europe.

You know she can't possibly be this stupid. She is quick to spot some things—other people's mistakes, yours in particular—good at manipulating people, organized about keeping precise lists of her complaints. Is she not trying to remember these things you're telling her? Could she be putting you on? The thought of this makes you angry, but the alternative—that she simply doesn't understand—is scarier. You feel that if she doesn't get this, it's somehow going to be your fault.

You arrive home early, expecting peace and time to reflect on the events of the previous night. But David's family is still there, Rick in your bathrobe in the kitchen, David asleep in your bedroom. Adelle wants to talk to you. In private, she says, leading you into the living room, where Janis Joplin wails from your stereo. You sit on an arm of the sofa in a tentative way; she sinks down into a recliner.

"I've been thinking," she says, "maybe we should push this wedding date forward just a little."

You shake your head hard. "No date," you say. "No wedding."

She shakes her head back at you. "Stop pretending, Cynthia. It's time to start planning for this."

"Why?" you say.

"Children."

"No. No children, no date, no wedding," you say, standing up to leave.

"Look," she says, "if David's going to marry anyone twice his age, I'd just as soon it be you."

"Thanks," you say, "but—"

"David's always been mature for his age, and you seem a little immature. And except for getting involved with him in the first place, you seem sensible enough. What I'm trying to say is just don't worry about this. Everything will work out fine. I just want you to know that I'm on your side, and we ought to start thinking about the children now because pretty soon you won't be able to—"

"Listen," you say, trying to reason with her, "there's insanity in my family."

She laughs at you.

"Really," you say, trying to sound convincing. "My grandmother was a schizophrenic."

"You're such a funny girl," she says, still laughing.

"My mother's an alcoholic. I have an uncle who's a diabetic transvestite. There's cancer in my family. I could tell you horror stories you wouldn't believe."

She's laughing harder now. You suddenly find yourself laughing with her, without quite understanding why, because everything you've said to her is absolutely true.

David opens his eyes, sits up on your bed, and smiles at you.

"David, please stop with this marriage business. It's really getting on my nerves."

He apologizes for having sprung it on you in front of his parents. "But we are getting married," he says. He tells you you'll get used to the idea, tells you it's part of your destiny, and destiny is something he knows to be true.

"Oh, come on," you say, rolling your eyes, but he continues over your objections. He tells you he's gotten more scholarship money than anyone in his entire school of 20,000 students; more, even, than the football players. He is undeniably a genius. His professors marvel at his ideas, ponder his opinions. Destiny, he says, is sheer logic. He has proven it in a mathematical formula which you would never understand. He respects you, he says, but don't try to debate logic with him. He has his limits, he says, and he's warning you about them now—if you try to fight with him, you'll always lose.

You know he's faking it, but on the other hand what he's saying seems so obviously absurd that you wonder at the possibility of it. You imagine him pictured in a physics book two hundred years from now. "David Clarisse," the caption reads, "the man who proved the existence of destiny." And then, at a corner of the page, a gratuitous picture of you: "Cynthia, the woman who fought him and lost."

It's a slow day at work. Lisa has bought a globe—from a salesman she felt sorry for—that she keeps on her desk, giving it a spin each time she answers the phone. In a single day, she has memorized the capitals of each of the fifty states. This, you find baffling.

She quizzes you on these capitals, pleased when she finally stumps you on Nebraska. "Not Topeka," she says, in the tone of voice you use when you're trying to be patient. "It's Lincoln, Nebraska; Topeka, Kansas." She purses her tiny lips together with an air of authority.

You retreat to your office and open the newspaper. Pleased is what you know you should be, yet you feel you've been let down. You were expecting more of a struggle, something the two of you would overcome together. Lisa's reform has come too easily; your crusade is over and you feel you've had no real part in it.

Rick is lounging around in the kitchen, wearing your bathrobe. Blue terry cloth, with white stripes—too small for him, too large for you. Jimi Hendrix is blasting out of the living room. "You know," Rick says, "I loved that man." He points toward the living room, indicating, you assume, Jimi Hendrix. "Why did he have to die?"

"Drugs will do it to you," you say, clicking your heels across the floor of the kitchen. You pick up some plates with crumbs on them, put them in the sink, and run water over them; pick up a sponge and start erasing stains from the counters.

"Most women don't understand," he says.

"Don't understand what?"

"Oh, about heroes, love, the broader perspective. But you, you're someone I can really talk to."

He asks you if you want a drink, which of course you do, so you sit there with him, sipping on brandy as he continues to mourn the passing of the sixties. Eventually, he gets out his pot. As you're passing a joint back and forth, you begin to tell him about an Arlo Guthrie concert you went to once. There were all these people selling drugs outside, calling out the names: "LSD! MDA! THC!" A man stood beside a fountain, staring into the water. "H_2O!" he called. "H_2O! H_2O!"

Rick convulses with laughter, which pleases you. Up until now, no one else has ever found this story amusing at all. But he continues to laugh until he's crying, which makes you a little nervous. "H_2O!" he keeps calling out. "H_2O! H_2O!"

This is how David and Adelle find you when they return.

"Water?" Adelle says. "Is that what you want?"

"Cynthia," David says, "are you all right?"

You're hanging off the side of the bed, with your head on the floor. Not the most comfortable position, but it's something David likes to do.

There's a knock on the door of your bedroom. You can't believe his parents have gotten in without your hearing them, but if you haven't heard them, they must have heard you. "Still awake, kids?" Adelle is saying from the other side of the door.

You push yourself upright, then into the bed beneath the covers. One of your legs is still on the floor when she opens the door. You leave it there, as though that's the way you sleep. You can see her silhouette wobbling in the doorway, like she's had too much to drink. "Well," she says, "I just thought I'd say good night."

"Good night," you say.

"Sweet dreams," she says, in a girlish tone.

"OK, Adelle," David says, "we've said good night already."

"*You* haven't," she says.

"OK, damn it, good night."

Adelle lets out a nervous laugh, clears her throat, and teeters backward, closing the door behind her.

David's fist jabs at a pillow. "Jesus," he says, "I can't make love now."

"Well fine," you say. "It's late anyway."

"No it's not fine. You want to, don't you?"

"Actually, no. Let's just go to sleep. Come on, it's late."

"No. We've got to talk." He's up on an elbow with his legs tensed, jerking the covers untucked from the bottom of the bed.

"Talk about what?" you say.

"Our feelings."

"Who can have feelings at three A.M.?"

"Don't you love me anymore?"

"Look," you say, "when are your parents going to leave?"

As you get to work in the morning, Lisa greets you at the door. "So, I hear you're getting married."

You scan the walls for hidden TV cameras. It's "Candid Camera" or "Twilight Zone"; you can't decide which. But no, there aren't any cameras.

"Who told you that?" you say.

"Your mother-in-law."

"She's not my mother-in-law."

"OK, so she's going to be."

"No. I'm not getting married."

"OK, I know, you wanted to keep it a secret, but it's not anymore. She seems really nice. We talked for a long time."

"You called my apartment?"

"Yeah, a couple of days ago. I was going to ask for a day off, but she told me it wouldn't be OK with you."

You go directly to your office and call your apartment. After several rings, Adelle answers and tells you she can't talk now, she's busy.

"Busy!" you say, "I'm the one with the job. I'm the one who's—"

"Look," she says, "I really have to go."

At lunchtime there's a surprise wedding shower for you, co-hosted by Lisa and Adelle. Most of the people you work with have gotten you presents. They fill up the coffee room, watching you open them. Sheets, trays, vases, appliances. Sorensen gives you a cheese board. Adelle gives you towels, "so you'll never run out when your relatives come to visit," she says.

You are numb, speechless, horrified. You suppose they assume that you are stunned at their generosity, at their thoughtfulness. And you have to admit to yourself that, in a way, you are.

Afterward, Adelle follows you up to your office. You sit behind your desk; she sits in the chair on the other side. "I shouldn't say this," she says, "but you know, I've always wanted a daughter like you." She gazes wistfully into your eyes.

You feel like someone's slipped some kind of drug into your coffee this morning; you're not sure how to react. Part of you is touched, but the other part feels like bolting out of your office. You watch as Adelle's face begins to drop. Suddenly, she is crying.

"What is it?" you ask her. "What did I say wrong?"

"Nothing," she says, with a sad little smile. "It's what you don't say."

Sorensen walks in, clears his throat, and offers her a mint. She looks up contritely, takes it, and thanks him. As soon as she smiles, he launches into a talk on the art of public relations, takes her off on a tour of the offices.

By the time they return, he's got her acting like she works for him. "You know what impresses me most about this office, Mr. Sorensen?" she's saying. "Everything's so polished, not a single thing out of place."

Sorensen blushes but he's smiling. "Yes," he says. "We like to keep things tidy around here."

You get home to find David asleep in your bed, Adelle sponging out the inside of your refrigerator. "What's going on?" you ask her.

"Just trying to keep things tidy," she says, looking pleased with herself.

"Where's the food?" you say.

"Well, I had to throw most of it out." She points to the opened garbage can. There are several white containers of Chinese leftovers on top, embedded in a layer of macaroni and cheese.

"Fellini," Rick says.

You ignore him. "That's all perfectly good food," you say.

"It looked old," she says. "Some of it seemed slimy."

"Just like a shot out of a Fellini movie," Rick says, still staring at the garbage.

"No it isn't! It's my food!"

Rick opens up one of the Chinese containers, takes out a chicken wing, and rips a piece of meat off with his teeth, takes a swallow of ginger ale out of a bottle on the counter, and finishes chewing.

"Look," you say to Adelle, "it's good enough for him to eat."

"Food! It's only food!" she says. "We'll get more. I've heard they sell it now in grocery stores."

"BUT THERE WAS NOTHING WRONG WITH THE STUFF I HAD!"

"I was only trying to help," she says, in a very small voice.

You head for your bedroom, like one giant storm cloud looking for another, slamming the door of the room behind you. David bolts upright on the bed. "I don't ask you for much, do I?" you yell.

He opens his mouth, you assume to disagree.

"Don't answer that," you shout. "It's not a question. So your parents come to stay for a couple of weeks. So it's a little crowded. So what, you think. Right?"

"Well, I—"

"Well it's more than a little crowded, David. It's claustrophobic. And now I suppose you're going to tell me how hard they've been trying to get along and do things for me and how I ought to appreciate that. But the truth is—"

"Cynthia," David says, "calm down."

"Right. You think I ought to mellow out. Why can't I bend just a little? Well, I'm too old for that, David. Don't you know that?"

"Well, no," he says, shaking his head. "Listen, I don't know what to say."

You don't know what to say either. David sighs and leaves the room. You take off your clothes, tossing them around onto different parts of the floor, then get into bed and sleep until David joins you later, his movements deliberate, careful to avoid touching any part of you. This infuriates you, and you lie awake seething. Your stomach growls; you imagine yourself as a woman made of lava, building up the heat of her resolve.

* * *

You've still got all of your shower presents in your car, and you know what you're going to do with them—give them back. And then you're going to go home in the afternoon and take a stand. You practice your delivery as you drive. "Out!" you're going to yell. "All of you out of here! This is my apartment and I like living in it alone. I like running my own life and I'm good at it. . . ." The speech continues; you go over it a few times until you're sure you've got it loud enough.

At the end of the day you're loaded up with phone calls. Everyone leaves before you do. It's all right; you'll give the presents back tomorrow.

When you arrive home, no one is there. You're no idiot. You can't be fooled this easily. They're going to jump out of a closet or surprise you in some other, horrible way. But there's a note next to the phone: "Finally found a room for the folks," it says in David's solid script. "Sorry things had to work out this way." Beside the note the yellow pages are opened to "Hotels."

You're stunned. "Where is everybody?" you say aloud. The speech you've planned suddenly seems as hollow as your voice now, echoing back at you. You look around for dishes to wash, counters to wipe, something to clean. But there seems to be nothing out of place anywhere.

Your towels are folded up in a pile in the living room, the albums now stacked neatly along the shelves beneath your stereo. You pull out a Laurie Anderson album and put it on your turntable. Actually, it's Arlo Guthrie, stuffed into the wrong jacket. You sigh but smile begrudgingly and let him continue. Alice's Restaurant.

Suddenly, the place seems very empty without them, as though there is too much space between things. You have to think for a minute to remember what it was you used to do when you came home from work to an empty apartment. You pick up your latest Jackie Collins novel, open it to the bookmark, then slam it down on the table. You can't imagine how you ever kidded yourself into believing that you liked being alone. You just got used to it, didn't you? Enjoyment is something entirely different.

You want to hear voices, you want color, activity, surprises. You want to be having a drink with Rick, listening to him go on about the past. Or talking with Adelle about your future—who else has ever cared enough to try to run your life for you? And you've been taking David for granted—haven't you?—fighting an involvement you've grown to depend on. You miss them now, all of them. Who else has ever paid so much attention to you? It's been years, you think. Years.

Shaking your head, you pour yourself a straight shot of brandy and sit beside the yellow pages, still opened to "Hotels." You start dialing. There are a lot of numbers, and though you feel kind of foolish, you're just going to keep calling until you find them and then you're going to bring them back.

TRAINSCAPES
by Lauren Belfer
(Columbia University)

Tonight Neil decides to rearrange the countryside. He positions the lamp to cast shadows across the landscape. He stretches out on the study floor. He concentrates, then moves the waterfall closer to the mountains. He adjusts the course of a river. He rotates the lakeside inn to give its guests a better view. The sticky scent of wisteria blows in from the porch.

Neil is an associate professor of medieval art at a women's college outside Philadelphia. Term papers are piled on his desk, but instead of reading them, Neil studies his current project, an HO-gauge scale interpretation of southwestern Pennsylvania in 1905, by his reckoning the year that the Chesapeake and Ohio Railroad first crossed the Youghiogheny River. After his parents' divorce when he was seven, Neil spent his summers at his uncle's farm a mile from the river. Although he can recall each detail of the local landscape, Neil doesn't bind himself to historical or topographical verisimilitude. He likes to think that he creates a trainscape the way someone else might write a novel.

When he's ready for the run, he attaches an American Flyer locomotive to a six-car freight train. The models are dented and old, a look which Neil gave them himself, because what train doesn't get battered every day of its run? Neil likes this particular freight train because of the hoboes he put into the cars. He spent days painting their khaki jackets and pants, even darkening the knee patches. The hoboes peer out the sliding doors, and their expectant faces remind Neil of his uncle. Neil watches intently as the train approaches Blue Rock Ledge. Just across the trestle, another hobo is poised to jump aboard.

After one run, however, Neil feels frustrated. This is his first spring in Philadelphia, and the dense humidity makes him restless. He debates whether to change the date of the scene to 1917. He would love to do a troop train: the high-spirited young recruits with their barely grown beards, the all-night card games, the clattering train rushing nonstop past country towns.

Neil remembers his own first trip abroad, when he was twenty-four. It's over two decades now since he strode down the marble staircase of Pittsburgh's P & LE Railroad Station, as sunlight poured through the stained-glass windows and sent flashes of color across his path. He stared out the train window all the way to New York, where he boarded the ship to Cherbourg.

He was a patched-together graduate student then. He'd just passed his Ph.D. orals with distinction, and he was surviving on fellowships. He paid his ship passage by lecturing on Gothic architecture. He always felt awkward on the ship, as if his collar were too tight or his jacket too thick. He kept glancing behind him, certain he'd done something wrong and wondering if anyone had noticed.

But it was that summer that Neil met Julia. He was working as a digger on his advisor's excavation of the second crypt of St. Martin. Julia, a graduate student from Columbia, was gluing together pottery shards. She wasn't pretty, so it was easy for him to talk to her. That first weekend, while Neil was still stumbling over his French and afraid to wander outside the set path between hotel and dig, Julia led him down the streets radiating from the church without hesitation or second glances. She walked into one shop after another and bought everything they needed for a picnic.

By the end of the summer, Neil's advisor had secured for him a temporary post available unexpectedly at Yale. Neil told Julia in confidence, and she told everyone else. Rumors abounded that Neil would be running his own dig in a few years. Neil's advisor was indeed negotiating with the French government for approval to begin work at St. Riquier, on the southern pilgrimage route. Neil would do the initial research for his dissertation, and if warranted, he would organize large-scale excavations later. The old boys have anointed their newest son, Julia teased, and she stayed close by him. The following spring, they married.

The diagrams and reports from St. Riquier are now stuffed into the space between the bookcase and the wall. Neil senses on his fingertips the gritty dust that covers them.

Thinking about Julia, Neil remembers that he needs a date for the end-of-the-year faculty dance on Saturday. He certainly can't bring a student to that. Not Sheri nor Tracy nor Emily, nor any of the other soft-faced creatures who fawn over him after class while he gathers his crinkled lecture notes and collects his scratchy slides from the projectionist. Trevor Matlin, his department chairman, has warned him twice this year about what he so tactfully described as "student affiliations."

"I myself care not a jot about your personal life," Trevor said in his Oxbridge cadences, "but the tenure committee doesn't appreciate this underage sort of thing." Trevor is an expert on Watteau and well versed himself, undoubtedly, in the corruption of minors. Boys, in his case.

Neil had seen Sheri this afternoon. She walked beside him down the corridor to his office and placed her hand on his arm to slow his steps. He could smell the scent beneath her loose dress. She seemed naked to him beside his well-tailored French suit.

They've become interchangeable, Sheri et al. They graduate (they can count on him for a good letter of recommendation), and new ones take their places. He doesn't flatter himself by imagining they care for him. He believes he's a kind of contest for them: they spend the night, then go off the next day to flaunt their sexual prestige over lunch in the dining hall. The worst part is that he never feels as if he's actually talking to these girls. Rather, he's playing out the role that seems to be expected of him, just as his lectures constitute a performance that's lately been getting a little shabby around the edges. No, he doesn't understand why committees are so quick to presume that he is the exploiter.

He retrieves from his desk the ledger reserved for women. Next to each entry, he has recorded the details of every date or telephone conversation. Paradoxically, the more names he collects, the fewer dates he gets—although he makes sure that the women involved never know this, as he plays on jealousy and works to create the illusion that he is the pursued, not the pursuer. His list includes married women, because he knows only too well that marriages do not necessarily last, and it would be a pity to lose track of a possibility. As a policy, however, he never has affairs with married women: he knows what that's like from the other side. So he calls the married women every few years to update their status, and if they are free, he asks them out. Julia is on the rotation, and he fully expects that one of these days she won't hang up when she hears his name. She has two children now with her second husband, but Neil doesn't mind children. He likes them, in fact. But he always locks the study door before they visit, because in his experience children don't show proper respect for model trains.

He checks his watch. 10:50. Shouldn't be too late to call. He starts at the beginning of the alphabet. Anson, Marjorie. Atlanta. He sees from his notes that she wasn't entirely forthcoming on the one night they spent together, but he remembers that she has the almond eyes of a Coptic painting.

"Margie, Neil here," he says into her answering machine. "The wisteria is blowing in the window and reminding me of you." Oh, no, he thinks as he hangs up. With a line like that, she'll never call back.

Next, Dunnington, Carol. Boston. Shy. Baked him oatmeal cookies on his birthday because he'd told her his mother did. Married three years ago, to a guy named Jim whom he knows from graduate school.

"Neil, is something wrong?" she asks. He hears a rustle and a click and imagines her sitting up in bed and turning on the light.

"Wrong? Not at all. Just calling to see if the bliss of marriage really—"

"Are you having a problem?" she asks. He hears Jim's voice questioning her urgently in the background. "Do you need to talk to Jim?" A friend, he realizes, she thinks of me as a friend. He feels embarrassed, caught in the midst of some despicable secret act.

"I lost track of the time," he stammers. "Is it eleven already? Well . . . I'm leaving for St. Riquier in a month. So I thought I'd check in." Jim gets on the other extension, and they talk about Jim and Carol's house, their garden, the baby on the way. The things that would shape and fill my life if I were still married, Neil thinks. He and Julia never had a chance to have children; she said she wanted to finish her dissertation first, and by then . . . Jim and Carol probably see her on the Boston academic circuit with the so very urbane department chairman who is now her husband. Neil waits nervously for them to mention her, wonders if he should ask about her, then fears that they don't even think of him in the same context as Julia, anymore. He hurries on to the next call.

Grant, Susan. New York. Ten dates, eight nights together, six years ago. He rereads his notation about the half-hour they spent on the edge of a bathtub while in the next room a party of overzealous medievalists discussed the Byzantine influences on the domed cathedrals of the Perigord. He held onto her hips, she held onto the shower curtain, and they managed, barely, not to topple over at the crucial moments. He should have thought of Susan before.

"Neil!" she says. "You were next on my list. I'm organizing the Chapel Hill conference this fall, and I'd like you to give a lecture on St. Riquier."

"Why don't you come down for the weekend and we'll discuss it."

"How about it? We're all waiting to hear what you're up to. Are you making the link to Sens? I warn you—if you don't, I will. How's the book?"

He glances at the manuscripts piled on the windowsill, flecked with withered leaves and bits of dirt from the flowering fuchsia hanging above. "You'll have to see for yourself when you get here this weekend," he says with a sardonic laugh.

"I'll put you down for, let's see . . . erotic iconography in monastic stained glass. That should entice you."

"You'll be interested to know that I've got an old-fashioned bathtub here," Neil says, "with a very wide and comfortable ledge."

"Neil," she says, as if she's finally noticed him, "that bathtub scene was an awfully long time ago. Can we just move on to the next phase now, please? Let me know about the lecture." She hangs up before he can respond.

He slouches in his chair. He'll have to work up something good for Chapel Hill. It's considered an honor to give a lecture there. Guaranteed placement in an obscure journal. Impresses the tenure committee. This is his second tenure-track position, so he should at least try to appease the committee. We had such confidence in you, the first committee said. We deferred your review year after year, waiting for the book.

He used to love conferences like the one at Chapel Hill. He and Julia would go as a team. They'd set off each morning for different lectures, then meet at lunch to exchange notes. He felt such a sense of ease, as if he belonged exactly where he was. But the last conference he attended, at Georgetown during spring break, seemed dominated by friends jockeying for the leftovers in next fall's job openings. At least his colloquium on the effect of the Crusades on the evolution of ambulatories turned out to be more interesting than he expected, and he even got a few laughs with his slide of—

The projectionist. That's it. Anna . . . something. M.F.A. candidate in drawing and painting at one of the Washington, D.C., universities, he can't remember which. Wanted to come to St. Riquier this summer as draftsman, the most important position on the dig and the only one that pays. Unfortunately, he already had a draftsman. A man, but a good artist nevertheless. He can start planning now for next summer, however. He put Anna's number and his notes about her into the dig file, instead of the date ledger, which is how he lost track of her. He rummages through the papers on the windowsill.

Palmer, Anna. Age twenty-five. Lunch after the colloquium. Good slide projectionist. He recalls that she always managed to get slide A on screen A, slide B on screen B, then change B while A was still up—no small feat in the world of slide projectionism, seven dollars an hour. And she wants something from him, which makes things easier. Three and a half minutes later, he has a date for the Saturday night dance.

He puts his feet up on the desk and reexamines the trainscape. It's still not quite right. There's something unnatural about it. The hoboes look a bit posed, perhaps. Neil's tempted to take it apart altogether, right now, and start the one he's been mulling over for months: a scene of his uncle bringing sheep to the farm. Of course, Neil's uncle never actually got sheep—couldn't afford to—but the idea of sheep seemed to keep him going year after year, until his death. Whenever there was a drought, or a drop in prices, he'd say, "Sheep next spring, Neil. Then we'll be in clover."

The sheep scene would be a massive project, and until tonight, Neil hasn't felt able to muster the energy. He decides to do a full plan on graph paper before dismantling the Chesapeake and Ohio Railroad crossing the Youghiogheny River. Most of his scene problems develop when he doesn't sufficiently plan in advance. He won't let that happen this time. Although it's almost midnight, he takes a pad of graph paper from his desk and begins work.

On Friday evening, Neil waits for Anna Palmer at the college train station. After a day of rain, the sky has suddenly cleared. The sunlight shimmers yellow on the trees. As the train approaches, Neil imagines Anna sprawled across his bed—thick dark curls cascading down her back, high-heeled sandals that she pushes off with her toes, long bare limbs stretched across his quilt. He searches for her among the tired faces getting off the train.

"Neil?" a voice asks. He looks down at a small young woman without makeup who wears a cotton print dress and flat shoes. There's a rim of darkness around her eyes. Yes. He remembers now. No wonder he put her in the dig file. Well, he'll just have to make the best of it. He decides to speed up his standard attack plan, to get the sex over with and leave time for train work afterwards. He arranged everything before he left for the station: the French dinner, the fine wine, the good china (from his marriage—he got to keep it because the department chairman let Julia buy a new set). Then after dinner, he'll give Anna a tour of the apartment that ends in the bedroom. He'll bypass the study, because he's noticed that women tend to find something odd about model trains. They don't say anything. They simply turn back to the hallway and pointedly admire his Viollet-le-Duc prints.

As they walk home, Neil discusses St. Riquier, as he always does with women.

"Why do you keep doing the dig?" Anna interrupts to ask. "Hasn't it gotten boring?"

Neil feels shocked, as if she's committed a diplomatic blunder. Doesn't she realize that she's supposed to be (or at least pretend to be) impressed? "Even small discoveries widen our understanding of the past," he lectures, "and each piece of evidence becomes a wellspring—"

"I don't care what you wrote on your last grant application," she says. "Why do *you* do it?"

Why you. Why I. He studies the light as it rakes across the facades of the old mansions that line the street, lending a precise geometry to the otherwise weary looking homes.

For years, Neil has hidden behind the dig's prestige. When fellow art historians ask him about St. Riquier, he earnestly discusses funding sources and hints at the conclusions he will explore in his book. With Sheri et al., he teasingly suggests that the real reason he goes to France each year is to meet the provincial jeunes filles, who are almost, but not quite, as pretty as they are.

During the early years of the dig, he found pleasure in designing a project to his own specifications. And he and Julia became parents to the young students who joined them. For the first time since his parents' divorce, Neil felt as if he were part of a family. The pain faded from the time when he let himself into a silent apartment each day after school; to fill the hours until his mother got home, and to block out the nameless noises of yet another new home, he studied for all he was worth. He still appreciates the irony that it was his loneliness that made him a scholar.

That first summer at St. Riquier without Julia, he panicked when he confronted the tables at dinner. Everyone seemed intimate with laughter and sealed off from him. He was the only one who didn't belong, he thought as he struggled to find an empty place. But gradually he learned to mask himself in charm, and to make the young women vie for his presence at their tables. He came to like the dig because it allowed him to be among people without being close to them. He's never lonely at St. Riquier, because he's surrounded by volunteers. But since he's the leader, people expect him to be standoffish.

"I like the independence," he says finally to Anna.

"You like being pompous," she replies.

"That, too," he says with a laugh, before he remembers that she doesn't have the right to challenge him. She's from the bottom of the list—in fact, she's not even on the list.

After dinner, Anna takes herself on a tour of the apartment. Neil doesn't like this. It's his apartment, he should direct the tour. She opens the study door with a brisk, "What's in here?" and he cringes. But when she sees the trainscape, she sits on the floor and disengages the American Flyer. "Where did you get this?" she asks. "My brother looked for one for years. He used to love model trains."

Neil stands with his hand on the doorknob.

"You might as well show me what others you've got," she says.

With a shrug, he opens the sliding doors on the bottom of the bookcase and takes out the shoe boxes in which he stores his collection. He keeps the rare engines in boxes padded with foam rubber and lined with white velvet. In regular boxes, he stores the models by subject: mail cars, bank cars, Pullman cars, and so on. He sits beside her on the floor as she examines the trains. Now that he is close to her, he sees the soft angularity of her body. The grace of her movements reminds him of the dance students he sometimes takes up with. He wonders why she doesn't touch him, the way the other girls do who even in his office lounge behind him with their elbows on his shoulders and their hands clasped across his chest. He feels oddly comfortable. Shyly, he points out the trainscape's landmarks and tells Anna about the sheep scene.

"Aren't you supposed to be writing a book?" Anna asks.

"Ah, the book." Neil laughs nervously. "Derailed," he says, mustering a smile. "Former wife blew up the tracks."

"Pardon?"

"Left. Nine years ago." He tries to sound both sarcastic and nonchalant. He has never told anyone his feelings about Julia, and he expects Anna to laugh. That's what Sheri et al. would do. They would presume that confessions were part of the standardized scenario. But Anna simply stares at him, as if she's actually stopped to listen to his words instead of moving on to the next line. He picks up a mail car and tinkers with the wheels. "I haven't published anything since then." He attaches the mail car to the freight train. "You see, she married a guy in the same field—don't ask who, I'm not telling," he says, and now Anna does laugh with him. "Full professor, wealthy family, very famous. In our own limited little world, of course."

"Didn't you want to take revenge by publishing the best articles anyone had ever read?"

"Can't say I thought of that. Seemed more like I didn't have much worth publishing." He studies the trainscape. "She has a family now."

"Do you want children?"

"I suppose so. Though kids always wreck a model train set." Suddenly he feels desperately the need to hold her, to reassure himself that he hasn't pushed her away by confiding in her. He places a hand on her shoulder and pulls her towards him. But she leans out of his grasp and points to the trainscape's field of poppies and wild mustard.

"Mustard is a whiter yellow than what you have," she says. "And poppies are more brilliant." He takes out the paints and mixes the colors until she is satisfied, then lets her repaint the field with a four-haired brush.

The next morning, Neil finds Anna on the front porch glancing through his train catalogues. Banks of lavender hydrangea shield her from the street, and sunlight flickers through the trees.

"Sleep well?" she asks with a smile. Last night, she settled herself into the guest room despite his best efforts to move her into his bedroom. No, he didn't sleep well.

"Too bad," she says, laughing. "Look. Sheep." He sits beside her on the swing chair and studies catalogue entries. Lincolns, Merinos, and Romneys. Straight and curly fleece. Tufted and untufted tails.

"I don't know what kind my uncle would have wanted," Neil says, hesitating over the pages. He can't focus on the choices. He feels warm and sleepy beside her.

"Since he's dead, you'll have to decide for yourself," Anna says.

After due consideration, Neil picks the Cotswolds because of the ruff around their necks, an Elizabethan touch that pleases Anna. Thirty lambs, fifty ewes, ten rams, seven pens, and turf enough to create five square feet of hilly dale. He chooses a sheering house and accessories, and five train cars designed for transporting sheep. He settles on an Australian sheep dog, which he will paint a color called "blue merle," which he once saw on a dog in France. "It's the kind of dog my uncle would have had, if he had known that such a dog existed," he tells Anna. Finally, he picks the slaughterhouse.

"Do you have to kill them as soon as you've gotten them?" she asks.

"It's just part of the landscape," he says.

He must admit, he feels proud at the dance when Anna impresses Trevor Matlin with her knowledge of Watteau's figure drawings. "He captures the turn of a hand better than any other artist," she says, moving her own hand in a kind of dancing imitation. She and

Trevor go off to the drinks table swept up in a conspiracy of figure drawings. Just like graduate school, Neil thinks, when a few passionate discussions of useless subjects were all he needed to get by from day to day. Back then, he studied Abbot Suger and the Neoplatonist philosophers of Gothic. They wrote that God is light. That the cathedral's soaring piers and sheets of light-soaked colored glass manifest the kingdom of Heaven. Neil was not religious, but something about this philosophy gave him comfort, and his dedication to it gave him a purpose. He surrendered himself to it, much as he surrendered to Julia, who seemed to unite the facets of his life. But gradually he came to suspect that Julia had other interests in Gothic besides the philosophy of light, such as contemporary philosophers of light. When the department chairman at Neil's university had an opening at his side, Julia applied, as if marriages were career steps, each one a move up the ladder to positions of ever-greater reward. And shortly thereafter Neil walked into a cathedral and experienced it merely as a job, like any other, and the radiant air only made him squint as he waited impatiently for the sun to shift.

One month later, the Saturday before he leaves for France, Neil sits at his drafting table and sifts through several years' worth of diagrams from St. Riquier. Anna is at his desk, doing charcoal drawings for her portfolio. With her safe beside him, accounted for, as it were, he feels free to resume the methodical work he gave up years before. He watches her as she draws. She seems rapt in concentration. The light from the window behind her illuminates her hair, as if she herself were the work of art, rather than the artist.

Three weekends, four nights together—that's how he would enter their relationship in his ledger. He would relate that on the second weekend, without his usual cajoling, teasing, or manipulation of jealousy and guilt, they simply remained together, as if that were the most natural alternative open to them. But he hasn't made any notes on Anna. Compared to his work, the careful note-taking seems pointless. He's been like a train with its switches crossed, he realizes, unable to move.

But as the day progresses, Neil keeps imagining what Anna will be doing at home while he's in France. Layout work at a magazine, she has told him more than once, caustically inquiring whether he could offer her a paying job in France instead. Yet he can't get his mind off the idea that she'll disappear if for an instant he looks away.

"I bet you'll be spending the next two months with a young stud while I'm slaving away at the dig," he says after dinner. That's the sort of thing he would say to Sheri et al., and he is sickened to hear himself saying it to Anna. He has made her an iced cappuccino, and the froth has left a line on her lip that he wants to kiss away. "Around July thirtieth, I'll get a postcard reporting that you've run off with a lifeguard and don't have time to write. Or maybe you'll be swept off your feet by your department chairman, in exchange for a hefty fellowship." He wants to nestle his face in the hollow of her shoulder and hear her reassurances. He gets up to clear the table.

"It's all right," he says from the kitchen. "Plenty of girls over there. French provincials—the best kind." He wishes she would tell him to stop.

"I had been planning to visit you for a week in August, as I think you may recall," she says finally.

He stands at the sink and scrubs the coffee maker. Yes, she planned to visit. That was the reason he went through a complex series of maneuvers last week to get Sheri (who won the undergraduate lottery to attend the dig) installed in the pensione room next to his: so that when Anna arrived, she would see that she couldn't take him for granted.

"Are you trying to tell me that you want to—'date other people,' I believe is the phrase—while you're away?" she asks.

"I'm not the one I'm worried about."

She comes into the kitchen and stands behind him. "Then you've created a false image of me," she says. "Why do you think you've done that?"

Clean the coffeepot, he tells himself. If he trusts her, he can see his future mapped out in quietude and comfort. That's what love is, or so he's read. The one other time he relied on that map of the future, his wife disappeared and left a blank space where towns and cities used to be.

That night Anna eases herself against him in the bed. She wraps her arms around his chest and pulls herself closer, fitting her body into the curves of his back, her legs against his, her feet molded to his ankles. She rubs her hand across his stomach and deep into his skin.

"It's hot," he says, shaking her off. "I've got to get up." She says something, but he doesn't listen. Her voice sounds to him like a radio band slightly off frequency, and he chooses not to twist the dial to make the sound come in more clearly.

He goes into the study and closes the door behind him. He locks it as an extra precaution and hopes that she hears the bolt turning. He opens the windows. The air is sweet and cool against his naked body. He sees a sickle moon when the breeze blows the leaves aside. Near the dig in France, there's an old quarry where he and his crew go swimming naked in the moonlight.

With his Swiss army knife, he meticulously slits open the package which arrived yesterday. He had planned to wait until he got back from his trip to open it, to save it for the letdown days he always feels when he returns home from the dig. But he will begin now instead. He takes the train models out of the box, then the pens and shearing house. Finally, he discovers the tiny sheep, each wrapped in fluffy cotton and surgical gauze. So small, so perfect, so pure. His fingers shake as he cradles their delicate forms.

He will paint them tonight. He mixes white with black again and again. He searches for that peculiar evanescent gray of the sheep he saw at Mont St. Michel on his first trip to France. He no longer feels distracted by the girl in the next room. He adds a touch of blue, a hint of yellow. The color is almost right.

THREE THOUSAND DOLLARS

by David Lipsky

(Johns Hopkins University)

My mother doesn't know that I owe my father three thousand dollars. What happened was this: My father sent me three thousand dollars to pay my college tuition. That was the deal he and my mom had made. We'd apply for financial aid without him to get a lower tuition, and then he'd send me a check, and then I'd put the check in my bank account and write one of my own checks out to the school. This made sense not because my father is rich but because he makes a lot more money than my mother does—she's a teacher—and if we could get a better deal using her income instead of his, there was no reason not to. Only, when the money came, instead of giving it to the school, I spent it. I don't even know what I spent it on—books and things, movies. The school never called me in about it. They just kept sending these bills to my mother, saying we were delinquent in our payments. That's how my father found out. My mother kept sending him the bills, he kept looking on them for the money he'd sent me, and I kept telling him that the school's computer was making an error and that I'd drop by the office one day after class and clear it up.

So when I came home to New York for the summer my mother was frantic, because the school had called her and she couldn't understand how we could owe them so much money. I explained to her, somehow, that what we owed them was a different three thousand dollars—that during the winter the school had cut our financial aid in half. My mother called my father to ask him to send us the extra money, and he said that he wanted to talk to me.

I waited till the next day so I could call him at his office. My stepmother's in finance, and she gets crazy whenever money comes up—her nightmare, I think, is of a river of money flowing from my father to me without veering through her—so I thought it would be better to talk to him when she wasn't around. My father has his own advertising agency in Chicago—Paul Weller Associates. I've seen him at his job when I've visited him out there, and he's pretty good. His company does all the ads for a big midwestern supermarket chain, and mostly what he does is supervise on these huge sets while camera crews stand around filming fruit. It's a really big deal. The fruit has to look just right. My father stands there in a coat and tie, and he and a bunch of other guys keep bending over and making sure that the fruit is O.K.—shiny-looking. There are all these other people standing around with water vapor and gloss. One word from my father and a thousand spray cans go off.

When he gets on the phone, I am almost too nervous to talk to him, though his voice is slow and far off, surrounded by static. I ask him to please send more money. He says he won't. I ask why, and he says because it would be the wrong thing to do. He doesn't say anything for a moment and then I tell him that I agree with him, that I think he is right not to send the money. He doesn't say anything to acknowledge this, and there is a long pause during which I feel the distance between us growing.

Just before he gets off the phone, he says, "What I'm really curious about, Richard, is what your mother thinks of all this," and this wakes me up, because he doesn't seem to realize that I haven't told her yet. I was afraid to. Before I came home, I thought of about twenty different ways of telling her, but once she was right there in front of me it just seemed unbearable. What I'm afraid of now is that my father will find that out, and then he will tell her himself. "I mean," he says, "if I were her, I probably couldn't bear having you in the house. What is she planning to do? Isn't the school calling you up? I can't imagine she has the money to pay them. Isn't she angry at you, Rich?"

I say, "She's pretty angry."

"I hope so," my father says. "I hope she's making you feel terrible. When I talked to her on the phone yesterday—and we only talked for a couple of seconds—she seemed mostly concerned with getting me to give you this money, but I hope that deep down she's really upset about this. Tell her it's no great tragedy if you don't go back to school in the fall. You can get a job in the city and I'll be happy to pay your tuition again next year. I'm sorry, but it just doesn't feel right for me to keep supporting you while you keep acting the way you've been acting, which to me seems morally deficient."

My mother is tall, with light hair and gray, watery eyes. She is a jogger. She has been jogging for six years, and as she's gotten older her body has gotten younger looking. Her face has gotten older, though. There are lines around her lips and in the corners of her eyes, as if she has taken one of those statues without arms or a head and put her own head on top of it. She teaches art at a grammar school a few blocks up from our house, and the walls of our apartment are covered with her drawings. That's the way she teaches. She stands over these kids while she has them drawing a still life or a portrait or something, and if they're having trouble she sits down next to them to show them what to do, and usually she ends up liking her own work so much that she brings it home with her. We have all these candlesticks and clay flowerpots that she made during class. She used to teach up in Greenwich, Connecticut, which is where we lived before she and my dad got divorced, right before I started high school. Every summer, she and a bunch of other teachers rent a house together in Wellfleet; she will be leaving New York to go up there in six days, so I only have to keep her from finding out until then.

When I get off the phone, she is in the living room reading the newspaper. She gives me this ready-for-the-worst look and asks, "What did he say?"

I explain to her that I will not be going back to college in September. Instead, I will be staying in the apartment and working until I have paid the school the rest of the money.

My mother gets angry. She stands up and folds the paper together and stuffs it into the trash. "Not in this apartment," she says.

"Why not?" I ask. "It's big enough."

"A boy your age should be in college. Your friends are in college. Your father went to college. I'd better call him back." She walks to the phone, which sits on the windowsill.

"Why?" I ask quickly. "He said he wasn't going to do it."

"Well, of course, that's what he'd say to you. He knows you're afraid of him." She sees I'm going to protest this. "Who could blame you? Who wouldn't be afraid of a man who won't even support his own son's education?"

"He said he doesn't have the money."

"And you believe him?" she asks. "With two Volvos and a town house and cable TV? Let him sell one of his cars if he has to. Let him stop watching HBO. Where are his priorities?"

"I'm not his responsibility."

"Oh, no. You're just his son, that's all; I forgot. Why are you protecting him?"

I look up, and my mother's eyes widen a little—part of her question—and it feels as if she is seeing something in my face, so I realize I'd better get out of the room. "I'm not protecting him," I say. "It's just that you always want everything to be somebody's fault. It's the school's fault. It's nobody's fault. It's no great tragedy if I don't go back to school in the fall; you're the only person who thinks so. Why can't you just accept things, like everyone else?" I walk into my bedroom, shutting the door behind me. I lie on my bed and look up at the ceiling, where the summer bugs have already formed a sooty layer inside the bottom of my light fixture. My ears are hot.

Our apartment is small. There are only the two bedrooms, the living room, the bathroom, and the kitchen, and so if you want to be alone it's pretty impossible. My mother comes in after a few minutes. She has calmed down. She walks over to the air conditioner and turns it on, then waves her hand in front of the vents to make sure that cold air is coming out. I sit up and frown at her.

She sits down next to me and puts her arm around my shoulders. "I'm sorry you're so upset," she says. As she talks she rubs the back of my neck. "But I just think that there are a lot of things we can do before you have to go and look for a full-time job. There are relatives we can call. There are loans we can take out. There are a lot of avenues open to us."

"O.K., Mom."

"I know it must be pretty hard on you, having a father like this." She gives me time to speak, then says, "I mean, a man who won't even pay for his son's school."

"It's not that," I say. "It's not even that I'm that upset. It's just that I don't want us to be beholden to him anymore. I don't even like him very much."

My mom laughs. "What's to like?" she says.

I laugh with her. "It's just that he's so creepy."

"You don't have to tell me. I was married to him."

"Why did you marry him?" I ask.

"He was different when I met him."

"How different could he be?"

Mom laughs, shaking her head. Her eyes blank a little, remembering. She was twenty when she met my father—a year older than I am now. I imagine her in a green flannel skirt and blue knee socks. "I don't know," she says, looking past me. "Not very." We laugh together again. "I don't know. I wanted to get away from my parents, I guess."

"Who could blame you?" I say, but I can tell from a shift in her face that I have pushed too far. Her father died two years back.

"What do you mean?" she asks, turning back to me.

"I don't know," I say. "I mean, you were young."

She nods, as if this fact, remembering it, comes as something of a surprise to her. She blinks. "I was young," she says.

I get a job working at a B. Dalton bookstore. The manager has to fill out some forms, and when he asks me how long I will be working—for the whole year or just for the summer—I say, "Just for the summer," without thinking, and by the time I realize, he has already written it down and it doesn't seem worth the trouble of making him go back and change it. Still, I go through the rest of the day with the feeling that I've done something wrong. It's the store on Fifth Avenue, and it's not a bad place to work. I am sent to the main floor, to the middle register, where old women come in pairs and shuffle through the Romance section. I eat lunch in a little park a block from the store, where a man-made waterfall keeps tumbling down and secretaries drink diet soda. There is a cool breeze, because of the water. It is the second week of the summer, and on returning from lunch I am told I will have Wednesday off, because it is the Fourth of July.

Riding the bus home, I begin thinking that maybe my mother called my father anyway. It's terrible. The bus keeps stopping and people keep piling in, and meanwhile I am imagining their conversation going on. If I could make the bus go faster, maybe I could get home in time to stop them. I try to make mental contact with the bus driver by concentrating. I think, Skip the next stop; but he, out of loyalty to the other passengers or simple psychic deafness, doesn't, and instead the bus keeps stopping and people keep getting off and on. Walking into our building, I get the feeling everyone knows. Even the people on the elevator scowl. Maybe if I had told my mother myself, I would have softened it somehow. What would upset her now is not only the money—although the money would be a big part of it—but also that I tried to put something over on her. I am almost afraid to open our door. "Hello," I call, stepping inside.

As it turns out, my mother isn't home. There is a note on the table. She has gone shopping. I look at the note for a while, to see if I can figure anything out from it. For example, it is a short note. Would she usually write a longer one? It isn't signed "Love" or anything—just "Mom," in the scratchy way she draws her pictures.

I hang my jacket in the closet and then turn on my mom's answering machine. There is one hang-up, and then a message from my father. It makes my whole body go cold. His voice sounds farther away than when we talked the last time. "Richard?" he says. His voice is slow. "This is your father. I just wanted to call to see how things were going. I had an interesting discussion with your mother this afternoon, and we can talk about it later, if you'd like to. Call back if you get a chance." Then there is the clatter of his phone being hung up, and then a little electronic squawk as the connection is broken, which the machine has recorded. I play it again, but there is no way of telling just what he and Mom talked about. I walk into the bathroom and splash cold water on my face and look in the mirror. Then I try reading my mom's note again, but all I can really make it say is that she has gone to the supermarket.

My mother comes home, carrying two big bags of groceries. She pushes the door open with her shoulder. "Can you give me a hand?" she says.

I stand up and take the bags from her and carry them into the kitchen. They are heavy even for me. I hold them close to my chest, where the edges brush against my nose, giving me their heavy, dusty smell. My mom stands in the dining area. She rests one hand on the table. She is wearing running shorts and a T-shirt that on the front says "Perrier" and on the back has the name and date of a race she ran. "Any messages?" she asks me.

I look at her, but I can't tell anything from her face, either. She looks angry, but that could be just because it was hot outside, or because there was too long a line at the supermarket. "I didn't look," I answer. "Don't you even say hello anymore?"

"Hello," she says. She picks up her note and holds it so I can see. "You can throw this away, you know," she says. "Or are you saving it for any particular reason?"

"No, you can throw it away."

"That's nice. How about you throw it away?"

"I'm unloading the groceries right now."

She puts the note back down on the table and then walks into the living room. I unload the rest of the groceries. There is a box of spaghetti, Tropicana orange juice, brown rice, pita bread, a few plain Dannon yogurts. I put everything away and then I fold up the bags and stuff them into the broom closet, where we save them for garbage.

In the living room I hear my mom turn on the machine. There is the hang-up and then my father's message begins again. "Richard?" he says. "This is your father." I walk into the living room. Mom is standing over the machine, one hand on the buttons. "Oh, God," she says, in a bored way when she hears his voice, and she shuts it off. Then she turns around and looks at me. I am standing near the wall. "Why do you have that funny look on your face, Richard?" she asks.

I shrug. "How was your day?" I say.

"Bad." She steps over her chair and sits down on the sofa. From the way she arranged herself, I can tell she is upset. She keeps her arms folded across her stomach, and there is something compressed and angry about her face. The way her lips are pressed together—and also something around her eyes. "You want to make me some tea?"

"What happened?" I ask.

"Nothing happened. I ran. I went shopping. I spoke to your father."

I pull a chair over from the table and sit down across from her. I count to five and then ask, "What did he say?"

She shakes her head and laughs through her nose. "Oh, God. He was awful, Richard. Just awful. Right when he got on the phone, he started asking if you'd found a job, and then when I asked him if he was planning to pay the rest of your tuition he laughed and said of course not. He said it was time for you to learn to take care of yourself. He said it was going to be good for you. I couldn't talk to him. Really, Richard, he was awful. I mean it. Just awful."

"I told you not to call him."

"Well, then, I was stupid, Richard."

"Are you going to call him again?"

"How do I know if I'm going to call him again? Not if he keeps acting that way on the phone to me. But I can't pay the school myself." Her lips go back to being tight, and she pulls her arms closer together, so that each hand curls under the opposite elbow.

It occurs to me that what's pressing down on her face is the money we owe the school. "Did the school call again?" I guess.

She nods. "Yesterday."

"Don't call him," I say.

"Thanks, Richard. You want to get me some tea?"

"How about 'please'?"

"How about throwing that note away? Or are you planning to leave it there till Christmas?"

The next day, I get the same feeling that she has called my father again. I go outside during lunch to phone her. It is very hot, and the undersides of my arms are soggy. I have to walk about two blocks down Fifth Avenue before I can find a free phone, and then when I dial our number there is no answer. I think I may have dialed the number wrong, because even if no one is home there should still be the machine, but when I try again there is still no answer. As I hang up, I catch my reflection in the shiny front of the phone for a second and I look awful, sweaty. The rest of the day is terrible. I can hardly work. I keep ringing up the paperbacks as calendars and the children's books as software. On the way home, I think that even if my father didn't tell her I will have to tell her myself. I'm afraid that if I don't something awful will happen, like we'll never speak to each other again or something. But when I get home she is sitting on the sofa, reading the newspaper with her feet up on a chair, and when I walk into the living room she smiles at me, and it just doesn't seem like the right time. I take off my tie and blazer and then pour myself a glass of milk and sit down next to her. She smells like Ben-Gay—a strong, wintergreenish smell—which is what she rubs on her legs after running.

"How was your day?" she asks me. She has a mug of tea on the cushion next to her, and when I sit down she folds the newspaper and picks up the mug.

"Fine," I say. Then I ask, "Did you go somewhere? I tried calling around noon, but there was no answer."

"I drove up to Greenwich," she says.

"Why didn't you turn on the machine?"

"What are you, the police inspector? I didn't feel like it, that's why."

"But why'd you drive up to Greenwich?"

She laughs. "I feel like I should have one of those big lights on me." She brings her arms very close in to her sides and speaks very quickly, like a suspect: "I don't know. I don't know why I went up to Greenwich." She drinks from her cup, which she holds with both hands. Then she shakes her head and laughs.

We eat dinner. When we lived in Greenwich, she used to teach art in the summers, too. They had a summer day program, with a bunch of little kids running around—I was in it, too, when I was younger—and she used to take them out into the fields and have them draw trees and flowers. She hated it. While we are eating, I get the idea that maybe this is what she went up there for, to talk to someone about this job. Dinner is cool things: tuna fish and pita bread and iced coffee. My mother has a salad. We don't talk for a while. All we do is crunch.

"Why'd you go up to Greenwich?" I ask her again.

She looks up at me, a little angry. The rule, I know, is that we don't talk about anything once she has clearly finished talking about it. "I felt like it," she says. Then she forks some more salad into her mouth, and maybe thinks that her response is off key, because she says, "I had a great idea while I was up there, though."

"What?"

"I thought we could go up tomorrow. You know, for the Fourth of July. See the fireworks. I thought it'd be a lot of fun."

"It sounds great."

"Yes," she says, "I thought you'd like that."

I sleep late the next day, and when I wake up she has gone jogging. She has left me a note saying so, which I throw away. She comes back sweaty and happy, drinking a bottle of club soda, and I ask her why she isn't drinking tea, and we joke, and it all feels very nice, until I remember about Dad and the money and her job and then I feel awful again, because it seems as if all our talking and joking is going on in midair, without anything underneath it to hold it up. We eat lunch, and then my mom makes some sandwiches and we get into our car and drive up the thruway to Connecticut. It's fun seeing the place where you used to live. We drive by our old house, and it looks the same, though there are some toys in the backyard and some lawn furniture—chairs and a big wooden table—which we didn't own. I get this funny feeling while we are in the car that we could still be living inside, as a family; that my father could walk out on the lawn and wave to us, or that if we stayed long enough we might see ourselves going past a window or walking over to sit at that big table. When we get to the high school, cars are everywhere, loading and unloading, families carrying big plastic coolers filled with food. I ask my mother if it was always this popular. "Yes," she says. "You just don't remember." We have to drive up the street about two blocks to find a space. By the time we have taken our own cooler out of the trunk, two more cars have already parked in front of us.

The fireworks are always held at the same place. The people sit on the athletic field and the fireworks are set off from behind the baseball diamond about a hundred yards away. Thousands of people are sitting on blankets or walking around and talking to each other. It's like a scene from one of those movies where the dam bursts and everyone is evacuated to a municipal building, only instead of all their belongings the people here are carrying pillows and Cokes and Twinkies. We find a spot right in the middle of the field. Some kids are playing a game of tag. They keep running through the crowd, laughing, screaming, just barely missing the people on the ground, which of course is part of the fun. When one of the kids brushes against my mother's shoulder I can see that she wants to stop him, give him a talking to, but I ask her not to. I remember when I would have been playing, too.

There is a black platform in the center of the baseball field, and after about three-quarters of an hour a presentation begins. A fireman and a policeman and a man from the Chamber of Commerce walk back and forth to the microphone and give each other awards, for safety and diligence and community service. Then they step down and a group of boys and girls collect onstage, most of them blond, all of them in robes. The man from the Chamber of Commerce, wearing his silver community-service medal, introduces them as the Royal Danish Boys and Girls Choir, "all the way from Holland." Then he leaves the stage, and though I imagine that the children will sing Danish folk songs, or maybe European anthems, what they sing is a medley of Broadway show tunes, in English, designed around the theme of a foreigner's impressions of America: "Oklahoma!" and "Getting to Know You" and "Gary, Indiana," though it is hard to make out the exact words through their accents.

By the time they have finished, the sky has turned dark blue, with the moon hanging just to one side. The policeman and the fireman return with the man from the Chamber of Commerce. "Good evening," he says. His voice echoes all over the field. "We'd like to welcome all of you to this year's celebration of the Greenwich, Connecticut, Fourth of July. In keeping with the spirit of this very special day, we'd like all of you to rise for the singing of our national anthem." My mother and I stand to sing, and there is something nice about being part of this wave of people, of voices. During the last line, there is a popping sound like a champagne bottle opening, and a yellow streak rises over the platform, nosing its way into the sky. The words "and the home, of the, brave" are lost in a chorus of "Oh"'s. We sit down again, en masse. I hand my mother her sweater. I can barely see her, but her voice comes from where I know she should be: "Thank you." The fireworks go off over the outfield, sometimes one, sometimes two or three at a time. Each one leaves a little shadow of smoke that the next one, bursting, illuminates. Some bloom like flowers; others are simply midair explosions, flashes. A few burst and then shoot forward, like the effect in *Star Wars* when the ship goes into hyperspace. Some are designed to fool us: One pops open very high in the air, sending out a circle of streamers like the frame of an umbrella; the crowd begins to "Ooh." Then one of these streamers, falling, pops open itself, sending out another series, and the rest of the crowd goes "Ah." Finally, one of those pops right over our heads, giving off a final shower of color, and the crowd whistles and applauds. The display gets more and more elaborate, until, for the last few minutes, there are ten or twenty rockets in the air at once, bursting and unfolding simultaneously. Everyone starts cheering, and the noises keep booming over us, making us duck our heads. The air smells like sulfur.

In the car, I am close to sleep. My mother is driving, outside it is dark, and I feel safe. The roads are crowded at first, but farther away from the school the traffic gets thinner, until we are driving alone down mostly empty roads. We seem to drive for a long time before joining up with the highway, where we become again simply one car among many.

"I'm working this summer," my mother announces after a little while.

I know, but I ask, "Where?" anyway.

"Here," she says. "At the school. I got my old job back."

"Mom."

She stops me. "I thought about it, and I decided that it really was important for me to have you in school right now. It was my decision to make, and I made it."

I turn to look at her. Her face is lit up by the meters in the dashboard. It's a surprise to remember that she has a body to go with her voice. I look at her profile, at her cheek, and at the skin underneath her chin beginning to sag. I remember how frightened she had been when we first moved to the city, how odd it had felt being in a house without my father's voice filling it, and how when we drove up to college for the first time last fall and she saw my name on top of my registration folder she walked out of the reception hall. I found her outside, on the main green, crying. "I can't believe we did it, we pulled it off," she said, meaning college.

"I just don't want to be a burden," I say now.

"You are," she says. "But it's O.K. I mean, I'm your mother, and you're supposed to be my burden." She turns to look at me in the dark. "I am your mother, aren't I?"

"As far as I know."

She laughs, and then we don't talk for a while. She turns on the air conditioner. I close my eyes and lean my head against the window. Every so often we hit a bump, which makes the window jiggle,

which makes my teeth click together. "I'm sorry you have to work,"
I say.

"Look, you should be. Don't ask me to get rid of your guilt for
you. If you feel guilty, that's fine. This was just important to me,
that's all."

Her using the word *guilt* frightens me. I sit up and open my eyes.
"What did Dad say to you on the phone?" I ask.

"Nothing. He said he wasn't going to pay for you. He said that
he was doing the right thing. He said you understood. Do you?"

"No."

She nods, driving. "That's what I told your father. He said you
should call him, if you want to. Do you?"

I laugh. "No."

She nods again. "I told him that, too."

She seems ready to stop talking, but I keep going. I want her to
tell me that it's O.K., that she missed working outdoors, that she
missed the little kids, missed Connecticut. "I just feel bad because
now you can't go to Wellfleet for the summer."

My mother says, "Let's not talk."

We drive. Through the windshield everything looks purple and
slick—the road and the taillights of the cars passing us and the
slender, long-necked lights hanging over the highway. We seem
sealed in, as if we are traveling underwater.

My mother reaches over and turns off the air conditioner. "There
is something I want to talk to you about, Richard," she says.

"What?" I ask.

She keeps her face turned toward the highway. "If anything like
this ever happens again, I want you to tell me immediately. Don't
make it so I have to find out myself. This whole thing wouldn't have
happened if you had told me about it in the spring. We could have
gotten loans and things. As it is, we're stuck."

I don't say anything.

"If you ever have anything to tell me," she says, "tell me when
it happens, O.K.? We're very close. You can tell me anything you
want to. O.K.?"

She looks over at me. I try to keep my face from showing anything,
and when I can't do that I look away, at my feet under the dashboard.
It is an offer. I can tell her or not. The funny thing is, I can feel that
she doesn't really want me to. If she has guessed, she doesn't want

me to confirm it. And though I am relieved, it seems to me that if I don't tell her now I never will, and this thing will always be between us, this failure, my father's voice embedded in static.

I look up. We are passing under the George Washington Bridge. "O.K.," I say.

P. M. R. C.
by Daniel Mueller
(University of Virginia)

Thanksgiving's over, which means Christmas, which means houses bedecked with bulbs! Which, to be honest, rivets me with as much anticipation as frog season, which is really only one day, or one night to be specific, usually in mid-June, when the frogs parade en masse across the cul-de-sac on top of East Hill. One cannot predict the actual date with much certainty, though Semen (his nickname!) has tried, deriving formulas from laborious hours of lunar observation and mathematic calculation. "Meloche," (that's his real name, Meloche) "you know what day it is?" He knows. We have discussed it with much riveting anticipation while making bombs, which are sometimes only Le Chefski's lunch bags filled with goulash, cherry cobbler, and peas. I hear him chortle, which means his parent is in the kitchen where the phone is, probably whipping up some sort of exotic bomb material, maybe crepe suzette, or squid in ink sauce, or chicken marmalade. "I'll see you on the cul-de-sac, nineteen hundred hours."

"Outside the gymnasium," he says, "by the ticket booth."

"I read you loud and clear," I say. His parent is without a cordless, but we have a system for understanding one another. We each make plans, but only the ones I make count. I click off and leave my room with the riveting posters of animal sacrifices, goats dipped in kerosene and torched, rabbits gutted and thrown out to the hungry mobs, neither of which have I had the opportunity to witness with my own eyes! About the best muzick to pass through this pleasant Wisconsin town was over a year ago now, some happy-go-lucky kids who called themselves "Abortion," *not* "The Abortion," or "Abor*tions,*" but "Abortion," singular, without an article, which in a humorous way is more graphic, and therefore better! than many of the names musical groups came up with in the past, names beginning with "The," or worse, pluralized. But, to be honest, the group in question was not all that different from many other groups current or defunct, which is to say, there was nothing that uniquely charming about them, which is to say that while their name was inspired, their poster is not on my wall!

Down the hall, where the charger for the phone is located, my own parent (her name is Candice) appears to be whipping up some of her own bomb material . . . out of the scraps of yesterday's pig, some cheddar filings, and two cups of elbow macaroni. "Allow me, Mother," I say. She is the most terrific parent a boy like me could wish for, and I use every opportunity to make her feel wanted.

"Would you?" she says. I take the wooden spoon from her hand *gladly,* because I know she has a lot to do in preparation for her date with Harold W. Lindstrom, M.D., who is more or less her boss, and with whom she has been fascinated since before her divorce from my other parent, Don. She is quite an attractive woman, I would say, despite her age (which is 38!), and I like her mostly for the active interest she takes in me and my doings. As always, she is frank with me about her plans for the evening and tells me the name of the restaurant where Harold W. Lindstrom, M.D., has made their dinner reservations (Geribaldi's on Rural Route K) and even writes down the telephone numbers where she may be reached in the case of an emergency (824–7658 and 234–0223, respectively). She asks me whether I'm doing something with Jon, which is not a name Semen, a.k.a. Meloche, goes by very often, but I understand whom she means well enough to answer, "Yes," and add, "we're thinking of attending the girls' gymnastics meet tonight. They're competing against *those* limber girls from Rotheschilde." Which is far from being a lie, since Semen and I have thought quite a lot about attending the girls' gymnastics meet, and what's more, the girls from

Rotheschilde *are* limber, especially one, whom you will meet shortly, once this true-to-life account has had a chance to unfold! Candice (my parent) winks at me and laughs, as if she can see in the twinkle of my eye the girl about whom Semen has had dreams (the thin, dark-haired gymnast whom you will shortly meet, whose name is Mona!), but I don't tell her, which is quite a different thing than lying! that what's causing my eyes to twinkle is the thought of Christmas lights, which is to say, all those cozy homes bedecked with bulbs.

"Honestly, you're becoming so mature," she says, which *is* the truth when one considers the kind of person I was a year ago, before I started hearing the words of artists like Blood Spot, Lung Wound, Sexual Knifing, and many others whom I will mention as the need arises—a person living in fear, afraid to leave the house, afraid to go to school, afraid to enter the world about which the aforementioned recording stars sing so poignantly! "We're like roommates," she says, and she's right, we are! which is another reason I like and respect her so much and try never to miss an opportunity to make her feel wanted. Which *is* not how it is with other of my friends, like Semen for instance, whose parents come down awfully hard on him at times, like when he comes home an hour late from a girls' gymnastics meet, or just comes home late.

In just her bathrobe, she leaves the bomb manufacturing center of the house we share, with the jars of oatmeal, millet, flour, the tins of spices and herbs, the pantry of canned fruits and vegetables and refrigerator of eggs, catsup, mayonnaise, cottage cheese! To be honest, as her hips sway past the trestle table on which, to date, perhaps a hundred bombs have been constructed! I see the raw sexuality men have found so attractive, and I am happy for her that she is unlike all the other parents I have ever met, like Semen's for instance, who has emaciated herself with diet pills, or Le Chefski's, who is a pig. And thinking about how nice it is to be able to see Candice so clearly, without any of the emotional coloring I have noticed in other kids' descriptions of their progenitors, I strain the macaroni in a colander, add a tablespoon of milk, stir in the hog bits and cheddar filings, and dump it all into a bag.

I wash the equipment in the sink and put it away in the cupboards because I know there is nothing more irritating to a parent, even one as happy-go-lucky as mine! than a counter covered with used dishes.

I walk down the hallway to her bedroom (she doesn't insist on my knocking before entering, and doesn't care if I see her nude, which I have many times! because she has a very nice body for a thirty-eight-year-old woman, and she should be proud of it!), but she is nowhere to be seen because she is in the bathroom showering for her date with Harold W. Lindstrom, M.D. I open the bathroom door and call to her through the beveled glass until she turns off the water on the Shower Massage, which I can imagine making her normally large nipples even more swollen and erect and red (because I have seen them in that state, many times!). "I'm leaving now, Mother. Thank you so much for starting the delicious macaroni and cheese with ham chunks. You always know just how to please a boy like me . . . by thinking of his tremendous appetite."

"You're welcome, Tommy," she says, addressing me by the most formal of my three names. People who know me kind of well call me Pass, because it's my last name, but people who know me really well call me Penis, because it's another *P* word (like Pass!), but mostly because of my own penis's monstrous size! "Have fun," she says.

"I want you in by ten o'clock," I say. "I'll be checking my watch every fifteen minutes."

She laughs, which is another of her many wonderful qualities. Were I thirty-eight myself and not related to her biologically, it would be her laugh, which is hollow and deep and as melodic as an oboe (which is *not* an instrument I am inordinately fond of ordinarily!), that would make me hard, which it kind of does anyway even though I am not thirty-eight and *am* very much related to her biologically in my role as son. In the entryway to the great outdoors, I put on my white World War II paratrooper's jacket, which Candice purchased for me at my request from the two very articulate and humorous old men who operate the war novelties shop that our city council is trying to push out of the pedestrian mall and into Harris Machinery, which is an abandoned brick building with busted windows five blocks away from any other merchant. It (the jacket!) cost $350 but luckily had a number of important selling points, one of which is the authentic .35 caliber machine gun holes (three) in a diagonal across the front and back, and second (the clincher as far as Candice was concerned) a thermal lining unsurpassed for warmth. Lucky for them (the two old men, whose names are Milty and Ak!), they have me living in this city with them, or else many of their highly descriptive and often amusing narratives of heinous war crimes and youthful debauchery would go unheard by anyone except them. I, with only limited access to funds my other parent (Don) makes available to our (now) two-atom molecular family, do everything I can to keep those two old men in business, which means buying their stock whenever opportunity allows, by which I mean swastikas, iron crosses, and army-issue knives that are spring-loaded and thus for display purposes only.

I pack the food at the bottom of the bag until it is a highly compressed, snowball-sized core and seal off the bomb with a wire twisty. Then I place it carefully at the bottom of one of my jacket's huge side pockets (another of its selling points! when Candice was thinking of dividing the $350 between a warm piece of winter clothing and a heavy-duty backpack for books). Soon I am out in the neighborhood admiring all the red, yellow, and green bulbs flickering on the snow-layered eaves and lawns, on my way to the cul-de-sac on top of East Hill, where on one night each June the frogs parade en masse and where, without much further ado, this adventurous and action-packed tale of bloodcurdling horror has its beginning. Semen is waiting for me under the street lamp, a chop suey bomb dangling between his legs, which he opens up and shows me, and so I open up my bomb for him, and for several long and pleasurable seconds we allow ourselves to be riveted by the thought of such desirable shrapnel—water chestnuts and macaroni, mushroom sauce and ham. I say, "Shall we get to the business at hand?" and he says, "I do believe it's time." Then we walk up the driveway to the porch of a two-story Dutch colonial.

On the other side of some very lovely taffeta curtains, a television is being watched, the volume turned up high, gunshots ricocheting from the cozy, fire-lit world of eggnog and naps into the cold, neon-lit world of intrigue. Semen balances across the upper rail of the balustrade like a cat burglar—he could've been a gymnast!—unscrewing bulbs that would scorch his fingers to raisins were it not for the thick, heat-resistant gloves we wear. While he works the entablature, I fill my pockets with bulbs from pine trees that punctuate the intercolumnation like a series of Spanish exclamations. "!Bombas como frutas! !Bombas como nueces!" We strip the cords of lights in less time than it takes a station to break, then move to the split-level ranch next door where we harvest another twenty-five bulbs from a wreath hung below the transom. "How many do you have?" I ask.

"Sixty or seventy," Semen says.

"Let's make it an even hundred apiece," I say, and so we do, with bulbs from a geodesic dome at the end of a long, wooded drive. Then we cut through the trees, cross Rural Route J, and take cover between the placard of Saint Alban's Episcopal Church and a fifteen-foot monolithic cross behind it. As Acuras, Mercedeses, and BMWs leave the church parking lot, we arc handfuls of light-bulb bombs over the sign and watch them explode off the shiny roofs and hoods. It is a spectacular sight, one for which Semen and I have waited nearly eleven months, and it is not a letdown, as very few experiences in life are, as long as one doesn't romanticize them into experiences they aren't, which is to say, Semen and I have remembered everything accurately—the pops! the sparks and flickers of globes impacting on metal. Every so often, a car stops, a door opens, but these are people dressed for mass, who are not about to risk life and limb in a high-speed foot chase over the snow, through woods and cornfields. Which is precisely why, when our arsenals have dwindled to fifty or sixty bulbs, we leave off for a while in expectation of more athletic enemy.

"Think we'll hook into some danger?" Semen asks.

"Be patient," I say. We sit in the snow, smoking fags, till the last congregant has pulled from the lot.

"Ready for some danger?" Semen asks. We stand up, each with a handful of bulbs, as a car comes up the hill with its high beams on, doing about sixty. We hurl about fifteen bombs over the sign before I even see that it is a blue Chrysler Le Baron. Explosions occur in front of it, behind it, and on it in a shower of pelts and sparks. "Direct hit!" Semen says. The driver slams on his breaks, which is what we have been waiting for, but the person who emerges from the car is none other than Harold W. Lindstrom, M.D.

"We gotta run!"

I grab Semen's throat. I whisper into his hair, "Stay calm."

Harold W. Lindstrom, M.D., steps onto the snow in his black wingtips with the slick leather soles. Through a knot in the wood, I see the collar of Candice's lynx stole, her pulled-back hair, one dangling gold earring. "The shenanigans are over," he says as

Candice purses her lips together in the light of the vanity mirror. "So you might as well come out and show yourselves." I hear Semen's frenetic, fearful breathing at my shoulder, which is a shame, for he cannot see the pale draining of potency from the face of Harold W. Lindstrom, M.D., nor enjoy the power of our concealment in the brittle network of shrubbery. "You can't fool me," says Harold W. Lindstrom, M.D., "I know you're behind there." His eyes are not on the sign, but on the huge, monolithic cross rising behind it. He takes a step backward as Candice lowers the electronic window.

"Come on, Harold," she says.

The wind flicks up his thin gray hair. Gray vapors rise from his mouth and nostrils. "Whoever they are, they need help."

"You don't even know where they are," she says.

"They're behind the sign." He points at us. "They're in between the sign and the cross."

"How do you know?"

"It's where the bulbs came from. The jerks threw Christmas bulbs at us." He swings his arms. "We could have gotten in an accident. Wouldn't that have been great. You know who'd be called from the hospital? Hedda, that's who."

Candice parts her lips in an expression of raw sexuality. "I saw them running," she says. "Dressed in black. They're behind the church by now, probably lying down in the cornfields."

"You saw them running?" he asks.

"Before you even stopped the car," she says. "Come on, Harold. We're late as it is."

He walks back to the car and inspects the finish. He runs his hands over the roof. I see him raise a fist at us. "You're a bunch of stupid jerks! You hear me? You ought to be locked up!" As he gets back in the car, I ease up on Semen's head, which has been like a nut in a nutcracker throughout the whole ordeal. Semen rubs his neck as the blue Chrysler Le Baron bears Candice and her date out of town to a place I have only heard about, Geribaldi's, where the waiters wear tuxedos, where the diners wash their fingers in tiny finger bowls, and where a 1977 vintage is served that Candice could not afford were it not for Harold W. Lindstrom, M.D., and the money he has made as an obstetrician and gynecologist. To be honest, I am thrilled for her, because my other parent (Don) was only the head mechanic at an imported auto garage and could only afford to take her to places like the Wagon Wheel Family Restaurants on Water Street and on East Franklin.

"Your mother is something else," Semen says.

"I know it," I say.

"I wish my parents would divorce," he says.

"Maybe they will," I offer halfheartedly, because I know they won't. Semen and I waste the rest of our bulbs on passing traffic. A college kid chases us into the playground behind the church and a little later, a police officer chases us into the cornfields. We outwait him, our stomachs on the frozen stalks, then we walk back to the road and stand on the shoulder for a car to come and receive our food bombs. Semen and I are not prone to lapses of nostalgia, but as we are standing there on the snow and gravel, our bombs dangling at our sides like hobo sacks, Semen asks me whether I think it will be a good frog season, and so I ask him what he means by "good."

"Will there be a lot of them?" he asks. "A lot of frogs?"

I tell him there's no way to know until the night of the parade.

"Last year," he says, "there were a lot of frogs. They came out four nights after the full moon. Also, it was after a winter of barely any snow. This winter there's a lot of snow. I wonder if that means they'll come out on the full moon, or maybe even before it. What if this year they come out in late May, before the end of school? If they came out on a school night, we might miss them altogether. Then the whole next year, we'd be thinking that if we had another winter with lots of snow, it would mean they wouldn't be coming out at all."

"That could never happen," I say.

"Why not?" Semen asks.

"Because if they paraded on a school night, we'd still see a few of the squished ones on the street the next day. And we would know that a winter with snow doesn't mean a summer night without frogs."

And for a long time it seemed as if anybody who was going any place had gotten there and that Semen and I might have to wait hours for them to return.

In this great world, I believe with Slit Membrane, Stomach Tumor, and Infected Gash that it doesn't pay to feel anything but glad, for, in the words of the late Thomas Jefferson (the lead singer of Cut, who shot himself in the neck with a Saturday night special while performing in Philadelphia), "However bad it gets, there's still no tellin' whose guts you'll see on the pavement tomorrow!" And it's true, at least in a metaphorical sense, for no sooner have I begun to sing the lyrics from the title track of Cut's album, *Fatal Surgery* (****1/2), than Semen and I see headlights at the bottom of East Hill. Each of us palms his bomb, and when the car (which reveals itself to be a cream-colored Mustang with drags) crests the top, Semen and I lob our sacks in front of it. Food explodes off the windshield. The car swerves to a stop, which forces us into the woods across the street from the church, where we look on from within the shadows of branches and tree trunks. "Know what?" I say, "I think we just nailed Le Chefski's brother's car."

"No," says Semen.

"Yes," I say, "I think we did." The Mustang rests there cocked on the shoulder, its headlights blazing into a cornfield, its taillights pulsing in time with our temples. We should run, we know, especially if it *is* Le Chefski's brother, who is six foot three, nineteen years old, and crazier than either Semen or I, which is precisely why we don't, why we stand there in the copse, trying to see through the side window whose face exists behind the headrest, whose cheek is otherworldly, dashboard green. "We might've hooked into some danger," I say, as the headlights blink off and the Mustang moves in reverse over the snow and gravel to the spot where Semen and I were standing when we lobbed our bombs. The inside of the car is now a cavern of darkness. The driver rolls down his window and out of it, like a probe, comes the long, black barrel of a shotgun (12 gauge!).

"Come on," says Semen, three trees away. "We gotta run!"

"Run and he'll pick you off like a turkey," I say.

"I don't care!" says Semen, whose boots have already begun to crunch through the layers of icy crust. Fire flashes three times from the end of the barrel in such quick succession I hear only one blast. Snow drops from the upper limbs as Semen, who is hardly more substantial than a shadow, drops to his knees and then to his chest on the white ground. I move from tree trunk to tree trunk to where Semen lies in a huddled mass. "I'm hit," he says. It's dark, granted, but I don't see any blood. I take off my gloves and feel his body with my hands, starting at the head and working my way down to the boots. I ask him, "Where?"

"I'm not sure," he says.

"Come on," I say. "Where?"

"I don't know!" he says.

"Penis!" I look up and Le Chefski is standing on the gravel in front of his brother's Mustang.

"Since when have you been old enough to drive?" I ask.

"Since Wayne gave me the keys," Le Chefski says. He trudges out into the snow.

"Where've you been?" I ask.

"All over," he says. "The gymnastics meet. Looking for you. My brother's having a party."

"At the farm?" I ask.

"Yeah," he says. "My parents came to town for a weekend at the Holiday Inn."

"Semen says he's shot," I say.

"Naw he's not," says Le Chefski. "I fired over his head."

"Maybe I'm not," says Semen, sitting up. "It sure as hell felt like I was!"

"You would be if I'd aimed at you," says Le Chefski. "But I didn't and that's why you're not. You want to come out to the farm? Mona's going to be there, but you better not mess with her, Pass. She's pissed at you."

"She pissed at you?" I ask.

"Yeah, she's pissed at me. She's pissed at Semen, too."

"But she said she was coming to the party. She said that to you?"

"Yeah."

"Why?" I ask.

"I don't know. I think maybe she has a thing for my brother."

"Wayne?" I say. Le Chefski's brother has been in eleventh grade for three years.

"She thinks he's nice."

"Him?"

"You want to come or not?"

"We're out of bombs," I say. So the three of us walk back to the road and get in the Mustang, me in the front and Semen in the back with the shotgun. Soon Rural Route J is flowing under our tires like a stream of hot, black coffee. Mailboxes and fence posts bend and converge to points on either side of us, like liquids pushed through huge syringes, and I am thinking about Mona and what she will say to me and what I will say to her, about the group Nasty Abrasion, and the idea for the riveting pep fest skit that came to me while hearing the poetry of their greatest single, ''Fetus in a Bag,'' off the *Buckets of Sperm* LP. In it (the song!), two lines are repeated for fifteen minutes and thirty-seven seconds.

> *My baby's got some death in her—*
> *Got to find me a cellophane bag.*
> (Copyright 1989 Mutated Music, Inc.)

Which gave me the vision of Semen dressed up as a pregnant Rotheschilde gymnast and Le Chefski as an abortionist. In it (the skit, performed this morning in the gym! before the screaming masses!), Le Chefski, wearing Mr. Johnson's white lab coat with a large *W* (our school letter!) emblazoned on his back, pushes Semen onto the basketball court in a red wheelbarrow. Mr. Morrell, our principal, is so relieved that someone has had the school spirit to put together a skit at all that he has decided to take a nap in his office, or so I assume from his absence at the fest! The kids, who are seated by grade level on the bleachers, are screaming, ''Kill Rotheschilde! Kill the Rotheschilde gymnasts!'' and for several long and pleasurable seconds, Le Chefski conducts them with a wire coat hanger, which he has bent into a baton and which, as a hush descends over the auditorium, he places between the spread knees of Semen, who is screaming in agony and shaking his long black wig better than he ever did in rehearsal! A number of teachers leave their seats and exit through the doors, which is their right! I hear Bunson, who is a kid we know, say, ''Go for it!'' and I am glad, for it's kids like Bunson who would never think of showing their support for our talented girls were it not for us! A bunch of kids have clumped in front of the exits. I see Mr. Morrel's head hovering behind the mob, on his face a scrunched-up look of consternation, which is one of the artistic effects we are trying to achieve! From a large grocery bag concealed in the folds of Semen's hospital robe, Le Chefski delivers the sickness for all to see, the metaphor for the Rotheschilde girls' notoriously bad performances season after season, which is to say, Le

Chefski reaches into the paper sack and orchestrates a great eruption of war novelties from between Semen's spread thighs. I see Mr. Morrel stumble over McEntire's foot, which is in a cast from a skiing accident, as debris falls to the floor around Le Chefski, debris in the form of Nazi armbands, hand grenade casings, iron crosses, machine gun shells, and spring-loaded knives! With an air of what can only be described as artistic snobbery, Mr. Morrel comes onto the gymnasium, grabs Semen and Le Chefski by the scruffs of their skinny necks, ushers them away to his office, where he gives them a lecture which lasts fifty-seven minutes by my watch.

At the intersection with Rural Route K, I see the sign for Geribaldi's ("Fine Dining. International Cuisine. Overlooking Phlox Lake. 8 Miles.") and imagine Candice seated across a candle-lit table from Harold W. Lindstrom, M.D., and so I ask Le Chefski if he has something to put in the deck besides country-western muzick, which are mainly songs about people cheating and being dishonest with one another, which I do not believe in. "Wayne listens to that death shit," Le Chefski says, "not me."

"He does?" I ask.

"Sure," says Le Chefski. "He's got tons of it. Bone. Skin and Spleen. Testosterone Catastrophe."

"He listens to Testosterone Catastrophe?" I ask.

"He goes to sleep to it," says Le Chefski.

"They're excellent," says Semen from the backseat. Le Chefski pulls the car onto a long gravel drive studded with pickups, Dusters, and El Caminos. Groups of older kids stand outside the house, their jackets and caps lit up by lights which radiate from every window. Le Chefski parks the car outside the barn, next to the shiny green corn harvester which Le Chefski leaves school early to operate every fall. I let Semen out of the back and hear the unmistakable guitar noise of Grim Reaper, the brilliant founding member of the group Blood and Bile, whose first album, *I Want to Blow Your Head Off*, shook the American charts by challenging all prior musical conventions! We walk over the stamped-down snow to the house past kids smoking fags and drinking from plastic cups. Le Chefski leaves Semen and me standing in the living room, among kids who try to pretend we're not there (because we're ninth-graders!), but I have a friend in Grim Reaper, who speaks to kids like me, "Splatter!

Fry! Splatter! Die!'' Which is when I see Mona in the kitchen talking
to Le Chefski's brother, Wayne.

She is wearing a black skirt and tights, her long, black curls
snaking down the back of her red letter jacket. "There she is," I
say to Semen, who began dreaming about her the night I told him
about her tongue, which was a week before Mona and I first fucked
and caused Semen to fall head over heels in love. "I'm going to talk
to her," I say to Semen, but when I get there, it's Wayne I address.
"This is a great party, Wayne," I say, interrupting his vivid and
interesting account of pig slaughtering, which is what the Le Chefski
family does when they aren't producing two of the world's all-time
greatest bomb materials—milk and corn.

"Yeah?" he says. "What's so great about it?"

"The muzick!" I say.

"Yeah?" he says.

"Yeah," I say. "Little Le Chefski tells me you listen to T.C. I've
got all three of their albums, *Uncomfortable Womb*, *Organ Donor*,
and *Amp U.T.*"

"*You* have *Amp U.T.*?"

"I had to order it from England. It's got 'Baring My Fang' on it.
It's got '(Give Me an Axe) Let Me Be Your Butcher.' It's got
'Clot.' "

" 'Clot'?" he says. I nod. It's a wonderful and riveting song
about bleeding from a heart wound, which is why it is one of Semen's
favorites. "God, I'd love to hear 'Clot' right now. You want to hear
something off *Organ Donor?*"

" 'Music Man,' " I say.

"I fucking *love* that song!" Wayne says.

"Put it on," I say.

"Mona, you wanna hear 'Music Man'?"

"Sure," she says, which is all it takes for Wayne to begin squeez-
ing himself and his fifth of sour mash through the kitchen of bodies
to the cabinet in the living room where the high-fidelity turntable
and tuner are located. Which is how it happens that I am left with
Mona, who is also a ninth-grader and who (because she goes to
Rotheschilde High School) knows even fewer of the people at the
party than I do!

"Well, I guess I'm a little disappointed in you," I say, which I know is something her male parent, Herb, says to her quite often, because she has told me so (many times!).

"Now I've heard it all," she says, which is what Lois, her female parent, says whenever Herb tells her he's had to work after hours at the window plant, which employs a large portion of Rotheschilde's male *and* female populace. "If you expect me to forgive you, you can just forget it."

On the other side of the house, Wayne lifts the needle off Blood and Bile, "Tell It Like It Is," as two fat droplets collect on Mona's lower lashes, which are good signs. "I'm not asking you to forgive me, Mona," I say, "because I haven't done anything wrong."

"Tell me about it," she says.

"No," I say, "*you* tell me. What have I done? I'd like to know."

She looks at me in disbelief. "The skit. I heard about the skit. Did you think I wouldn't find out?"

"I knew you would," I say, "I was going to tell you myself. I thought you'd see the hilarity of it. You, Mona, of all people."

"Tommy," she says. "I told you about my abortion. I trusted you. How could you think I'd find that hilarious?"

Wayne drops the needle on "Music Man" and people cover their ears, everyone, that is, except Mona and me. "It wasn't you I was making fun of. It was the frivolity of human passions. I mean, don't you see the least bit of hilarity in a gymnastics squad of sexually prolific females? The whole state knows over half the girls on the team have had abortions. Half the girls, Mona. You want to know something else? You're not to blame."

"Oh yeah?" she says, "who is?"

"No one's to blame," I say. "People can't help doing what they do." I put my arm around her shoulders and her head shakes against my World War II paratrooper's jacket. "Me. I was only demonstrating school spirit."

"You're fucked!" she says.

"No," I tell her, "the world's fucked!" I tell her it's not me, but the fucked world she sees *in* me.

"God, Tommy, I love you so," she says, and the two of us weave through the labyrinth of bodies, past Wayne on his way to the kitchen, past Le Chefski, who taps me on the shoulder as we pass through the door and says, "I hope you know what you're doing, penis head."

We pass Semen, who is standing under a tree, a cup of beer in either hand. We pass kids smoking and drinking in small groups, pass the Mustang and the shiny green corn harvester, to the stone wall behind the barn where at least two other couples are clenching. In the darkness I unbutton her letter jacket and slide my hand under her Dacron shirt. "God, I've missed you," she says. "I thought you didn't want to see me again." I spring the single hook of her bra, which is a much simpler garment than the four-hook, underwired, ultrasupport bra Candice wears. "The only reason I came, I hoped you'd be here, Tommy, I hoped." *I'm a music man*, I say. I take her silver giraffe earring in my mouth, cup her breasts in my palms, then I pinch and twist her nipples, which are not as tough and erect and swollen as Candice's get when she places my fingers on them, saying, twist them gently, gently, yes, like so. *Got gland in my hand*, I say. I suck Mona's tongue, then she sucks mine, as I slip my hand under the elastic waistbands of her skirt and tights. Then Mona pulls her face away. "Tommy," she says, "we've been honest with one another. I've told you everything." I find her clit. That's a clit, darling! It is about a third the size of Candice's. *I'm a man, a music*. I press it with my finger. "Wait. I've got to tell you something." I rub it gently. Yes, like that. It's almost like a pickle, isn't it? Ribbed, look at it. Wet, touch it. Candice is like a huge kosher dill compared to Mona. "Listen to me." *Gonna rip me*. "I let Wayne Le Chefski come inside me."

"Wayne?" I say.

"Yes," says Mona, wrapping her arms around my head. "Do you hate me?"

"When?"

"This afternoon, before the meet. I thought you hated me . . . I thought." I keep rubbing her and she opens her legs a little.

"A girl should experience everything," I say. Don't ever try to restrict a woman, Candice said.

"I don't love him," Mona says, taking my monstrous penis in her hands. Do unto others, Candice said, as you would have others do unto you. We rub each other gently. "Do you love me?" Mona asks. "Say you do. Say it. Say it. Say it."

"I love you, Mona," says Wayne Le Chefski. He is standing in the snow, next to the pigsty, the shotgun propped against his shoulder. "I love you!" he says again, and as he does, the other couples break from one another and look on from beside the barn. Kids who were outside the house gather around Wayne Le Chefski and us. "Come on," says Mike Schleuter, who is the captain of the football team, "put the gun down, Wayne." I see Semen standing next to the corner of the stone wall, both of his cups refilled with beer. From the house comes Testosterone Catasrophe, "Mary . . . I wanna, wanna, wanna eat your heart!" I kiss Mona on the ear, walk up to where Wayne Le Chefski is standing, stoic, like a statue, and plug the barrel of his shotgun with my thumb.

"Go ahead. Blow me apart, Wayne."

"Pull out your thumb!"

"Please," I say, "blow me apart!"

"Please," he says, "pull your thumb out of the barrel."

I do, and he fires, and Mona splatters against the wall of the barn. I am recounting the truth of what happened November 24, 1989, at approximately 11:15 P.M., at least insofar as words are ever capable *of recounting the truth.* Yet, the particulars of Mona's death are not what interest me. What does, and what should interest you—if you have read this far and not just turned here by accident!—is that a group of lobbyists in Washington, D.C., composed of parents, church leaders, and the wives of two prominent U.S. senators called the Parent's Music Resource Center is trying to make it impossible for kids like me to purchase audio and video recordings like the ones I have either alluded to or mentioned by name—because they believe such works of art are contributing to the corruption of our nation's youth. As a youth, I maintain such works of art are only as corrupt as the world they depict, our world, the world you and I share! In a matter of a half page, if you will bear with me, I will describe in graphic detail how the buckshot entered Mona just below her rib cage, what she said as she looked down at the shotgun hole in her black Dacron blouse, how the crowd dispersed and Wayne Le Chefski and I were arrested by the police. But you must bear in mind as you read—that I am only able to do so because of songs like "Sweet Surrender" by Open and Gaping, "Love Me Tender" by Sick Fuck, "(What Do You Get) When You Fall in Love" by Proud Felch, songs I have listened to hundreds of times, without whose imagery I would be left groping for words. Or worse, be forced to use frogs as a metaphor, the only creatures besides Mona I have ever seen splatter (!), one summer night each year, off car doors, bumpers, and grilles—when Semen and I have collected enough of them off the cul-de-sac to make it worth our while. Frogs barely the size of a human appendix! Is that how you would have me describe a ninth-grade girl's disembowelment and death? Clearly, we must *band* together, no pun intended, and fight against the fascists who want to restrict our rights (rights granted in the Constitution of our great nation!) to appreciate the art of our choice!

Wayne Le Chefski pulls the trigger and fire flashes from the barrel past my right shoulder and for several long and pleasurable seconds, about thirty of us stand there in a semicircle staring at Mona, unaware that anything extraordinary has even happened. At first not even Mona is aware. She says, "Let's leave," but when she tries to pull herself from the wall and can't (because the buckshot has more or less plastered her to the stone!), that's when we see the bulge in her blouse, which is really a hole, from which an organ is attempting to spill! "Oh my god, oh my god, oh my god," says Mike Schleuter. Two or three kids scream. Some scramble back to the house, some back to their cars. A couple of boys put their arms under Wayne Le Chefski's shoulders and help him away over the snow a step at a time. In the midst of the excitement, I walk over to Mona, whose thin nyloned legs prop the rest of her body against the side of the barn like the stand of an easel.

"Look," she says when I am standing before her, "I'm giving birth."

"No, you're not," I tell her.

I help her with the buttons of her blouse, help her pull the tattered Dacron away from the edges of the hole and from around what looks like a shiny, blue head. "Feel," she says and places both of my palms on the soft, hairless scalp. "Is it a boy or a girl?"

"I don't think it has eyes, a nose, or mouth."

"I don't care," she says, "I love it anyway," and as her shoulders begin to shake, I feel her baby's head jiggle and turn of its own accord. "It's coming," she says. "Help it come, Tommy."

I place my hands on either side of its soft head, where it should have had ears, and feel its thin neck between my fingers. "Pull, Tommy." I pull, but it won't come, so I reach in and take its warm, entangled body in my hands.

"I don't think it has any arms," I say.

"I don't care. It's ours, Tommy. It's ours." As I pull, its body unravels into long, fleshy tubing, which I raise in my fists and show to Mona. "That's its umbilical cord, stupid." I feel our baby breathe and cry. "You have to cut that, Tommy. Do you have a knife? Find someone with a knife. You have to cut it or it'll die!"

I look for someone with a knife and see Semen standing by the corner of the barn, his body doubled over, spilling beer onto the snow from his mouth. "You all right?" I ask him.

He shakes his head.

"You have to cut it!" Mona cries.

"You have a knife, Semen? A pocket knife or something?"

"Can't you bite it off?" Mona asks. I let go of the glistening blue head, and it hangs outside her blouse by a second neck, which curls upward into the hole. I take a step backward as more and more of its "umbilical cord" unravels through the opening, coiling onto the snow between her shoes. I kneel in the warmth, put my mouth to the hard juncture, and sink my teeth into the fibrous tubing. There are sirens, red and blue flashing lights. Mona tries to cradle the baby, but its second neck prevents her from lifting it very high. My face is covered with her warmth. The tissue snaps, a granular, black liquid spews from the severed end of the hose onto my face, onto my White World War II paratrooper's jacket, as Mona pulls the baby free.

"There," I say. I hear a long, loud cry, like the wail of a newborn baby, but it is only Semen, who has watched Mona pull her own stomach out of the hole and rock it in her arms. Five police officers round the corner of the barn. Two of them pull me away from Mona, wrap my arms around my back, and force my face into the cold stone. They tell me anything I say can and will be used against me. "I've got nothing to hide," I tell them. They slam my head into the wall. I tell them it's nobody's fault! I tell them I can explain everything! that Mr. Morrel signed the form! he didn't know what was in the skit, but he signed the form anyway! my mother made me irresistible to women! she showed me how to touch them! how to make them peal with rapture! my father was no good with women! my mother told me how he'd just lie there after he shot his load in her! how he'd go to sleep like a fish! Mona wanted a baby so much it affected her mind! her parents were mean! her mother put her hand on the burner when she was just a little girl! her father touched her places she didn't want to be touched! Mona told me so many times! but then, they can't help it if their own parents raised them that way! their lives are hard, too! Wayne Le Chefski only wanted a girlfriend! Mona only wanted love and affection! Mr. Morrel's so overworked! he only wanted a nap! Milty and Ak don't want to lose the glory that once was theirs as fighting men of our great nation! don't make them move into Harris Machinery! my mother has my best interest at heart! she doesn't want me to grow up to be a loser with women! Mr. Morrel only wants our girls to do well on the balance beam, horse, and mat! Wayne Le Chefski's parents have got enough to do feeding the hogs and milking the cows without worrying themselves over two wild and reckless sons! even Harold W. Lindstrom, M.D., is trying to be a good second husband for Candice! even if he's married to someone else! he can't help that! why just last week he gave me twenty dollars from his wallet, without which I'd have had to wait to buy the new Pus L.P.!

"Shut up!" says Wayne Le Chefski. He is sitting next to me in the back of the patrol car. "They can't hear a word you're saying! They've got us in the cage!"

I try to grip the wire screen that separates the front and back seats, but my wrists are restricted by steel cuffs. On the other side of it is an inch-thick pane of soundproof glass, through which I see the two police officers smoking pipes. As we move toward town, they draw the smoke through the stems in unison, and it leaves their mouths in tiny crests which swirl before the lit-up dash, thickening the haze in which they work.

SHIT HAPPENS
by Michael Drinkard
(Columbia University)

A roommate, like a brother, you can't choose yourself. And by the look of the redheaded guy nailing a boot heel to the bedroom door—a harmonica fitting snugly in the faded slot in the back pocket of his Levi's, a pack of Camels rolled up in the short sleeve of a T-shirt with the words SHIT HAPPENS stenciled on the front—Sylvan thinks somebody upstairs has made a mistake. Or pulled names out of a hat.

"Alabama," the redhead says, offering a freckle-covered hand.

"Napa," Sylvan says. "Fifty miles northwest of Sacramento, if you know where that is."

"No, I'm not from Alabama, I'm from Tennessee. I'm called Alabama on account of my accent."

Like a rubber band, Sylvan thinks, stretched out and snapping on the b's and t's. Maybe a Tennessee accent has more twang, maybe less. Somebody once told Sylvan he had a guitarist's accent, whatever that is, and he doesn't even play. Alabama does, if that amplifier blocking the hallway is any indication. Sylvan hopes he's not a bar-chord-and-blues-scales man.

"Sylvan," Sylvan says. They're still shaking hands. "Sylvan Park."

"Your parents hippies?"

"They both have short hair," Sylvan says. "But my sister kind of is. Or used to be." Beads and Joni Mitchell and *One Flew Over the Cuckoo's Nest*. Now she's grown-up, a first-year resident at the UCLA medical center. And soon to be a mother. "Uncle Sylvan" has a ring to it, but implies . . . something. Oldness, hairy arms, ironed clothes. "Why, are yours?"

"No. It's just that your name sounds lyrical."

Lyrical? Sylvan realizes that his own name probably seems to Alabama as exotic (or Californian-hippy-dippy) as, say, Gaia, Wolfgang, or Heaven.

"I guess Sylvan is better than Otto. Get it? Auto Park? Ha!" Turns out Alabama's an exchange student, here to finish up a degree in English, a language he doesn't really speak but heck they were handing out fellowships. His real name is Thoburn Downs Whitaker III, which sounds to Sylvan like a sports page headline, and he grew up in a mansion outside Nashville, with two brothers, one sister. His mother is a congresswoman and his father runs a chain of tanning parlors, he thinks.

"What do you mean, you think?"

Alabama shrugs, sucks his cheeks furtively, looks kind of sullen. "He's got his fingers in lots of pies." Many other students at this school brag about their fathers' being in one version of Mafia or another. But usually they're not so sheepish about it. Why the big mystery?

Alabama changes the subject, grins broadly again as he tells Sylvan he's an exchange student from Princeton, knows Latin and Greek, hates the Romantics except for Blake, and came to California because he wanted to see if people really say "gnarly" and "bitchen." "Long drive, though, and when I finally make it here, paradise, but my car door won't open."

Too much information for Sylvan to absorb at once. Somebody upstairs definitely screwed up. Here he is, seriously Earth Sciences for one thing, a nonsmoker for another, the opposite of—what Alabama says he is and appears to be with his grizzly red whiskers, arms pumped up from hammering the boot heel, and now jumping around on one leg and blowing metal noise from his blues harp. What kind of SHIT HAPPENS anyway?

Maybe he should have moved off campus this year. But student

housing is close to the labs and not that far from Tres Ojos, conve-
nient, still the best deal in town. The campus is so spread out. The
university has a policy of no-buildings-higher-than-the-redwoods, so
you come upon them like a discovery. Ansel Adams was a creative
consultant in designing the campus. Mood was his thing. "Consider
public safety but also consider the basic mood of the place." Sylvan
likes that, *the basic mood*.

This particular cluster of apartments was built just two years ago,
mod. Crisp lines, all white walls with purplish pipes, the exposed
plumbing and skylights keeping things honest, roofs all slanted the
same way and spotlit at night, making the place look like a Holly-
wood studio lot, all props and facades. Especially this week, with
orientation booths giving out cookies, lemonade, and safe-sex kits,
banners decorated with banana slugs saying WELCOME, music coming out of every open window, and blue and yellow helium-filled
condoms riding the breeze. New students in shorts smile at each
other, everyone carrying boxes of books, stereos, sleeping bags,
personal computers, and houseplants. Mood.

"Fine sight." Alabama stops playing harmonica. He's looking
out the window at a pair of legs. The girl they belong to is bending
over a box packed with Cheerios and peppermint tea, toilet paper
and a teddy bear. "You sudsworthy?" Not waiting for an answer,
which he won't get anyway because Sylvan doesn't understand the
question, Alabama jams the harmonica back into his pocket, does
an emptyhanded drumroll on a dictionary, and walks toward the
kitchen.

The whole inside of the apartment is open, kitchen and living
room and dining room combined into one, clean with the smell of
paint and sunlight. Probably not for long.

Alabama opens the refrigerator, which contains a case of beer and
a hunk of cheddar, along with Sylvan's package labeled SEAWEED.
He tosses Sylvan a beer, the can cold and sweaty. Bubbles tingle
the back of Sylvan's throat, the quenching making him thirstier.

"Always this hot?"

"Gets hot a lot here. Even hotter yesterday," Sylvan says, remembering the bull episode with Teo. What a nightmare. At least he got
his job back. Even if Phyllis was being weird. Asking him about his
sperm like she was serious. Why him? Millions of stud types around;

millions. One right here, as a matter of fact, this roommate who's unrolling cigarettes from his sleeve.

"Smoke?"

"Rather you didn't inside."

"Why not?"

"I like fresh air."

"Understandable. Good to nip these things in the bud." Alabama rolls the Camels back up into his sleeve and begins eating sunflower seeds instead, spitting the shells into a sack, sometimes missing.

Vacuum cleaner headaches and slimy carpet. Oh well, there are worse things. What is it Sylvan's mom tells him? "An ideal situation teaches you nothing." "You know yourself by the concessions you make." "Heaven is for dead people." She's always making up aphorisms along with the *et als.* and *comb. forms* and *fill in the* _____s for the Sunday crosswords she composes for the Oakland *Tribune.*

"Geology?" Alabama asks, pointing to the bookshelf bending under the weight of Sylvan's textbooks. *Geology, Hydrology, Volcanology,* and *A Look at Planet Earth,* all thick as dictionaries. "Or fossils?" He jerks a thumb at the Napa Park Wines crate packed with Sylvan's special collection: deer antlers, a string of pink and green iridescent feathers, a single human vertebra, and a chunk of molten glass. Other stuff is tucked underneath: a box containing a bluebelly lizard pelt and a rattlesnake rattle, a tin of shark teeth, his own baby teeth, a pearl shaped like a tiny peanut, various quartzes and pumice stones, the talon of a white-tailed kite, and a large magnifying glass.

"Museum of Natural History in a wine crate, goddamn."

"I just collect this stuff. But yes, my major is Earth Sciences." Sylvan tells him how he has just spent the summer in the White Mountains mapping terrain and charting wind erosion. Now he's back in Santa Cruz to finish his senior thesis.

"Earthquakes?"

"Yeah. Volcanology and sand migration and seismology. You know, plate tectonics."

"Toast. Here's to the collision of continents." Clunk of half-full beer cans. When he smiles, Alabama has perfect teeth except for two, the front and canine turned sideways, an imperfection making him seem, in some way, trustable.

* * *

"Hate to do it, but I gotta ask a favor." Alabama swallows the last of his beer. "Orientation meeting started five minutes ago, and I don't know where the English Department is yet. How 'bout a tour?" He picks up his dictionary as if to take it along, but then sets it back down.

On the way across campus, Sylvan points out the library that looks like a giant microchip plunked down in a redwood glen, piano-equipped practice rooms, the sorrel clover that tastes sweet this time of year but sour in the spring—the same plant they pour vinaigrette over in San Francisco and call New California Cuisine—and the exact spot under a fallen madrone where last year he found an Amanita Muscaria, bright red with fuzzy white polka dots, violently hallucinogenic.

"Smell this." He hands Alabama a bay leaf, half limy, half minty, and ultra aromatic. If you inhale deeply several times in a row, sparks go off in your head. Sylvan knows because little Teo tricked him into doing it last year. "Crumple it up first."

Alabama shuts his eyes and takes long, nose-drawn breaths. Suddenly he gasps, squinches up his face in a closed-mouth yawn, and puts his hands against his temples. "Speed of light."

It's a couple of moments before he can open his eyes. And grin. "More kick in this leaf than in the smelling salts they gave out for high-school bootfa—football." He sniffs again to make sure, yep, oughtta get his pop to package it, make a mint, get it? and retire for life. He stuffs several in his pocket. "Gonna send 'em home, seriously."

By the time they reach the English Department, students are already coming out the door with syllabi, bibliographies, course descriptions, wine and cheese. Alabama lays a hand on Sylvan's shoulder, raises an eyebrow toward the girl they saw earlier, the legs, the Cheerios, the teddy bear.

"My lucky day. She's English."

He introduces himself, pouring on the Southernese, and asks what he missed. Nothing. He didn't think so, but what about those papers? Plenty more inside, wine too. Her name is Monica, and she's got big eyes, brown, polite, and bored. She's obviously used to this, deflects lots of unwanted attention, gives directions to strangers too often. Alabama hands her a few bay leaves to smell.

"O my fucking God—"

What language, and a face that looks about to explode. Now she watches Alabama with different eyes, and agrees to come over tomorrow night. "Be neighborly," Alabama puts it, and "Bring your roommate."

Sylvan takes Alabama, who won't know the difference, the long way home. There are so many trees and ravines and curving paths that you can't see much sky. Hard to tell what direction you're heading when there are no shadows to judge by. People know this without knowing it. Getting oriented can take several weeks on this campus—huge, sprawling as a natural park, but better, fewer rules, more mood.

Sylvan has gone to progressive (though now the word is its own antonym) schools all his life. Hardly any rules at all. He learned video editing and t'ai chi, as well as the basics, in classrooms furnished with air pillows instead of desks.

The path comes out on an open hillside that has a view of all Santa Cruz. Tres Ojos, in the distance, looks close enough to touch. Kids are playing on the playground. He can make out Wolfgang (red hair), Astrid and Humberto (inseparable), and Adonis (trying to climb the fence and escape). No sign of Teo or Phyllis.

"I work there starting Friday."

"Baby-sitting?"

"No." The guy obviously has no concept. "I take the kids on field trips."

"Cool." Alabama squints.

"The lady who runs the place—" Sylvan stops. Maybe she doesn't want anybody to know. Artificial insemination could be kind of a scarlet letter. The only reason he could ever treat it lightly is because he knows he's not going to say yes. "She's a nice lady."

"Nice or *nice*?"

"She's an okay person." An okay person?

Beyond Tres Ojos: more hilly neighborhoods, then downtown itself, highlighted by the roller coaster standing like a Tinkertoy structure on the boardwalk overlooking the bay, which shines today like brushed metal.

"Injuns?" Alabama points to the row of tepees in the foreground, setting off the campus farm. "Or just decoration?"

"They grow organic stuff."

"Organic stuff gives me the farts." Suddenly Alabama's leg skates out in front of him and he almost goes down. His heel leaves a slimy yellow skidmark. "Mercy!"

"Banana slug," Sylvan explains. "They're pretty common around here." Bright yellow like ripe bananas—though farther north they're often green—and about six inches long, banana slugs creep about the redwood forests leaving behind glazed trails of slime. The slime, now smeared across the path, and all over the bottom of Alabama's sneaker, works as both an adhesive and a lubricant. A slug can stick to Teflon, and slither unscathed over the sharpest barbed wire.

Using a handful of leaves, Alabama cleans the yellow remains off his shoe.

"It's the school mascot," Sylvan says. "Major issue, though, even made *Time* magazine." The chancellor wanted sea lions, but in the end, the students voted seven to one for the slug, calling it symbolic of the university's philosophy: noncompetitive, no grades, emphasis on tutorials, mostly liberal arts, but with access to the finest scientific laboratories, which in Sylvan's case happens to be California itself.

Banana slugs' sex lives are extraordinary. And, given Phyllis's strange request yesterday, Sylvan thinks that particular characteristic may somehow reflect Santa Cruz's image as well. Although banana slugs are hermaphroditic—each slug possessing both male and female sexual organs—they must mate with one another to reproduce. Finding a partner is like hunting, and occasionally a slug will shoot dartlike spears into a potential mate. Slug penises grow as large as half the body length, and sexual entanglements may last a couple of days.

"You have the banana slug, at Princeton we had Brooke."

"Careful." Sylvan points out some poison oak, dry now, the glossy red leaves turning brittle, but not harmless. It will be just sticks in a couple of months.

"So that's the stuff." Alabama has read a warning in a campus brochure. "Do firemen really die from breathing the smoke when it burns?"

"From the inside out."

"Hey, I like that." He takes a pen from behind his ear and writes on the back of a syllabus. "Not the concept, but the turn of phrase."

"Are you a writer?"

"I'm writing, aren't I?" He bends over, closer to the oak, eyes going wide from a squint.

Even in the fall, the plant is dangerous. Sylvan has seen people messed up. His field partner Rusty, for instance. Last year when they were measuring the sediment (which Rusty spelled "sentiment" in lab reports) pouring out of Waddell Creek for a sand-migration study, he got wrapped up in a whole plant that must have come unrooted during the storm and was floating downstream along with black foam, logs, and twenty-seven gallons of silt per cubic foot per minute. Sylvan had to rip the plant off, thankful for his thick neoprene gloves, and help Rusty to the shore, where he stripped and went right back into the river to wash off the oils. To Sylvan: "Any soap?" To the bush: "Fuck you. Not really." To the sky: "Please, no."

Three days later Rusty was laid up—"the bed feels like nails"—his head the size of a basketball and his eyes puffed almost shut. What little of them Sylvan could see was red like split tomatoes. And his lips, cracked, secreted the same yellowish crusty stuff that came from the sores on his arms. Doctors gave him cortisone injections, but those didn't seem to help. The red scars lasted for months. Eventually they healed completely. Hard to believe that something so evil-looking could vanish without a trace. That Rusty's head, so deformed, had returned to normal.

Now Alabama is putting his hand in the oak.

"Don't!" Sylvan says. Great. A fool for a roommate. He can see it now: Alabama fat-headed and sick for weeks. Oozing all over the apartment.

"Wondra!" Alabama extracts something from inside the plant. He delicately holds a piece of green paper as if it were a butterfly wing. "Fifty ducats." It's a fifty-dollar bill. Unbelievable. "Charter our party fund." He walks on his toes, giddy now, more with the discovering than the discovery, eager to "go exploring." He wants to follow the "real life" deer trail that Sylvan knows loops around the firehouse and leads back to student housing.

The trail winds down a hillside through a fern grotto, the glades brown-fringed and dry. The air gets dusky under a canopy of madrones, gauzy-lit, and smells like dried sap. Sylvan probably wouldn't have noticed but there's also a heavier scent, wet wool, from behind a charcoaled tree stump. A wild animal skeleton lies stretched out on its side, the flesh having sunk into the ground, where clusters of deathcaps feed on its compost. Hide and hair stick to the ribs and in tarry patches along the spine. The skull is pretty clean though, the teeth enamelly and predatorial.

"Bobcat. Didn't die of old age." Sylvan wouldn't mind saving the thing, reassembling it with wire, showing it off in his apartment. In fact, that's what he's going to do. "I gotta run back and get a bag to collect these bones."

"I'll hang here." Alabama squats and scribbles more notes on a folded syllabus.

It's dark before Sylvan has labeled each bone, bagged each paw separately, and numbered each rib and vertebra. While he finishes up, Alabama sits cross-legged under a tree and smokes. "Mama or papa cat?"

"Don't know."

"What do they eat?"

"Prairie dogs, jumping mice, lizards, stuff."

"How'd it die?"

"Don't want to know."

"Why not?"

"Don't know." Sylvan places the ziplocked bags inside a green tight-mesh net and puts that inside a backpack.

"Rubber gloves freak me out," Alabama says, watching Sylvan peel them off.

"I'm used to them from the lab. Give me those." He points to a couple of cigarettes Alabama has crushed out in the dirt. Even one butt would ruin *the basic mood* of the place. He crumples them up into the disposable rubber gloves and bags the whole mess.

"I would have offered to help."

"I know that," Sylvan says, glad Alabama didn't make him have to say no.

"Can't you make that look somehow normal?" Alabama asks.

Sylvan is boiling the bobcat skull and teeth in a soup kettle. He has already boiled the rest of the skeleton, and various bones are soaking in bleach trays set out on his bedroom floor.

"Monica's coming over." Alabama's spitting sunflower shells into an empty beer can.

"So?"

"She's a pretty girl." Girl, the way he says it, rhymes with virile. "I just don't want her to get the wrong impression."

"Then why disguise things?"

"She's bringing her roommate." Alabama winks. "Besides, it sorta stinks. How 'bout it? Make it look like soup."

Sylvan can't smell any stink, but Alabama's pinching his nose and fake-barfing. "All right, all right, it's soup." Why waste a chance to be a good roommate? He throws a clove of garlic, an onion, and some carrots into the pot. Curious how doing somebody a favor makes you like them more. Vegetables won't damage the bones in any way he can think of, and they'll make the apartment smell good.

"Boastable?" Alabama asks.

"What-able?"

He underhands Sylvan a beer, then "boasts" one himself from the stockpile of imports paid for with the "party-fund fifty-spot." Alabama has his own language. Last night he "bagged up" at bedtime, and this morning he "bogged down" in the bathroom. Anything undesirable is a "cheese product," and the opposite is "a wondra" or "a boon." When he's let down it's "much to my dismantlement," and he's fond of "-ism" and "-worthy" as suffixes, so when he's hungry he's "munchworthy," and when he's philosophical, "that's lifism."

Now, while Sylvan stirs with a wooden spoon, Alabama chants: "Double, double, toil and trouble, fire burn and cauldron bubble. Shakespeare. Now comes the good part. Cool it with baboon's blood, then the charm is firm and good." Alabama empties Sylvan's package of SEAWEED into the soup.

Fifteen minutes before nine, Alabama pump-sprays some mousse and runs an Ace comb—the fine-tooth black rubberized kind Sylvan used to carry in his back pocket before he stopped combing period—through his hopeless red hair. No two strands the same length, each hair has a different curl. The total effect is that of an exploded seedpod.

He pulls on a pair of turquoise cowboy boots, tucking in jeans that have a crease like a chalk line down each leg. With a sleeveless T-shirt finishing off the outfit, Alabama looks tight and together, and standing next to him, Sylvan feels tall, clunky, out of control in the elbows. Hard to believe he used to be a shrimp—the shortest person in the fourth grade, and fifth, and sixth, all the way up to high school, when he suddenly had a "growth spurt." Almost a foot in two years, leaving stretchmarks on his knees and hips. He spent most of those two years sleeping or eating multiple helpings of roast beef. Now he's more than six feet tall, sensitive in the ribs, always too hot or cold. He also has perpetually bruised shins from knocking them on lab stools, and he can't sleep on his side because of pointy hipbones.

Alabama caps the mousse. "You don't need any of this."

Sylvan's hair is curly and yellow and "too pretty for a boy," women (but thankfully not Phyllis) have told him all his life. His eyelashes are the same yellow, now bleached white from a summer above timberline, and he can see people looking at them instead of his eyes during conversations. Alabama may have the same problem with those reddish lashes, but at least his eyes themselves are darker—hazel with green specks, and on his right eye, a green fleck even outside his iris.

"What?" Alabama blinks rapidly. "Do I have a pimple or something?"

"Nothing." Sylvan looks down. His jeans are bunched at the knees and hips, they sag at the crotch, and the cuffs pile onto his hi-tops. Outdated and sloppy, but all clothes are like that on him. Except for cutoffs, anything he wears looks, somehow, borrowed. He takes a tooled leather belt from Alabama, who cautions him that vanity is the worst insecurity but running a tight ship is a different story, and tucks in an old Hang Ten shirt, red with thin white horizontal stripes. Less awkward-looking now, but still so damn tall. Why would Phyllis choose him? Unless she wants a geeky kid.

The windows are steaming up and the room's beginning to smell good.

"Home cooking," Alabama says as the doorbell rings.

Monica comes "via UCLA" and is here to do graduate studies in Comparative Lit, which, Sylvan thinks, is an airy thing to study.

Real dissections of imaginary frogs. She has an ambassador for a dad, and a certain prettiness that turns to beauty in photographs. Snapshots are lying all over any available table, since Alabama somehow, and for some reason, persuaded her to go next door and bring back her photo albums. God knows why. He seems kind of hung up on Family.

Monica's roommate, Dawn, wants to talk politics, especially since it appears Monica has lived in more than a few geopolitical hot spots, but nobody's interested.

Here she is seven years old, eating papaya in Grenada. Here she is at fifteen riding a camel in the Sudan. And later, a seventeen-year-old standing on the White House steps with Dad and the president of Yemen. She acquires a strong jaw and cheekbones in the photographs that she doesn't have in real life, and her brown eyes look as if they're asking your name. Twenty-two and very right in a bikini.

"No brothers or sisters?" Alabama asks. She shakes her head no. "I got a whole slew of them." He looks at Sylvan. "Hear that, buddy? Three brothers and a sister. Expect visitors."

"I thought you said two brothers."

"Did I?" Alabama points to his own temple and shakes his head. Then he holds up a snapshot of Monica blowing out eleven birthday candles.

Damn. Sylvan remembers it was Emma's birthday last week. He always forgets hers, she never forgets his. And now that she's pregnant he wants to be extra nice to her, as if she were his younger, rather than older, sister. What could he get her? Baby spoons? A rattle or something? Or maybe something doctorish, since she's a full-fledged resident now.

"Mmmmm," Dawn says. "Smells good in here."

Sylvan watches Alabama force back a grin by concentrating on Monica's pictures. "All these exotic locales and you're not smiling in a single one."

She explains by smiling. Bulging cheeks, ears that tip back, one eye squinting shut. Goofy.

"Heavens," Alabama says, employing the accent. "Not your run-of-the-mill saycheeser."

She goes into a seizure of laughing—swallowing giggles and spraying a fine spit mist that everybody politely ignores, except for Alabama, who makes a show of wiping his cheek with the back of his hand. Now they all laugh, laughing at themselves for feeling bad about laughing at her.

But when the laughing stops, they all avoid each other's eyes.

"What's that high-pitched buzzing?" Monica asks. A thin, fried-sounding whistle comes from nowhere, everywhere, impossible to say how long it's been ringing before she noticed.

"It's the light." Sylvan points to the fixture on the ceiling.

"Smoke detector," Alabama says.

"Sure is loud," Dawn says.

"Why'd you make us all hear it?" Alabama asks.

"I couldn't stand to bear it alone," Monica says.

Dawn has the face of a dog straining at the end of its leash. She follows Sylvan into the kitchen, where he's going to get another round of beers and some chips. She's wearing denim down to the boots, which have pockets sewn over the ankles. A copy of *The Female Eunuch* by Germaine Greer sticks out of one. Dawn's a History of Consciousness student specializing in Women's Studies. Born and raised in Fresno, she moved to Santa Cruz because, she says, "It's an antenna for the country as a whole, the westernmost point on the frontier of Western civilization, picking up on the first tremors of new cultural zeitgeists."

In the other room, Sylvan can hear Monica saying something about "Bugs Bunny speaking Swahili." And Alabama saying, "In Nashville when it rains the sidewalks get foamy." Dawn meanwhile has Sylvan cornered while she explains her "White Blob Theory of Western Civilization." The white blob standing for men, virginity, the president's residence, sperm, the vast middle class for Chris-sakes, everything powerful and oppressive. While she talks, the fingers of one hand pick at a janitor's key chain holding at least two dozen keys. "It's the subject of my dissertation."

"Congratulations." Sylvan can get away with saying this and not sounding mean. After all, she's right, in a way, about women getting the short end. He basically agrees with her. But just now he's thirsty and she's standing between him and the refrigerator. He squeezes past and takes out four beers, grabs a bag of chips off the counter, and walks back into the living room.

Monica is talking about growing up an only child, living in hotels or in houses just like them, sandbagged for protection against exploding trucks. The only thing to do was watch a lot of TV (emphasis on the T) and read. "I read *Peter Pan* in four languages."

"Wasn't Peter Pan allegedly murdered by a crazed individual right here in California?" Alabama asks.

It had been all over the newspapers during the summer. Peter Pan, age unknown, a San Francisco address. One of the casualties in a mass murder reminiscent of the Night Stalker, the Hillside Strangler, Helter Skelter, etc. This one involved videotaped tortures and meat-hooks. Sylvan doesn't want to laugh, but can't help it. The way things connect up is very strange.

"Murder capital of the world right here," Dawn says, referring to Santa Cruz's string of never solved ax murders, a series of hitch-hiking dismemberments, and a psycho who went on a rampage with a homemade bazooka (six tennis-ball cans soldered together shooting wood screws and nails as shrapnel) at City Hall.

"But before I read *Peter Pan*," Monica is saying, off on her own track, "I always thought of grown-ups, who I spent a lot of time with, all of it really, as g-r-o-a-n-u-p-s."

When Sylvan was four his father had brought home a red lump of hard plastic and put it on the kitchen table. It had ugly blue and yellow veins. This, Dad explained, was a heart. The size of your fist. Chunks of it pulled away, revealing, in cross section, ventricles, valves, the aorta. Not at all the heart Sylvan had pictured beating inside his own chest, a sweeter color red valentine that had nothing to do with blood. What a disappointment this was, the plastic human heart lying next to the salt and pepper shakers. What you had to look forward to in life.

"What's 'rimming'?" Alabama asks nobody in particular. He's pulled a safe-sex pamphlet out of a pile of books and papers on the floor next to the couch. "Oh, I see. 'Applying the tongue to the anus.' Considered unsafe."

Sylvan watches Monica and Dawn try to retain their composure. They do a good job of it, mainly keeping their eyes to themselves.

He wonders if there's anything in the pamphlet about artificial insemination. Safe unsex. Sylvan chuckles to himself, wishing some-body were here to share the joke, and wonders what Phyllis is doing. Is she still at work? What does she do in the evenings? What's her favorite food? Her sex life like? What *do* lesbians do? He should take a look at that pamphlet.

"I'll be." Alabama's crazy without being rude. He scratches an eyebrow. "Wouldya look at—hum, never would've thought of doing *that*. Imagine putting a telephone—forget it." A moment later he snaps shut the booklet. "Practically every kind of relations—even normal ones between consenting adults—is considered high-risk behavior."

Everybody looks down. It is impossible to be silent now without hearing that high-pitched buzzing.

"My, doesn't that soup smell wonderful," Dawn says. "Aren't you gentlemen going to offer us any?" She's pressing her fingertips down on the last crumbs of potato chips at the bottom of the bag. Anybody else, and this gesture would be endearing.

"Absolutely," Alabama says. "By all means. It'd be a pleasure. We would have already offered, but truth is, we haven't unpacked any bowls or spoons yet!"

He has to be joking, rubbing his stomach like that.

"Don't bother," Monica says. "We'll just go next door for them."

"More chips too," Dawn says. Even her eyes look denimy.

"What next? Open a can of Campbell's?" Sylvan asks. They'll be back in five minutes at most.

"She's fully me." Alabama is still looking at the door.

"You can't feed them that stuff. Make them sick." Though it probably won't. The skull, clean to begin with, has been boiling long enough to kill any bacteria, viruses, or single-celled etceteras that may have been malingering.

"What do you think of Ms. Denim?" Alabama asks. "She your type?"

"Include me out." Sylvan's beer is empty, but he lifts the can to his mouth anyway, and watches the skew fleck of iris drift across the white of Alabama's eye.

"What are you looking at?"

"Germs. Patches of hide. Clots of who knows what. Go ahead, eat it if you want, but I'm not having any." He settles back into the sofa. Maybe Alabama's bluffing. "Boast me."

"Dare me?" Alabama asks.

"Just throw me a beer."

Alabama tosses him one, and gets one for himself. He also takes out a head of broccoli and adds it to the pot along with salt and pepper. "Smells like heaven."

"Heaven is for dead people."

He slurps from a wooden spoon, dips for a carrot, brings it to his lips, blows on it, eats it. "Not bad. Needs a little more salt."

Watching, Sylvan's stomach growls.

"Did you see how I made her smile?"

"You're going to feed her that soup, aren't you?"

"She's hungry. I like her." Alabama can get away with it. They'll eat it and love it and never know the difference.

Sylvan remembers going fishing one time with his cousin Gary, who was six feet eight and big in every way. Sylvan was seven years old, a shrimp, and not having much luck, not having any luck with his line. So he went in search of a new spot. On the far side of the cove he found a foot-long catfish floating belly up in the shoals. He grabbed the fish and shook his wrist so it appeared to be wriggling violently. "Gary! Gary! Look! I caught it with my bare hands!" He ran towards his cousin, but just when he got close he fake-tripped and let the fish go flying. It splashed into the lake with a hollow plop. Fantastic, Gary had said. Bare-handed. But after being so easily faked out, or, worse, letting him get away with the lie, Gary seemed not so big anymore.

"You tell them or I will."

"Absolutely," Alabama says, smiling, displaying those sideways teeth, trustable.

Monica's got a box of Figurines and two crocks, and Dawn has chips and another pair of crocks. Sylvan does not like this pairing-up dynamic—Monica holding her own and Alabama's is okay, but Dawn holding hers and his is not. That everybody acts as if they don't notice makes it seem even more absurd, and slightly insidious.

"You girls have yourselves a sit," Alabama says, setting the coffee table. "I'll dish you some soup."

"Women," Dawn says.

"Pardon?"

"*Women*, not girls."

"Doesn't take special powers to see the obvious."

"It's just that we're not *girls* any more than you're *boys*."

Alabama sucks his bottom lip, considering. "How about 'faces'? Hey, Face. How's that?"

Monica changes the subject. She starts talking about the crickets and Indian summer, how outside the air smells like toast, which reminds her how hungry she is. She hands over the crocks and makes her eyes go like butterflies. "What kind of soup is it, anyway?"

"Bobcat," Alabama says.

"Hmmm," Monica says. "I think I had that once. Now I remember, at the World's Fair in Vancouver. Or maybe it was venison."

"Made with real bobcats?" Dawn asks.

"Don't worry," Alabama says. "They're not on the endangered list, are they, Syl?"

Sylvan catches up with Alabama in the kitchen. "Stop this."

"I told them the truth."

"No."

"What no?"

"No no."

"Dude." Alabama shakes his head and clicks his tongue. "I wouldn't serve them anything I wasn't eating myself."

"You're serious."

"A girl with a normal appetite is rare nowadays."

"You're—"

"I'm told people tell me I'm crazy."

Monica and Dawn come into the kitchen, ask if anything's the matter. "Can we be of help?"

"Sorry. Can't eat the soup," Sylvan says, uncrossing his arms, trying to look relaxed, like he knows what he's talking about without having to talk about it. A trick of body language he learned from Phyllis, the way she deals with a classroom of four-year-olds.

Monica's openmouthed, Dawn's stewed, and Alabama's examining a thumbnail. Nothing makes Sylvan feel worse than putting somebody under the gun, having to see them squirm. He'll do anything to prevent another person's humiliation. Alabama deserves this, though. Monica may hate him, but at least she'll see him for what he is.

"Because—" Sylvan says. "I made it special. It's mine."

Alabama smiles the smug smartass smile of a successful bluffer, the women collapse into bad posture, and Sylvan feels like the Bad Guy who's really the Good Guy. There's no way he can say anything now. About the bobcat skull, the real situation here (what kind of person would salvage a bobcat skull and then boil it with vegetables?). How nothing is the way it seems. How this kind of shit happens when a wrong impression gets out of hand.

"You coulda told us before," Monica whines.

Dawn says, "Finally, a man cooking, and he hogs it all for himself. It figures."

"All right, all right. Go ahead." Partly because they're being such whiners, but mainly because now he wants to see Alabama eat it.

"Yum!" Dawn says.

"Are you sure?" Monica asks.

"Absolutely." Shades of Alabama in that assurance.

Alabama himself now looks a little freaked. His lips are parted in an involuntary, barely perceptible sneer. And his eyes are wide.

"Really. Alabama'll dish it up for you."

They all sit around eating bobcat soup, except for Sylvan, who has poured himself only half a bowl and pretended to eat one spoonful. But even when Alabama gets to the bottom of his crock and is forced to accept seconds from the girls, so helpful, Sylvan can take no pleasure in the revenge. He's too old for this, should be moving past dorm-room pranks, past hanging out with people not of his choice. Toward doing exactly what he wants with people he can, well, call his own.

HORIZONTAL LIGHT
by Chris Spain
(Columbia University)

Pop . . . Pop . . . Pop. Early in the morning the toads hug the pavement, looking for yesterday's sun. When I hit them square they bust like balloons, and when I just graze them they exhale like old people sighing when someone has died too young. I zip past hissing anhydrous ammonia tanks, white as buffalo leg bones, and accelerate to get out of Texas before the asphalt is gummy from the heat.

It has been one hundred degrees in Muleshoe for a month. I have worked the whole summer for my uncle, irrigating feed corn and painting grain silos and fertilizer bins. When I paint I paint everything white, and try not to think about Leigh. But she is in that paint, pale as the triangles of skin that her swimming suit shades from the sun.

It takes me twenty-two minutes to cross the Oklahoma Panhandle, and then it is Kansas until after lunch. I'm leaving before harvest, heading back to see Kris and Leigh. The plains of Colorado look like Texas until the mountains jump out of nowhere. Twenty miles from Fort Collins I see the pile of whitewashed rocks that shape a big *A* on the foothill above the stadium. It used to stand for the Aggies of Colorado State University. They're not Aggies anymore, now they're Rams. Kris and I have been talking about adding two S's to that A ever since we were kids. Only thing is it would be a lot of work.

At the farm Kris has planted barley right up to the road and it's ready for a combine. The lawn has just been cut and the mower squats in the clippings. Kris and Leigh are on the back porch.

"Hey," I shout.

"Yahoo," says Kris.

Skinny as a Mexican chicken, Kris has knotty farmer's muscles. He's got on ragged overalls and there are streaks of sweat running from his armpits. I hug him and walk to Leigh. She looks like she is watching a movie that she just decided to walk out of. She squeezes my hand and I kiss her, giving her a faraway hug. She has that same talc-like smell, and there is no hair on her arms which are covered with fine white scars.

"Hi," says Leigh.

"Missed you," I say to them.

"We missed you too," says Kris.

I look at the mountain which is turning blue as the sun tries to get behind it.

"You just get in?" asks Kris.

"Straight off the highway."

"From Texas?"

"Tex ass."

Kris's mother hugs me and tells me how much she missed me. How she thought about me when the TV said how hot it was in Texas, and how she wished I had stayed in Fort Collins. She fixes iced tea and we sit at the table next to the bay window.

"Where's your dad?" I ask Kris.

"Getting trucks to bring the cattle down from Soapstone." I don't mind the old man not being around, he's not too fond of me.

"Isn't it kind of early?"

"We're ready to cut barley," says Kris. "We'll let them graze the stubble."

Kris asks me if I want to help fix a fence before it gets dark. I bring in my bag which has my work clothes in it and Kris's mother tells me to put it in the upstairs guest room. She says the bed is made and I am welcome to stay as long as I want. I tell her I will only stay a night or two, until I find a place in town. I put on my boots and go back downstairs. Kris and Leigh are together on the porch; they burst apart like startled pheasants.

"Let's go," I say.

We walk to the barn, booting up swirls of dust with our feet. Kris says it hasn't rained in three weeks. We throw a come-along, wire, and fence posts into the back of the Impala that Kris uses as a pickup. It's strange driving to the field with Leigh between us and her leaning toward Kris, but reaching to touch my knee so that my whole leg is nervous. We hit the bar ditch and head across the bottom where we always get stuck when it rains. The fence follows the lay of the land, separating the alfalfa and barley. I have fixed this fence about a hundred times. The alfalfa is long and nearly ready for the last cutting. Kris stops where the barbed wire is torn away from the posts. It's curled on the ground like a scorpion spiking itself in the back. The small cloud of earth following us swallows the car and then drifts across the field. The sun is low and bounces off the mountain and the little snow that always makes it through August. We open the doors but stay in the car. It's the choice part of a summer day, after it has started to cool off and some wind comes down from Wyoming.

"Better do it," says Kris.

We put our gloves on, cut away the bad wire, and pull up the crooked fence posts. Leigh walks into the field to sight the fence line for us and she waves to me when I've got it right. When I wave back she is already looking off toward Greeley.

"How was Texas?" asks Kris.

"Hot," I say. "Corn grew so hard the fumes made me high."

"Hot," says Kris.

"How about here?" I ask him.

"Just about a regular summer," he says.

"How's things with Leigh?"

"It's been good."

"She looks awful good."

I wallop a new fence post with the sledge while Kris holds it at the base. The deep clay thumps, and soon I'm sweating. I arch my back and give all my body to the hammer. I want to show Kris and Leigh my summer muscle. The thud of each swing shakes me to my shoulders. When the post is in, Kris grabs my biceps and squeezes hard.

We get the five strands strung tight as banjo strings. I pluck them with a pair of pliers and listen to the twang bounce between the fence posts. We have set the fence straight and it looks right. Leigh is on the hood of the Impala, and Kris and I stretch out next to her. On the inside of her right knee she's still got this beauty of a scar from when we dumped my dirt bike riding up the canyon. She got her leg stuck under the muffler and I couldn't get the bike off her before I smelled the skin burning.

"You still got that scar," I say, pointing at it.

"I got this feeling it's not going away," she says.

The sun is giving that long horizontal light, a light that makes it seem like the colors are coming from the inside. We are silent, like we are seeing it all for the first time.

When that light is gone I strain to keep the feeling. A song I remember from somewhere comes on the radio. Leigh stands on the hood to dance, bouncing the shocks. We watch her, smiling and letting our heads roll back and forth on the windshield. I get up to dance with Leigh, and we rock the car and bump our hips.

"You hear something?" I ask Leigh.

Kris turns down the radio and I hear the shouting better but I can't locate where it is coming from.

"GODDAMN."

It's coming from the beans. I see Kris's dad, his arms flapping in the air like a crazy man and his feet coming off the ground. He looks like a silent movie, only I can hear him.

"GET OFF THAT CAR."

"Who said that?" asks Kris.

"I think it's your dad, he's in the beans."

"CRAZY DRUNKS," shouts Kris's father.

I jump from the car and help Leigh down. Kris takes a long look at the bean field.

"That's dad," says Kris.

"You think we're in trouble?" asks Leigh.

We watch the old man walk back to the house. Kris says not to worry, the folks are going out for dinner and will be gone soon. We stay in the field until they leave. It's late summer so even when the sun is gone the warmth stays. I put my arms behind my head and close my eyes and breathe in the smell of Leigh.

We drive up to the house and park by the water well. It is quiet except for the hiss of big trucks on the highway. The floodlight on top of the barn is on. It's above the basketball goal, and the shadow of the rim spreads like a water stain on the dirt.

"Game?" asks Kris.

We look in the tool shed for the ball. It's kind of flat. We try to locate a needle, but we don't find one. Leigh sits under one of the dying oak trees to watch us. When Kris takes it to the basket the first time, I know we're not holding back.

"One nothing," says Kris.

We play until we are sweating hard and tied at tens. Then Kris drives on me and smacks me in the mouth with his elbow as he goes by. I hear my teeth chatter and I come down holding my jaw. He knows he has hurt me and he stands next to me as I lean over, spitting blood on the ground.

"You right?" he asks.

I straighten up and wipe my mouth on my shirt. Leigh is walking toward the house. The grass is still tall enough to make her look barefoot.

"I'm going to see what there is for dinner," she says.

Kris holds the ball against his hip and watches her.

"She's mad," says Kris.

"Your ball," I say.

I'm no good with my hurting mouth. Kris has me down point-thirteen when he pulls up for a jumper. He's a skinny bastard but he has the best-looking jump shot of any white person who's ever left the ground. He goes up and I go with him. He's holding the ball way above his head and his wrist is cocked, loose and easy. He's still going up when I peak, and he keeps going like he is going to jump right through the sky. I owe him a good foul. Down I come and there is Kris, silhouetted against the mountain, sweat glistening off his body, and I realize I am probably seeing the most beautiful thing I will ever see in my whole life. He lets go of the ball and I don't even turn because I know it will click the net.

"Game," says Kris.

"Game," I reply.

We sit on the slab of the empty corn crib, and lean back against the wire.

"Guess you're slowing down, old man," says Kris.

"I was just letting you look good in front of your woman," I tell him.

We find Leigh sitting in the kitchen, in the dark, staring out the bay window at nothing but dark.

"You want to know who won?" asks Kris.

"No," she replies.

"He won," I say.

Kris turns on the light and we sit at the table with Leigh. I think she has been crying. I can't tell if Kris notices.

"What do you want for dinner? There's meat," says Leigh.

"Why don't we do a barbecue?" I say.

"I'd like that," says Leigh.

Kris and I go looking for charcoal. Kris says they had barbecues all summer long. I tell him that in Texas we never did find the grill, it was just that kind of summer. We go through the barn and the garage and don't find a bit of charcoal. Finally we end up getting out the axe to shave splinters from some winter wood.

"This'll be a real barbecue," says Kris.

Messing around the wood pile I find cedar scraps. There isn't anything I would rather smell burning than cedar. I bust the wood with the axe. Somehow I jolt myself and my mouth starts bleeding again.

"What?" asks Kris.

"Mouth's bleeding again."

I leave Kris to finish the wood and I go to fix my mouth. When I get to the house I don't even stick my head in the kitchen but go straight to the downstairs bathroom. I'm nearly through cleaning my mouth when I see Leigh standing in the hallway watching my reflection in the mirror. I don't say anything but finish and then go out in the hallway and look at her.

"How are you?" I ask her.

"Same as always."

She always says that, she would say that even if she had just won a million bucks.

"How's your mouth?" she asks.

"It's nothing."

"I don't think he meant to do it," she says.

"He didn't mean to do it."

We go to the kitchen and I sit down and watch Leigh cut the meat. We can see Kris dumping an armful of wood into the grill.

"That new muscle looks good on you," says Leigh.

By the time we have a decent cooking fire going Leigh has had the steaks ready a long time. We put the meat on and soon it's dripping and making flames burst up from the coals. Kris hangs a speaker out the kitchen window and we sit back in lawn chairs, listening to music from when we were in high school. We have a couple beers and by the time the meat is cooked I'm feeling better.

Leigh finds some leftover potato salad in the refrigerator and we end up having a real meal. When I finish eating, I prop my feet up on the grill. The heat feels good through my boots. Leigh says she wants to take a shower. I think she is trying to give Kris and me some time alone, either that or I am just making her nervous.

Kris and I walk to the corral, kicking at the stones on the dusty earth. We lean against the long wood and watch a jackrabbit sniff the air. When Kris sighs the old jack takes about a ten-foot leap and is gone.

"Olympic jackrabbit," says Kris.

The moon is up and hanging out east like a peach.

"You want some watermelon?" asks Kris.

We stumble around the tomato stakes and squash in the garden. I hunker down to the ground, pulling at the clods of earth with my hands. I can feel this dirt in me, under my fingernails, in my breath.

"I guess I better be leaving tonight," I say.

"You don't have to."

"Your dad's never too happy with me hanging around," I say. "After that car bouncing he'll probably be looking for it."

"I got a monster," says Kris, and I hear him pop the vine. It's a clean snap, the kind that tells you the melon is ready.

When Leigh finds us our faces and bellies are covered in watermelon juice, and we are surrounded by seeds that look like june bugs crawling on the cement. Leigh looks great. She's the only girl I know who would look good stepping out of a car wreck. She has her hair wrapped up in a white towel, like some kind of wild Arab woman. I tell her I'm not staying.

"Where are you going to stay?" she asks me.

"I'll find a place, somebody'll be home."

Leigh sits between us, not close to either one of us. We sit for a long time.

ZORRO
by Steven Barthelme
(Johns Hopkins University)

It was a big, dark place with white walls and tall rattan chairs, full of lawyers, fraternity boys, people on dates, drug dealers, and some nights, when a Mexican band played, laughing, flashy Spanish types, and us, always us, there for hours at a corner table drinking and talking about nothing in the darkness, and the waitresses were these stunning women still going to college but pushing thirty, in long black nylon dresses, cut on the bias, who brought double Glenlivets and said, This was a mistake, to give us the drink free.

Now I'm standing in my mother's kitchen, thinking about Maria, wondering, Why don't we ever go there any more? In the living room Mother is shouting. When she's on the pills she is always shouting, after she washes them down with Smirnoff, Finlandia, Gilbey's. This is really not my job; I could be home in bed, watching the trees in the backyard, with Maria. It's my father's job, which he escaped by dying. But it's bitchy of me to complain about his shirking this one job.

"Bobby!" she says. "Did you forget how to find the living room or something?"

Every week my mother calls long-distance, usually drunk, manu-facturing reasons I don't listen to any more, and every weekend I get in the car and drive down here. Austin to Houston on Friday. Home to Austin on Sunday. Three hours each way.

I spin the top onto the vodka, put it back into the cabinet, and take my drink in with me, sit on the low, flat lounge my father built. Near one end the red fabric has a dim, almost invisible stain which I've stared at for twenty years. It's where they put his head. Maybe it's not even there. Across the room, in front of the wall which is all windows, my mother sits in the big armchair, her blue eyes half-closed. There's no smile.

"How come *you* can drink?" she says, pointing. "How come? How come you can lecture Mommy with your left hand and slosh down vodka with your right?"

I look past her, out at the yard and a tall Lombardy poplar planted when they built the house. I used to stare at that, too, for hours, home sick from school. When I was getting better, she'd bring me steak cut up in pieces and a baked potato, the official recovery food. No one was afraid of grease around our house. Maria says, They're going to have to stick balloons in your arteries, eventually.

"Hey," my mother says. "How come?"

"Well it's because I don't do such a thorough job of it as you do, Momma. Look, I'm going home."

She sets her glass down on the table beside the big chair. "It's Saturday," she says, wet eyes. "I'll sober up. We can garden. Tomorrow. All I have to do is go to bed." She looks at me. Now she's smiling. "With plenty of money wrapped up in a five-pound note." She laughs, then stops. "Don't mess with me, kid, I was here before you were born." She takes another drink.

It's half past eight; the summer sun is just setting. The light on the back terrace is orange. When the telephone rings, we look at each other.

"Twitchy," my mother says.

I stand up, hesitate. "Hey, you get on the phone again, and I'm driving back tonight. I'm long gone."

"I love it when you're macho," she says.

"I'm serious."

"Oh, I love it when you're serious, too."

I get the phone in the back bedroom. My suitcase, on the floor, is yellow cowhide, new, from Best.

"Are you okay, Bobby?" Maria says. "It's bad this time?"

"It's okay. How're things up there?"

"Nine rings before you pick up the phone—it's bad," she says. She tells me what the cat's been doing, what was in the mail, that there's nothing on TV, her hair is wet. She was up until five last night, couldn't sleep.

"I'll call you back at eleven," I say.

"Well, I'm going dancing," she says. "With Jonathan. So I won't be here."

"Yeah, well, have a good time. Incidentally, who the hell is Jonathan?"

She laughs at me, long-distance. Someone else's conversation starts leaking into ours, then fades. "Jonathan's gay," Maria says. "The new guy at the clinic. I told you about him, but as usual you weren't listening. I'll be back at two, if you want to call."

"I'll be asleep. Before you're through dancing."

"Robertito," she says. "Don't be silly." The other conversation comes back. We say goodbye, and after Maria hangs up I listen to a woman talking about someone named "Val," until the dial tone comes on. When I go back in to the living room, my mother says, "I heard it all," and then, "She's bi, isn't she?" An hour later, she's asleep.

Late, at quarter to three, I call my house in Austin and there's no answer, so I go out the sliding-glass doors and stand in the backyard with a drink. The ice cubes are loud in the darkness. Then the sirens; sirens all night now, not like when I was a kid. It's a big yard, and the trees are big. The poplar is old now, but in the dark it's not friendly; it's not even familiar.

In the bathroom before I go to bed, I make the mistake of opening the mirrored medicine cabinet and there they are, a half-dozen brown plastic bottles. They weren't here the last time. Three different doctors' names, two pharmacies, old dates.

Your reserves? I think. The other bathroom might be too far away? The next morning I'm just getting up when she's coming home from church.

I get some eggs and bacon, sit at the table reading the Sunday *Chronicle*, switch to the *Post*, checking bank ads in the business section because the agency, in Austin, has just gotten a small bank. Stupid really, because all bank ads are the same, but it gives me the illusion of doing something. My mother looks like my mother again.

"How was Mass?"

"I'm going to join one of those copperhead religions," she says. "At least they still believe there are things which can't be explained." It's an old conversation, a favorite. "Pretty soon we'll receive Communion from an automated teller." She looks out the back windows. "Have you got time to help with the yard? I know you want to get back to Twitchy. Why don't you ever bring her with you any more?"

I look at her.

"Oh, c'mon, I was just kidding her. All I said was, 'It must be nice getting paid to yak with people.' She's too sensitive."

"As I recall you said some other things. The 'cheap spic' stuff was real winning."

"Bobby, I never said that, and you know it." She shakes her head, really hurt this time. "I don't remember ever—"

"Momma—"

She walks out of the kitchen. A few minutes later, she comes back. "Will you stay?" She's patched together a motherly demeanor with Mass and aspirin. With her hair pulled back in a blue and white bandanna, she reminds me a little of Patricia Neal. Her voice is very beautiful.

At first she doesn't want me to climb the trees at all, and then she worries about me climbing in boots, and then she doesn't like me kicking the dead limbs down instead of sawing them. When I hit a green one in the top of a tallow tree, the limb bounces and I slip. The air seems thinner up here.

"Bobby! You'll fall," she says, squinting, fifteen feet below.

"I'm not going to fall, Momma. I'm not graceful, but I can handle it. Me and this tree go way back." My father would've cut the limbs, dressed them with that black junk.

We do another tallow and an oak which leaves me with something in my eye and a hundred tiny scratches on my arms. I stand with her on the terrace, rubbing at my eye, point over toward the poplar, although it's really all trunk.

"That one?"

"Honey, it's straight up in the air," she says, wiping her forehead with the bandanna. "Let it be." She fades away, then says, "It was only seven feet when we planted it."

"Another shrine."

"What does that mean?" she says, angry.

"Nothing." She's staring, she won't let me out of it. "It's another shrine to Pop. Like the couch you've never had re-covered. Like the stain on the lounge."

I can't tell if her laughter is real or not. "Honey, that's coffee. You mean the stain on the end? It's coffee." She smiles quickly.

"Yeah, and you knew exactly which stain I was talking about."

"My Lord." She turns to go in. "It's coffee, honey."

When I leave, she's standing on the driveway. She wants me to look at her car again, it's still not right. I tell her I can't.

"You're not coming next weekend," she says. Her expression changes. She leans on the car and says, "He wasn't any damn hero, you know. Ruined my goddamn life in twenty seconds. And you— He left you, too."

"Left? Momma, he didn't leave. He killed himself." The car rocks when I turn the key and the engine fires. I look up. "It was a long time ago, Momma. You don't have to . . ."

She leans in, kisses my hair.

Out of town, I push the air conditioner to MAX, put on a Tom Petty tape, and turn it up so loud my eardrums hurt. Rock and roll: curettage of the brain. After an hour or so, around Flatonia, I switch to Beethoven, some symphony I taped off the radio, a sort of mental intensive-care unit.

As the car rolls into Austin, I think of taking another route to the house, through downtown, by the bar we used to go to, but I'm tired, the traffic's bad, too much noise.

When I get to our house, there's an Alfa out front with the top down. Birds are eating berries in the tree above it, and the Alfa, which used to be solid white, now looks like a Pininfarina dalmatian. Jonathan is a weight lifter, in a T-shirt, with curly hair. He opens the kitchen door, and our cat, Cholo, who's been trying to trip me all the way up the driveway, slips in ahead of me. Jonathan introduces himself, as he's leaving.

"He's not as gay as I thought," Maria says. "But don't worry, he slept on the couch." Her hand goes to her hair. She looks at me and shakes her head, slowly.

"Okay."

"You look terrible," she says.

"Couldn't you have flushed him before I got back?"

"It's nice to have you back." She's wearing a loose, light, faded white nylon dress with black swirls printed on it. One I've always liked.

"You look great."

"Gracias."

"But, listen, no more overnight visitors when I'm out of town. Okay? I'm old-fashioned. You said you were going dancing. Give me a break."

"I can't sleep in an empty house."

The cat bounces from floor to chair to the tabletop and I slam my hand down. "Cholo!" He hits the floor running, hits the wall on his way down the hallway toward the back of the house. His feet slip on the hardwood floor. I look at Maria, look down.

"He'll be okay, Bobby," she says. "He's not that fragile." She gets up and goes to the refrigerator, fills a glass with ice and Diet Coke, and hands it to me. "I'm sorry," she says.

"Me, too." I pull out the chair next to mine. "Sit over here and talk to me. I want to listen to you talk."

Later, when I wake up, nude, it's bright in the bedroom and black outside; moths are tapping the window. The clock on the bedside table says 3:00 A.M. Maria's not there. I pull on some jeans and wander into the kitchen.

"Work tomorrow," I say, staring into the refrigerator for a beer. I sit down across from her, pull out the end chair for Cholo. A peace offering. He jumps up, yawns, sits primly looking from Maria, to me, to Maria. The crickets, outside, are loud.

"You shake now when the phone rings," Maria says, not looking up. "Your hands shake. Did you know?" She reaches for my beer; she's wearing one of my old shirts and the cuffs flop around her hands as she pours beer into her glass.

"Work tomorrow."

"You're a mess, Bobby. They're not happy with you at work, either, I bet. You've got to decide."

"What's to decide?"

"About your mother." She looks up. She can stare like no one else I've ever known. Brown eyes. She's Mexican and Irish. Her name was Mary, but she went down and changed it when she was eighteen. Her mother called her Maria.

I stand up and take her hand, lifting her away from the table.

"She needs help, Bobby. I have some names, therapists, in Houston; they're good people."

"Give me my shirt back."

There's one day of peace before my mother calls, drunk, Tuesday night. She's gotten the car fixed.

"Only they cheated me," she says. "They just smeared grease along the edges of the hood and wrote me up the prettiest invoice you'll ever see."

"Mostly they don't cheat you. They're usually just incompetent."

"Then I'm happy that they didn't touch anything, right?"

"Momma, when I was working for Lancaster this woman left us a VW, and I drove it around the block and then went into his little office and told him there was nothing wrong with it. Lancaster just looked up from the desk, and said, 'Well, then it oughta be easy to fix.' "

"It's a parable," she says. "She's me. I'm her. Right?" She laughs.

"There's nothing wrong with that car."

"I love parables," she says.

Wednesday evening at five past six, the telephone rings. Maria looks at me and says, "We could get an unlisted number." We already have an unlisted number.

"I'm sober," my mother says. "It's six o'clock. I'm bored stiff."

"Have you seen any people this week?"

"You mean the Senior Citizens' Picnic? Bingo?"

"You're laying it on a little thick, Momma. You're only fifty-two. Find some good-looking man and take him dancing. Get down. It's what everybody else does."

"Did you change your mind about coming down this week?"

"Next weekend? Can't. Weekend after."

"How come when we get on this subject, you start talking in syllables?" I can hear the ice clink in her glass. Then there's silence. She says, "That was loud, wasn't it?"

Maria stands watching me talk on the telephone until I hang up. In jeans, she looks like candy. She walks out the kitchen door, slams it, and I hear her car door slam. I wait for the car to start. It doesn't.

Two minutes later she walks back in the door. We stand in the kitchen like Alan Ladd and Jack Palance. It's stupid.

"You think you're doing her any good?" Maria says. "You're not. You're encouraging it. If you didn't run down there every time— Who do you think you are? Zorro?" Her eyes get sort of flat, and don't blink. "She needs treatment, Bobby. You can not fix it."

"What do you suggest? Handcuffs? Anyway, I owe her."

"Bullshit. You don't owe her this. You don't sleep. You're always wired, or brooding. You shake like—"

"Hey, save it for the office. Some oedipal stuff, some R. D. Laing, and that guy in Philadelphia, what's his name? Christ, I'm getting advice from Philadelphia."

"There's no fun any more, Bobby."

"Jonathan's fun, right? You ride around in that little white car pretending you're Isadora, right? You expect fun?"

"It shouldn't be all grief."

I sit down. I think, Something's surely wrong because I've gotten myself into one of those arguments where the woman is right. This should never happen. I hold my forehead with my hand, start listening to my breathing. She's just standing there, on the high ground.

"I'm sorry," Maria says. "I feel terrible." She puts her hands on my shoulders, rubs my neck. "Could we talk about puppies or something?"

For a week nothing happens. The weekend passes. I lay out from work a couple extra days, get some sleep; we barbecue in the backyard, plan to go out Friday night. We even watch a little television.

Late Thursday night, after we've gone to bed, the telephone rings. It's not my mother. It's a guy who says he works in the emergency room at Ben Taub, another doctor. "She's all right," he says. "My name's Matthew. I want you to talk to me when you get here. Don't ask for me. Just look. I'm taller than everyone else." They apparently picked her up downtown in a department store, passed out. He says "lacerations," "sutures," other things. I go into the bathroom and splash water on my face. No one goes to the downtown department stores any more.

Maria's sitting up in bed when I get back in the bedroom. "Is she all right?"

I nod. "She's in the hospital."

"Maybe somebody there can help her."

"I'm going down."

She looks at the clock. "Now?" She reaches over and twists the clock so I can see it. It's two o'clock. "Bobby, I don't want to argue. I can't take this any more."

Rumpled, bleary-eyed, black-haired. She is straining to wake up. I walk around the bed and kiss her forehead. "Go to sleep. I'll be back in a couple days. Hold on a couple more days."

"A couple years," she says. She's crying; I leave anyway.

The highway looks strange and clean, and except for a few semis and speeders, it's empty. One of my headlights is messed up, no low beam. I spend three hours with trucks flashing their brights in my eyes, then a half-hour getting across town.

The hospital corridors have an odd brand-new old look. A dozen people sit in the hall outside the emergency room, filling out forms. It's a slow night, Thursday. I look for Matthew.

He has a beard, not a good beard, thin, manicured, gray like rats' fur. He takes me into an empty room.

"She's fine," he says. "She's either in I.C.U. or upstairs in a room." He hands me a piece of paper from the pocket of his white jacket. "I'm not giving you this. You never even heard of me." He pauses to let some footsteps pass outside, in the hall. "Memorize them."

"I can remember." I'm sitting on a bed. He's standing. He doesn't look so tall. They must have a short crew.

"The top name is a doctor on the west side. He's a quack. He's got a drug clinic over there, biofeedback, mind control, Rolfing, vitamins they get out of skunks—sixties shit. Sex, too, probably, he's a pretty boy. Whatever. He gets results."

"What about—" I say, pointing to the other name on the paper, not wanting to say it out loud. We're playing CIA.

"She's the meanest, sleaziest malpractice lawyer in town," Matthew says. "She also gets results. Dropping her name to whoever prescribed all this junk for your mother will cut off the supply, at least for a while."

"There're three or four of them."

"So?" he says, shaking his head. "Tape the calls." He shakes his head again, and laughs, a squeaky little laugh. "I liked her. But

I just spent six years in Guadalajara. Can't handle it. This is my bit; this is all I can do."

He takes the paper from me, tears a strip off the top, the "Rx," and hands the rest of it back. "Here," he says.

"Hey, how come everybody knows what to do but me?"

"You need therapy," he says, and laughs. The pale yellow door closes gently behind him.

They aren't releasing her, and I can't see her until tomorrow, so I find my car and leave. There's an Alfa in the hospital parking lot, and I notice two others on the freeway out to the house. At the exit I want, the one for my mother's house, I don't turn, I stay on the freeway and watch the big green signs sail overhead. Another ten miles and the roadsides are littered with signs for developer suburbs. Passing them in the darkness, I feel free. I'm going home.

Ten more miles and I'm staring into complete darkness; my headlights have cut out. I get the car onto the shoulder, get out, and somebody blows by me at eighty in a truck. The air is wet and cool. I check the fuse, under the dash; jerk the headlight switch in and out; pull the hood release. At the front of the car, I hit each headlight with my fist—nothing. Twist the wiring harness behind the bulbs. Look up and down the highway. Another half-hour, it'll be daylight. I can wait. I reach up for the hood and slam it. The headlights come on. I remember my father.

In the clear, dark countryside, I remember my father, the strangers standing around after they carried him in and put him on the lounge. There was an inch-high gap under the door to the bedroom where I was sequestered while they stood around, making arrangements, smoking cigarettes. The floor was white tile. I remember helping him replace some of the tile once, the way he patched together two pieces to make one with a linoleum knife and the cigarette lighter he used to carry, a big Zippo, and how the patch was perfect and how I was amazed.

For years I tried to build things the way he did, so they came out perfect, as if they had been made by machine. I couldn't. Every saw cut was crooked. Wood split. Bolts stripped. Paint ran.

Just once, I think, before you left, you could have made a mistake, could have broken something or left a sloppy edge somewhere, if only to let me know it was all right.

You poor stupid son of a bitch.

It's a divided highway. I run the car across the median strip and head back toward my mother.

After four hours' sleep, in my old bedroom, I get on the telephone, arrange for a nurse. Then I call the doctors. When they call back, I slip in the lawyer's name. They don't seem to care. One doesn't even call back. I call Austin, no answer. I try to read *House and Garden,* the *New Republic,* then settle for *Time,* watch TV, pan-fry a steak, eat alone, call again. In the afternoon I pick her up, bring her home. There's a small patch of gauze under her chin on the right side and a magnificent white bandage covering half her upper arm, right arm. She goes to sleep. The nurse arrives and smiles a lot. I call Austin all day, get no answer. I write my mother a note, throw it away.

"Look who's here," she says, sitting up in bed, when I go in to see her. I take a fifth of vodka. There's more gauze on the fingers of her right hand.

"I'm jumping ship," I say. "My suitcase's already in the car," which is a lie, actually, because I didn't bring one. If I had brought a suitcase, it would be in the car. "You learn anything, recently?"

"I'm sore," she says. "Like that?"

"No, I mean like it's not all fun."

"A speech," she says. "I love speeches." She shifts her weight, and winces.

I sit on the bed. "I always thought you killed him. You didn't. You're not even killing me, although that's what it feels like. You're killing yourself, though, just like he did." I put the vodka down on the shelf beside the bed, along with the name of Matthew's clinic, on a new piece of paper. "Try this place. Please."

"It's a grandstand play, Bobby."

"I can't fix it, Momma. Nobody ever fixes anything anyway. Nobody ever ruins anything, either. Patching, is what you do." She's looking at me; I'm wondering whether I'm lying.

"You're your father's son."

"Not yet, I'm not."

"Sure," she says. She smiles at me. "Could you bring the Collins mix?"

On the telephone again before I leave, I imagine the cat, Cholo, sitting on the corner of the bedspread, on the bed, watching it ring.

In the car, on the highway, watching the cows and fields and Stuckey's pass, I think, I can't sleep in an empty house either, and I try to bring a woman's face and the smell of her hair into my mind, but all I can do is remember that dark bar, and wonder what it was we used to talk about for hours at that corner table in those tall high-backed rattan chairs, and remember how she used to laugh. Maria.

APPROXIMATIONS
by Mona Simpson
(Columbia University)

In my family, there were always two people. First, my mother and father. Carol and John.

They danced. Hundreds of evenings at hundreds of parties in their twenties. A thousand times between songs her eyes completely closed when she leaned against him. He looked down at the top of her head; her part gleamed white, under and between the dark hair. He rubbed her back, trying to rouse her, but she became indistinct, blurring against his jacket. He hugged her imperceptibly closer, moving his hand in slower circles on her back, but when he talked it was to someone else over her head. He closed a big hand on her ear.

How do I know this? I don't. But there was a black-and-white snapshot with my father staring at someone outside the frame. I was looking at the picture when, for some reason, I asked my mother where he was.

I was young, only four years old, and I had no memories of my father. I must have been repeating a question someone else had asked me. My mother was ironing. It was 1960 and all her summer clothes were seersucker and cotton. Her hands stalled over the iron when I asked the question.

"He's gone," she said, not looking at me. The windows were open. A string of hummingbirds moved on the lilac bush outside. "But," she said, gathering her cheeks, "he'll be coming back."

"When?"

For a moment, her mouth wavered, but then her chin snapped back into a straight line and she pushed the iron over the perforated pink-and-white fabric again.

"I don't know," she said.

So we waited, without mentioning it, for my father. In the meantime, we got used to living alone. Just the two of us.

Other people asked me questions.

"Any news from your Dad?"

"I don't know."

"You must miss him." Other mothers got maternal, pulling me close to their soft, aproned bellies.

For a moment, but only for a moment, I'd let my eyes close. Then I jerked away. "No," I said.

Saturday nights, we went ice-skating. We wore skin-colored tights and matching short dresses made out of stretch fabric. We skated in tight concentrated figures, our necks bent like horses', following the lines of an 8. Then, when the PA system started up, we broke into free skating, wild around the rink. My mother skated up behind me and caught me at the waist.

"This is how you really lose the pounds," she called, slapping her thigh, "skating fast."

I was always behind. Jerry, the pro, did a T-stop to impress my mother, shaving a comet of ice into the air. They skated around together and I had to slow down to wipe the melting water from my face.

When the music stopped, my mother pulled me over to the barrier, where we ran our skate tips into the soft wood. She pointed up to the rows of empty seats. They were maroon, with the plush worn down in the centers.

"See, when you're older, you can bring a boy you're dating here to see you skate. He can watch and think, hey, she's not just another pretty girl, she can really do something."

She peered into my face with a slanted gaze as if, through a crack, she could see what I'd become.

Taking the skates off, on the bench, was all joy. You could walk without carrying your own weight. Your feet and ankles were pure air. The floors were carpeted with rubber mats, red and black, like a checkerboard. In regular shoes, we walked like saints on clouds. The high-domed arena was always cold.

The first time we heard from my father was 1963 in the middle of winter. We got a long-distance phone call from Las Vegas and it was him.

"We're going to Disneyland!" my mother said, lifting her eyebrows and covering the mouthpiece with her hand.

Into the phone, she said she'd take me out of school. We'd fly to Las Vegas and then the three of us would drive west to Disneyland. I didn't recognize his voice when my mother held out the receiver.

"Hello, Melinda. This is Daddy."

I shrugged at my mother and wouldn't take the phone. "You'll know him when you see him," she whispered.

We waited three days for our summer linen dresses to be dry-cleaned. "It's going to be *hot,*" my mother warned. "Scorching," she added with a smile. It was snowing dry powder when we left Illinois. We only saw white outside the airplane window. Halfway there, we changed in the tiny bathroom, from our winter coats to sleeveless dresses and patent leather thongs. It was still cool in the plane but my mother promised it would be hot on the ground.

It was. The air was swirling with dirt. A woman walked across the airport lobby with a scarf tied around her chest; it trailed behind her, coasting on air.

My mother spotted my father in the crowd, and we all pretended I recognized him too. He looked like an ordinary man. His hair was balding in a small circle. He wore tight black slacks, a brown jacket, and black leather, slip-on shoes. His chin stuck out from his face, giving him an eager look.

He had a car parked outside and my mother got into the front seat with him. We passed hotels with bright blue swimming pools and the brown tinge of the sky hung over the water, like a line of dirt on the rim of a sleeve.

My father's apartment was in a pink stucco building. When we walked up with our suitcases, his three roommates were crowded on the porch, leaning on the iron bannister. They wore white V-neck

T-shirts and thick dark hair pressed out from under them. I hadn't seen men dressed like that before.

"He told us you had long blonde hair."

"You look like your Dad."

"She's prettier than her Dad."

When my father smiled, the gaps between his teeth made him look unintentionally sad, like a jack-o'-lantern. He looked down and I felt he was proud of me. He touched my hair. I loved him blindly, the feeling darkening over everything, but it passed.

My mother stepped up to the porch. "Don't you want to introduce me to your friends, too?"

My father introduced each man separately and each man smiled. Then my father gave me a present: a package of six, different-colored cotton headbands. I held it and didn't tear the cellophane open.

My father worked as a waiter in a hotel restaurant. We had dinner there, eating slowly while he worked, watching him balance dishes on the inside of his arm. He sat down with us while my mother was sipping her coffee. He crossed one leg over the other, smoking luxuriously. My mother leaned closer and whispered in my ear.

"When are we going to Disneyland?" I asked, blankly, saying what she said to say but somehow knowing it was wrong.

My father didn't answer me. He looked at my mother and put out his cigarette. That night in the apartment, they fought. My father's roommates closed the doors to their rooms.

"So, when are we going," my mother asked gamely, crossing one leg over the other on a dinette chair.

His shoulders sloped down. "You were late," he said finally. "You were supposed to be here Monday. When you didn't come, I lost the money I'd saved."

"In three days, how? How could you do that?"

"On the tables."

"You, you can't do this to her," my mother said, her voice gathering like a wave.

They sent me outside to the porch. I heard everything, even their breath, through the screen door. There was a box of matches on the ground and I lit them, one by one, scratching them against the concrete and then dropping them in the dirt when the flames came too close to my fingers. Finally it was quiet. My father came out and opened the screen door and I went in.

They set up the living room couch as a bed for me. They both undressed in my father's bedroom. He pulled off his T-shirt and sat on the bed to untie his shoes. My mother looked back at me, over her shoulder, while she unzipped her dress. Finally, she closed the door.

The next morning my father and I got up before my mother. We went to the hotel coffee shop and sat on stools at the counter. I was afraid to ask for anything; I said I wasn't hungry. My father ordered a soft-boiled egg for himself. His eyes caught on the uniformed waitress, the coffeepot tilting from her hand, a purse on the other end of the counter. The egg came in a white coffee cup. He chopped it with the edge of a spoon, asking me if I'd ever tasted a four-minute egg. I ate a spoonful and I loved it. No other egg was ever so good. I told my father how good it was hoping we could share it. But he slid the whole cup down, the spoon in it, without looking at me and signalled the waitress for another egg.

Walking back to the apartment, he kicked sand into the air. There were no lawns in front of the parked trailers, but the sand was raked and bordered with rows of rocks. My father's black slip-on shoes were scuffed. He was holding my hand but not looking at me.

"So we'll go to Disneyland next trip," he said.

"When?"

Suddenly, I wanted dates and plans and the name of a month, not to see Disneyland but to see him. Taking long steps, trying to match his pace, I wanted to say that I didn't care about Disneyland. I dared myself to talk, after one more, two more, three more steps, all the way to the apartment. But I never said it. All I did was hold his hand tighter and tighter.

"I don't know," he said, letting my hand drop when we came to the steps in front of his apartment.

On the plane home, I was holding the package of headbands in my lap, tracing them through the cellophane. My mother turned away and looked out the window.

"I work," she said finally. "I pay for your school and your books and your skates and your lessons. *And,*" she said in a louder whisper, "I pay the rent."

She picked up the package of headbands and then dropped it back on my lap.

"A seventy-nine-cent package of headbands."
It wasn't fair and I knew it.

The next year my mother went back to Las Vegas without me. She and Jerry, the ice-skating pro, got married. She came back without any pictures of the wedding and Jerry moved in with us.

She said she didn't want to bother with a big wedding since it was her second marriage. She wore a dress she already had.

My mother and I spent all that summer in the arena, where Jerry ran an ice-skating school. All day long the air conditioners hummed like the inside of a refrigerator. Inside the door of my locker was a picture of Peggy Fleming. Inside my mother's was Sonja Henie. In the main office, there were framed pictures of Jerry during his days with Holiday on Ice and the Ice Capades. In them, he didn't look like himself. He had short bristly hair and a glamorous smile. His dark figure slithered backward, his arms pointing to two corners of the photograph. The lighting was yellow and false. In one of the pictures it was snowing.

We practiced all summer for the big show in August. The theme was the calendar; the chorus changed from December angels to April bunnies and May tulips. I couldn't get the quick turns in time with the older girls, so I was taken out of the chorus and given a role of my own. After the Easter number was over and the skaters in bunny costumes crowded backstage, I skated fast around the rink, blowing kisses. A second later, the Zamboni came out to clear the ice. I stood in back before my turn, terrified to go out too early or too late, with the velvet curtain bunched in my hand.

My mother came up behind me every show and gave me a push, saying "now, go" at the right time. I skated completely by instinct. I couldn't see. My eyes blurred under the strong spotlight. But one night, during the Easter dance, my mother was near the stage exit, laughing with Jerry. She kept trying to bend down to tie her laces and he pulled her up, kissing her. Finally, looking over his shoulder, she saw me and quickly mouthed "go." I went out then but it was too late. I heard the Zamboni growling behind me. I tried to run, forgetting how to skate and fell forward, flat on the ice. My hands burned when I hurried up behind the moving spotlight and I saw that I'd torn my tights. The edges of the hole on my knee were ragged with blood.

I sat down on the ice backstage while the music for my mother's number started up. I knew it by heart. Jerry led my mother in an elementary waltz. She glinted along the ice, shifting her weight from leg to bent leg. Her skates slid out from her body. She was heavier than she had once been. She swayed, moving her head to glance off the eyes of the crowd. Under the slow spotlight, she twirled inside the box of Jerry's arms.

I quit skating after that. When my mother and Jerry went to the rink I stayed home or went out to play with the other kids in the neighborhood. The next year I joined the Girl Scout troop.

Eventually, my mother stopped taking lessons, too. Then Jerry went to the rink himself every day, like any other man going to a job.

One Saturday, there was a father/daughter breakfast sponsored by my Girl Scout troop. I must have told my mother about it. But by the time the day came, I'd forgotten and I was all dressed in my play clothes to go outside. I was out the front door when my mother caught me.

"Melinda."

"What?"

"Where are you going?"

"The end of the block."

"Don't you remember your Girl Scout breakfast? You have to go in and change."

I didn't want to go. I was already on the driveway, straddling my bike.

"I don't feel like going to that. I'd rather play."

My mother was wearing her housecoat, but she came outside anyway, holding it closed with one hand over her chest.

"He took the day off and he's in there now getting dressed. Now, come on. Go in and put something on."

"No," I said, "I don't want to."

"Won't you do this for me?" she whispered. "He wants to *adopt* you."

We stood there a minute and then the screen door opened.

"Let her go, Carol. She doesn't have to go if she doesn't want to go. It's up to her."

Jerry was standing in the doorway, all dressed up. His hair was combed down and wet from just taking a shower. He was wearing a white turtleneck sweater and a paisley ascot. I felt sorry for him, looking serious and dressed up like that, and I wanted to change my mind and go in but I thought it was too late and I flew off on my bike. None of the other fathers would be wearing ascots anyway, I was thinking.

My father called again when I was ten, to say he wanted to take me to Disneyland. He said he was living in Reno, Nevada, with a new wife. He and my mother bickered a long time on the phone. He wanted to send a plane ticket for me to come alone. My mother said either both of us went or neither. She said she was afraid he would kidnap me. She held out. Finally, they agreed he'd send the money for two tickets.

Around this time, my mother always told me her dreams, which were about things she wanted. A pale blue Lincoln Continental with a cream-colored interior. A swimming pool with night lights and a redwood fence around the yard. A house with a gazebo you couldn't see from the road.

She had already stopped telling Jerry the things she wanted because he tried to get them for her and he made mistakes. He approximated. He bought her the wrong kind of record player for Christmas and he got a dull gold Cadillac, a used car, for her birthday.

Before we went to California, my mother read about something she wanted. A New Sony Portable Color Television. A jewel. She wanted a white one, she was sure it came in white. In the short magazine article she'd clipped out, it said the TVs were available only in Japan until early 1967, next year, but my mother was sure that by the time we went, they would be all over California.

Jerry took us to the airport and he was quiet while we checked on our luggage. When we got onto the plane, we forgot about him. We made plans to get my father to buy us the New Sony. It was this trip's Disneyland. We'd either win it or lose it depending on how we played.

At the airport in Los Angeles, we met Velma, my father's new wife. She was a good ten years older and rich; her fingers were full of jewelry and she had on a brown fur coat.

This trip there was no struggle. We went straight to Disneyland. We stayed in the Disneyland Hotel. The four of us went through

Disneyland like a rake. There was nothing we didn't see. We ate at
restaurants. We bought souvenirs.

But knowing the real purpose of our trip made talking to my father
complicated. As I watched my mother laugh with him I was never
sure if it was a real laugh, for pleasure, or if it was work, to get our
TV. My father seemed sad and a little bumbling. With everyone else
around, my father and I didn't talk much.

"How's school?" he asked, walking to the Matterhorn.

"Fine," I said, "I like it."

"That's good," he said.

Our conversations were always like that. It was like lighting single
matches.

And I was getting nervous. We were leaving in a day and nothing
was being done about the New Sony. The last night, Velma suggested
that I meet my father downstairs in the lobby before dinner, so the
two of us could talk alone. In our room, my mother brushed my hair
out in a fan across my back.

I was nervous. I didn't know what to say to my father.

My mother knew. "See if you can get him to buy the TV," she
said. "I bet they've got one for sale right nearby."

I said I hadn't seen any in the stores.

"I think I saw one," she said, winking, "a white one."

"What should I do?" I knew I had to learn everything.

"Tell him you're saving up for it. He'll probably just buy it for
you." My mother wasn't nervous. "Suck in your cheeks," she said,
brushing glitter on my face. She was having fun.

I didn't want to leave the room. But my mother gave me a short
push and I went slowly down the stairs. I tried to remember everything she told me. *Chin up. Smile. Brush your hair back. Say you're
saving for it. Suck in your cheeks.* It seemed I was on the verge of
losing one of two things I badly wanted. With each step it seemed
I was choosing.

I saw my father's back first. He was standing by the candy
counter. Whenever I saw my father I went through a series of
gradual adjustments, like when you step out of the ice rink, in
summer, and feel the warm air. I had to focus my vision down
from an idea as vague as a color, to him. He was almost bald. The
way his chin shot out made him always look eager. He was buying
a roll of Lifesavers.

"Would you like anything?" he asked, seeing me and tilting his head to indicate the rows of candy arranged on the counter.

I thought for a wild moment. I could give up the plan, smile, and say yes. Yes I want a candy bar. Two candy bars. He'd buy me two of the best candy bars there. I could stand and eat them sloppily, all the while gazing up at my father. If I smiled, he would smile. He would bend down and dab the chocolate from my mouth with a handkerchief moist with his own saliva.

But I didn't say yes, because I knew it would end. I knew I'd remember my father's face, soft on mine, next year when no letters came. I would hate my best memory because it would prove that my father could fake love or that love could end or, worst of all, that love was not powerful enough to change a life, his life.

"No," I said, "I'm saving up my money."

"What?" he said, smiling down at me. He was unravelling the paper from his Lifesavers.

I gulped. "I'm saving my money for a new Sony portable color television," I said.

He scanned the drugstore for a moment. I think we both knew he was relinquishing me to my mother.

"Oh," he said finally, nodding.

We didn't get the Sony. On the way home, neither of us mentioned it. And when the plane landed, we didn't call Jerry. We took a taxi from the airport. When we got home, my mother collapsed on the blue-green couch and looked around the room disapprovingly. The suitcases were scattered on the floor.

"You didn't say one big word the whole time we were there," she said. "Here, you're clever. You should hear yourself kidding around with Jerry. You say three-syllable words and . . . There, you didn't say one smart thing in front of him. Let me tell you, you sounded dumb."

She imitated a dumb person, stretching her eyes wide open and puffing air into her cheeks.

She sighed. "Go out and play," she said. "Go out and play with your friends."

But I just stood there looking at her. She got worse. She kicked off her shoes. She began throwing pillows from the couch onto the floor.

"Not one big word. The whole time we were there," she said.

"And you didn't smile. Here, you're sharp, you're animate. There you slumped. You looked down. You really just looked ordinary. Like any other kid around here. Well, it's a good thing we're back because I can see now this is just where you belong. With all the mill workers' kids. Well, here we are. Good."

She was still yelling when I walked out the door. Then I did something I'd never done before. I walked down to the end of our road and I hitchhiked. I got picked up by a lady who lived two blocks away. I told her I was going to the arena.

From the lobby I saw Jerry on the ice. I ran downstairs to my mother's locker and sat alone, lacing up skates. I ran up the hall on my skate points and I ran onto the ice fast, my arms straight out to the sides. I went flying toward Jerry.

He was bending over a woman's shoulders, steering her into a figure eight.

A second later he saw me and I was in his arms, breathing against the wool of his sweater. He put a hand over my ear and told his student something I couldn't understand.

A few seconds later, when I pulled myself away, the student was gone. I stopped crying and then there was nothing to do. We were alone on the ice.

I looked up at Jerry; it was different than with my father. I couldn't bury my face in Jerry's sweater and forget the world. I stood there nervously. Jerry was still Jerry, standing in front of me shyly, a man I didn't know. My father was gone for good and here was Jerry, just another man in the world, who had nothing to do with me.

"Would you like me to teach you to do loops?" he asked quietly.

I couldn't say no because of how he looked, standing there with his hands in his pockets.

I glanced up at the empty stands around us. I was tired. And cold. Jerry started skating in tight, precise loops. I looked down at the lines he was making on the ice.

"I'll try," I said, beginning to follow them.

EYE WATER
by Jennifer Coke
(Sarah Lawrence College)

Eye-water (tears) is an archaism elsewhere, but not in Jamaica . . . Similarly, *mouth-water* is saliva. It may well be, however, that both these expressions are loan-translations from African languages: Ibo and Mandingo have just these combinations.

—FREDERIC G. CASSIDY, *Jamaica Talk*

I shouldn't have been surprised by Melody and Donald's getting together. The Neville Lewis fiasco should have prepared me for anything. Hindsight. It's not necessarily a terrible thing; it keeps you humble. It holds up your past like an x-ray to white light, and shows you exactly how dumb you can be. I'm pretty sure now that I wouldn't have slept with Neville if Melody hadn't won the beauty contest.

By this time we had moved to Kingston. Mama had prodded Daddy into accepting a professorship at the university the year Melody started high school. She nudged him by subtle references to Carl Moncrieffe's success. Mama, Daddy, and Uncle Carl all had gone to college together, and something about Mama—the way she held in her stomach and smoothed her dress, the way she averted her gaze when she saw him—dropped a hint that Uncle Carl and Mama had been lovers. One day while we were taking turns hand-beating butter and sugar for one of Mama's lead-heavy cakes, Melody came right out and asked Mama if she used to go out with Uncle Carl. Mama cracked a couple of eggs into a bowl and said yes, but that was a long time ago.

Melody wasn't satisfied. "Well, how come you didn't marry him? He's sooo handsome."

You could tell by Mama's face that something had happened that she wanted to dismiss. Her vagueness seemed too contrived. She measured out a teaspoonful of rose water into the mixture. "Oh," she said in a careful voice that held neither happiness nor self-pity, "I met your father. Every girl on campus was after him."

Well, that was hard for us to imagine. It was hard to imagine even after we'd checked out a sepia photograph of Daddy dressed to the nines in his double-breasted flannel suit with lapels a yard wide and pants that could have saved his life if he'd jumped from a plane. There was Daddy, chin up, squinting into the lens, a Panama hat worn gangster-style on his head, and a proud and proprietary foot up on his big-nosed car. But he didn't look like any silver-tongued Cassanova to me.

So, Daddy had either swept Mama off her feet, or with his legendary sterling grades promised her an extension of the life they had known on campus. Knowing Mama, I'm sure she found identity in the glow of Trevor Ward's success. Old sweet-talking Daddy must have had her in the moonlight, spinning out his life dreams, and she must have fallen hard for it. I can just hear Daddy telling her that he was going into politics; you never know, maybe run for prime minister when Jamaica became independent from Britain. Mama had always told us that even back then Daddy had known the country had to go that route. But young Jean Beckford couldn't have known that somewhere along the line, Daddy's fear of achievement would make him sabotage any chances at success.

It was a shame Daddy spent half his life not doing anything particularly rewarding to him. Daddy was brilliant. We heard it often from the people who heard him speak; we heard it from his students. He wrote long manuscripts that he had to be coerced into submitting for publication, but he loved the double-bass roar of his voice and he'd give speeches without anybody asking him twice. He loved the way birdlike women would shyly give him damp handshakes and flutter up compliments to him after those speeches. But Daddy, Ph.D. hot in his hands, opted to settle for the first safe job he found—headmaster of some rural boys school. Meanwhile, Uncle Carl set out to build his construction empire, and Mama with her bright eyes was left with dreamdust. So, all she need do was mention seeing one of his trucks or relay an invitation to his house for dinner, and Daddy would wake up the next morning with his insecurities in bed with him. He'd be insufferable all day.

Mama knew this and wasn't above using a little emotional black-mail. She'd imagined herself a city girl, shopping at Nathans in Kingston with the girls, going as a family to the Christmas Panto-mime or the ballet at the Little Theatre. So when another long letter of invitation to join the faculty from the University of the West Indies arrived at the house, Mama decided she wanted to salvage some of those fantasies she had had in college.

"Did you see the mail?" she asked Daddy gently at dinner.

"I saw it," he growled.

Mama ladled some meat and gravy over his rice.

"Well, what did Errol have to say this time?" Errol Paisley was a classmate of theirs who, to hear them talk, stayed near the bottom of the class. As these things go, he was now dean of the faculty of Political Science Studies at the university.

"Same thing."

"You're a fool if you don't take that job, Trevor. They're not going to keep asking you."

"I told you before, Jean. You're not getting me to live in Kings-ton."

"Well, you can live here by yourself the rest of your life," she said, and set his plate down hard in front of him.

Daddy said nothing.

Melody and I pretended we were invisible. The last thing we wanted was Daddy's hostility to arc over and zap us. This was a new and private squabble; we hadn't heard this script before. Melody touched my knee lightly with a cold big toe. I chugged my lemonade and focused on my plate, waiting for Daddy to hiss his teeth and tell her to stop her nonsense. He didn't.

"I don't know why the hell I married you," Mama said finally, laying Uncle Carl on the table, activating the tension that had run through their married life all these years.

Daddy got up instantly, crashing his chair to the ground, and went to listen to the BBC News. I got up and righted Daddy's chair, and the women of the house ate in silence. It wasn't more than three months later that we moved to a house abutting the university campus in Mona Heights, a pretty development with streets named after flowers.

Those were good days. Downtown wasn't just a park in the middle of town with a chiming clock tower and a rusty cannon phalanxed by a bright hemorrhage of Canna flowers. Kingston was bustle and policemen blowing frantic whistles at traffic. I can't begin to tell you how urbane Melody and I felt living in the low concrete house, its flat roof railed off by decorative wrought iron to provide a cool place for nighttime entertainment. We loved the row of trees flanking the path-sized sidewalk that Daddy had a man whitewash halfway up their trunks. We even found pleasure in watching the gardener push a rattling lawn mower over our hybrid carpet of a lawn, instead of hacking at long, half-breed grass with a sickle like he'd done in Black River. And I swear every morning for weeks we walked around in that dazed fugue state between waking and sleeping because we were up as soon as the sun touched our beds. We didn't want to miss anything. There was so much to learn from our new friends who knew so much and who took power from our moon-eyed delight of the city. Town kids didn't wear play clothes. When good clothes faded, they simply stopped wearing them. And town kids our age had outgrown the four o'clock rural convention of showering, changing into freshly pressed clothes, putting ribbons in out new braids, and going for a walk. After a while Daddy stopped telling his town kids that we looked like ragamuffins and that we couldn't come to the dinner table until we looked tidy, and Mama stopped wearing anything floral which she thought broadcasted that she'd lived in the country.

I don't know what I was expecting from this move to Kingston. I guess somewhere in the back of my mind I was convinced that by some miracle I would suddenly become this new, popular person; I was bound to start meeting boys. Well, it took me four years, but I met Neville Lewis.

Neville was in our carport taking shelter from the rain on one of those October days when it rains so hard people stay home without apology. "It rained" was good and sufficient excuse for missing work or school. I peeked out at him waiting out the storm, watching the heavy scrim of rain run, watching the cruel water trampling the blossoms, swamping the lawn, eroding the road, drowning the city. He stood there shivering in his wet clothes and his soaked-through shoes. Mama took pity on him and sent me to invite the poor boy in for a towel, bully-beef sandwiches, Guinness Stout mixed with milk, and newspaper for his shoes.

I couldn't believe it. Neville wolfed the sandwiches in exactly four bites. The food was like an enormous tumor in his left cheek. I could even hear his long jawbones squeak as they knotted and strained.

"That slipped down good, boy," he said, handing me back the plate. "This damn rain made me miss my lunch. Maybe that's a good thing. There's ain' nothing worse on this earth than lunch on campus."

"You're welcome," I mumbled. "Anytime." God. I was seventeen and I still felt nervous and thick with boys. Mama had done me an injustice by sending me to an all-girls school. I tried again. "You sound like you're from Barbados," I said.

"Oh, now you're insulting me. Do I look like some round-face Bajan boy? No, man, I'm from Trinidad. Steel band, carnival."

"Blood pudding." I pretended to gag.

"If you ever tasted it, girl, you wouldn't be doing your face like that." He looked at me for a second. "Hey, listen, you like jump-up?"

"You mean dancing to calypso till you drop?"

"Now you're talking. Look here, the boys are planning a fete, real Trinidadian jump-up, steel band, costumes, everything."

I couldn't picture myself doing anything like that, and my face must have shown it. "That's too wild for me," I said looking out into the rain, trying to hide my face.

"You Jamaicans don't know how to have a good time, I'm telling you. This is going to be like back home."

This copper-colored boy was stepping in the shit already. College kids from the other islands, Trinidad, Barbados, Antigua, even the littlest of islands, liked nothing better than to take potshots at Jamaica, and it was beginning to get on my nerves. They compared the food, the weather, the politics, the temperament of the people to their own, and we invariably paled in comparison. I decided to take him down the only way I knew how. Go the intellectual route.

"Come now, you're forgetting something, man. We have a different history here. We're British and Anglican, not French and Catholic. We don't need a big blowout before Lent like you and your stupid carnival."

Neville crossed his arms and gave me the kind of smile you give a six-year-old sure of her facts. If there was someone else in the room, he'd have nudged them and shared a private snicker.

I knew this, but I was on a roll, I couldn't stop. And at this point I couldn't care less what he was thinking. "Every year around carnival time you hear about a bunch of people getting killed and all that. We just aren't as rowdy as you Trinidadians, you know." I said *Trinidadians* like I'd say *assholes* but either he didn't get it or he was getting used to the slur.

Neville tugged on his red moustache and arched an invisible eyebrow. "You don't have to tell me, girl. I know."

"So, how come you're planning this fete from October?"

"Never too soon to start planning fetes, man. In fact we're having a little one Friday night."

"Oh, dry run."

"Well, sort of." He smiled. "We like to practice and practice till we get the drinking down just right."

Okay, I might have liked Neville because he could make me laugh and he could take his insults.

"Listen," he said, his tongue a metronome. "You think your father will let you go?"

So this was how people got asked out. I had a date. Me. I forgot about Neville's jingoism. I forgot his wet lips. I even forgot what he looked like. Our conversation was a tape I played a hundred times in my head, before I went to sleep, on the bus, in the shower. I combed through a wardrobe that held nothing but rags, it seemed, and I knew the panic Cinderella must have felt. But Melody lent me her new pink dress, styled my hair, and told me I was going to look fabulous.

Neville came early. Melody looked at his long, copper face, at the self-consciousness bowing his concave body, at his pointed toe shoes. "Your boyfriend is here," she told me, avoiding my eyes.

My boyfriend. How sweet those words were, and how soon they soured and curdled. One look at Melody's face told me everything I didn't want to know. I could almost see her shaking her head and telling me that I could have done better than that. But she went willingly enough to get him a soft drink, and to run interference while Daddy checked out his pedigree. Daddy could be brutal on Melody's young men, giving them the third degree until he found out who their parents were and where they lived, then he'd go disappear behind the evening newspaper. But Neville got him talking about a history syllabus, and Daddy warmed right up to him. One less worry off my mind.

I finished dressing and called Mama to my bedroom. I was shaking. The zipper on the dress was stuck halfway down. I couldn't find my left shoe.

"Calm down, sweetie pie, let him wait," Mama said. She fumbled with the back of the dress for what seemed like hours and I could feel myself relax as the zipper finally sang its way up. Mama gave the dress a few final pats, and spun me around.

"Look at my pretty daughter," she said. "I just hope that boy is worth it."

Melody's dress was tight, but I was beginning to feel sophisticated. My lipstick was the exact shade as the dress, I was wearing high heels, and I was going to a dance with a college boy. I was so nervous it felt like my throat had grown fluff. I rushed to the kitchen to get a cold sip of water.

Edna, the maid, let out a thin wolf whistle, crossed one arm over her middle, and with the other cradled her cheek in surprise. "Miss Monica, is you that?" she asked in patois. "You look so sweet. You look like film star."

I walked into the living room tall as a bride. But in the fifteen minutes it took me to finish dressing, Neville had not only set Melody aflame with an invitation to the big fete in March, he had asked her to enter the beauty contest that would cap the party, the big bang. He was sure he could get her a sponsor. He was sure she would win.

I felt like old flowers. I have never again in my life felt as ugly as I did at that moment.

"I didn't know you had a sister," Neville accused me as we drove to the fete.

"Yes, she's exactly two years younger than me. We even have the same birthday. She'll be sixteen. I'll be eighteen."

"She's younger than you? You sure?"

"Course I'm sure."

"She just seems older." He shook his head. "You two don't look anything alike."

"Yeah, I know. I've heard that all my life."

"She's nice. Not as serious as you."

Damn, there it was again. New acquaintance, ancient comparison. Translate serious as less fun. I sat there feeling counterfeit in Melody's party dress that had grown so tight the waist was digging into my skin. I had nothing to say. I just looked out the window. The sliver of moon in the curdled sky looked like a nail paring. If I'd had the guts I'd have asked Neville to turn the car around and take me home. I couldn't think of anything to say to him that was witty or clever. Luckily, he did all the talking and all I had to do was nod.

We lived a half mile away from the campus, but I'd never even set foot in the student union. It wasn't anything like I pictured from Melody's stories. It was nothing more than an open-air, gym-sized concrete area, with a long counter that could serve either as a bar or concession area, and a huge stage. The place was fenced in by a rough, ten-foot concrete wall topped by embedded bottle shards that threatened serious laceration to riffraff gate crashers. We could have killed ourselves on the small metal tables it was so dark. Apart from the lights on stage the only other light came from the soft, throbbing flames of candles in meshed glasses. Neville led me over to where his roommate, a short Trinidadian Indian named Singh, had pulled several of the naked, gray tables together. There was the usual bored acknowledgement of introductions. I scraped a metal chair up beside Singh's date, Ellen, a thin, nervous girl who pawed him with her eyes and talked to him in baby talk.

"Want something to drink?" Neville asked me. I heard myself ask for a beer. He returned with beers for everybody at the table and excused himself. As one of the organizers of the fete he had to see to the gate receipts, make sure there was enough booze. He'd forgotten to tell me that. Singh also disappeared after a while, so I found a friend in Ellen who seemed a little in awe of me after finding out that Daddy was Professor Ward. By then I'd chugged my first half a bottle of beer, realized that I was getting drunk and it wasn't unpleasant. So by the time I'd emptied the last of the suds into my glass, Ellen and I had become giggling buddies.

"I don't know what it is about West Indian men," she said. "But they always leave the girls and go off to I don't know where. You ever notice that?"

"Well," I said. "I've never been out with Neville before. It's our first date."

"Oh, that's right. You'll really like him. He's a sweetheart."

So Neville wasn't an all-time loser after all. People liked him. I sat back and enjoyed the warm alcohol buzz. It was as if the rhythmic steel-pan timpany had reeled me into some kind of meeting place for charismatics. The Trinidadians in one raucous voice sang out the hook line of every calypso, grinning at the obsequious double entendres, and everybody seemed to be dancing in some other hot, hazy world. It was wonderful. But I was content just to watch them; I couldn't quite trust my feet. Neville came over from time to time and taught me to do the jump-up, hands in the air, do whatever you wanted with your body. And more than anything I didn't have to spend the night wondering if anybody would ask me to dance. I was on a date. Even Singh asked me to dance. Before I knew it, Neville had pulled me into him for the traditional slow last dance, and I found myself following as easily as when Melody insisted that she teach me to slow dance.

"We ought to do this again soon," Neville shouted over the music.

I smiled and nodded like some idiot savant. So the date hadn't been that bad for him after all; he wanted to see me again. I felt as if I'd aced an exam. Neville left the motor running as he walked me to my front door, gave me a tentative wet kiss, then writhed his cold tongue into my mouth.

"Thanks for a great time," I whispered. I was having a hard time breathing.

"My pleasure. Listen, tell your sister I'll be talking to her more about the contest. Maybe I'll come by tomorrow night."

He did come by the next evening and subsequent evenings and the pattern was set. When Melody didn't have a date, the three of us sat on the roof talking until decorum sent Melody to bed, and

Neville turned to kissing me. On these nights Melody came off as the wiser, more worldly sister and I took on the role of the younger sister by default. Melody had graduated with her O levels and Daddy had found her a job as some kind of executive secretary for a friend of his at Desnoes & Geddes, the distilling company. She was so damned grown up at sixteen, and she reveled in the pleasure of buying me little presents with the money she earned. Sometimes when we were alone, though, she still wanted to bounce ideas and fears off me. For instance, finding the cocktail dress for the beauty contest took on the urgency of planning a wedding, except I wasn't going to be a bridesmaid and Daddy refused to pay for any of the expenses. Melody was almost sick with worry.

"I'm just skylarking," she told me.

"You'll win," I told her, sure that either Margaret McFarland with her high cheekbones, or Debbie Pershad with her heavy mane of hair and dimples would. Skepticism bred from familiarity. We never seriously thought she could win.

"I'm just going through this stupidness for nothing. Tomorrow I have to run back to the dressmaker, again. Come with me?"

"Melody," I said, tired of the whole contest. "Relax. Just wear the dress Carole sent you, and be done with it."

"You just want people to laugh me off the stage, that's all." Our older sister Carole had sent a dress that might have been *haute couture* in Paris, but was too *haute* for Jamaica. Melody thought it was the ugliest dress she'd ever seen in her life. To me, it rustled quiet sophistication and class.

Melody ended up wearing a long, emerald, water-patterned tafetta dress that fit like skin through the bodice to the skirt, a full and rustling parachute that she had to be reminded not to pick up when she walked. A short, pout-mouthed professional came in and did her hair and makeup, and she looked like a bona fide beauty contestant. My sister Melody looked like she'd walked right off the cover of *Woman's Own* magazine.

Mama, Neville, and I were alone in a sea of people as we watched Melody clip clop across the stage, her behind working like a show horse. We whooped and clapped as she walked up to an unseen mark and rocked her feet into a quasi–third position ballet pose. Mama blew her kisses and grabbed my arm tight as we watched Melody's legs tremble in her stilleto heels.

"My Lord, she looks like a big woman," Mama whispered.

"She's going to win, Mrs. Ward. I'm telling you she's going to win," Neville yelled. "Just you watch."

"Like a big woman," Mama said again.

"Go Melody," I yelled, hands cupped around my mouth.

Neville put his fingers in his mouth and let out a long, piercing whistle that made my ears ring. I nudged him with the sharpest place on my elbow. He kept on looking to the stage, then looking at me with proud, shiny eyes as if he had personally molded her from clay and breathed life into her.

The winner of the Mona Heights Beauty Contest was Miss Melody Ward, daughter of our own Professor Ward, her first prize an all-expenses-paid Caribbean cruise, and a year's supply of Colgate and Palmolive products.

Mama went home to wake up Daddy with the news and to leave the dancing to the young people.

Neville was crowing. He told her she'd win. He knew she'd win. He'd bet the boys on his floor she'd win. He danced so hard in celebration that his half moons of sweat expanded until they took over his shirt. Melody, out of gratitude, a sense of obligation, danced with him briefly until her current boyfriend jumped in to claim his prize and Neville sought me out to dance.

Finally, he was giving me some attention. Annoyance had puffed me up, but I knew I didn't dare pout. I had the feeling that if I wasn't on my best behavior he would dump me, and I'd be back to going to bed at nine o'clock on Saturday nights. A boyfriend was the ticket I needed to double date, to be on par with Melody. Besides, Neville had served notice on me. He talked incessantly about how Ellen had been giving him trouble, and that if he were Singh, he wouldn't stand for any of that rubbish. So, naturally everything he did was fine with me as long as we could go out, as long as I had a boyfriend. And in the five months of our relationship I lived in dread that he'd tell me he didn't want to see me anymore.

I swallowed my anger and clung to him. I breathed in the wet, fish-smelling sizing of his new shirt, hating the wet cloth against my cheek, but enjoying being mashed against him, enjoying the faint underlying whiff of Aqua Velva. I was dancing with my baby. I could feel his heart beating as loud as a cheap clock. I could hear his breath coming out thin and fast and wheezy. He kissed the top of my head once and mashed me closer. Something inside of me swelled and burst and something liquid ran fast and delicious through my body.

By this time I'd been letting him feel me up through my blouse. In the movies I'd been running my hand way up on his leg and giving him a little squeeze. I'd even let him slip a rude, long-nailed finger under the elastic of my underpants. We never discussed the gradual sexual progression, and he hadn't asked me to sleep with him. So that night when Neville suggested we walk over to his dorm, I never planned on anything much more than a series of mouth-numbing kisses in the dark, maybe some heavy petting.

Ha. Up in his dorm room Neville peeled off his wet shirt, unzipped his trousers, hopped out of them, and skinned his jockeys over his too-lean hips. He stood butt naked before me. His penis seemed so far out of proportion to his spare body; I could count every rib. He came toward me grinning, like a proud but shy teenaged flag bearer in a parade. He gave me a kiss with his rubber lips, and walked me backwards over to the bed.

"What're you doing?" I whispered.

"Shh, relax, I just want to touch you." His hands were cold. "Don't worry. I won't put it in." His breath was metallic from a combination of a day's worth of rum punch, beer, and excitement and my mouth felt sticky and tight from his kisses.

He took my hand and made me squeeze his penis. I could feel the blood rising; I felt my own sweet contractions.

"Feel how much I want you."

"We'd better go back. C'mon Neville, stop."

"Please, you can't leave me this way. Please."

I decided what the hell. I didn't want this yet, but I didn't want to come off whiny and juvenile. Besides Melody had long lost her cherry and wore her status like a badge. Neville also had a way of cajoling me into doing things and going places I knew we'd catch ten tons of grief from my parents for, by insinuating that I was less fun than my sister. I was tired of dealing with the sting of comparison. But it seemed there was no getting around it. Mama compared Daddy to Uncle Carl, Daddy and Mama wanted Melody to be like me, and Neville wanted me to be Melody.

I lay wooden on the bed and allowed him to take off my clothes. He fished under the bed and came up with a condom. His hands shook as he took it from the foil and snapped it on. He made the same twisting motion you use on a childproof medicine cap on my breasts and jammed his penis into me harder than I thought he needed to. I didn't think it would hurt much. I don't know what I was expecting, but I wasn't ready for the red, tearing, persistent pain that wasn't anything half as fun as his fingers had been. It didn't seem worth doing. Three involuntary cries tore out of Neville. He collapsed on me with his full weight and was quiet. I think he snored on my chest for a while, then he jerked up suddenly and slapped me on my bottom.

"C'mon, we better get back, girl," he said. His voice was rusty from cheering for Melody. "Your sister will be looking for us."

He yanked the rubber off and sailed it through the window into the blue night. My legs were shaking from the unaccustomed position, from regret, and I sat there shaking on the hard, narrow bed. Tears grouped and trembled against my lip, and I didn't care about biting them back.

"Don't start with the crying," Neville warned. But he held me while I blubbered. "Shh. It's all right." He picked up my underwear from the floor and handed it to me. "C'mon, now, put your clothes on."

I muffled my face in the pillow. He should have sailed me out the window with the Trojan. I felt that disposable. So I just sat there and bawled till my throat got hoarse. I was crying because my body had been taken so casually, because of the pain of that new knowledge, because Melody had won the contest, because somehow I knew that my love affair, like the contest, was over, and because I knew that Neville Lewis tolerated me but loved my sister.

THE LETTER WRITER
by M. T. Sharif
(Boston University)

A dervish who stopped in the town for a loaf of *barbari* saw Haji the letter writer and proclaimed, "Mark my words. Today that man inscribes cards and papers. Yet he will live in a seven columned house. And seven concubines will attend him. And seven servants will obey his every wish." Saying this he gathered his bundle and disappeared.

Gossip spread faster in Rostam Abbad than lice on a donkey's testicles; the dervish's words created a sensation. Drinking tea in coffeehouses, people of different persuasions debated the issue hotly. All referred to the one house of opulence they knew, the Shah's summer mansion, Shady Palace. Though no one approached it to peer through its gates, in this shady place in the mountains, the informed assumed there were many rooms, many columns, many mirrored *darbars*. Here the consensus ended and arguments ensued. Some said, "Haji has eyes the size of hubcaps. Made for ogling over extravagances, we tell you." Others said, "You propose that he will occupy a home resembling the King's?" The local pundit said, "Haji's a fool. He cannot tell a *mullah* from a mule." So the rumors persisted and his future intrigued people.

Haji ignored the sudden interest in his affairs, muttering, "A businessman has little time for chatter." Then he looked right and left, and startled passers-by with a lusty call: "Hurry. Hurry. Petitions. Affidavits. Money orders drafted here."

His professional apparatus consisted of a few pens and quills, some papers, a Koran, and colored pictures of the Prophet. Resorting to these pictures, citing the Holy Book, waving his material in the air, all day he accosted people. *"Agha.* Yes you, chewing beet leaf. Are you deaf? Commission a card for your wife, children, or mother-in-law." He coaxed another, "Madame. Lady in the see-through veil. Are you married? Have you a father? What would he say if he saw you dressed like this? A postcard for your suitors?"

He scolded those who obstructed his view. He concocted, for a few *toomans,* a eulogy or a curse-letter. He directed traffic. At all times he advertised an impressive array of services: "Hurry. Hurry. Checks. Wills. Notarized papers. By special arrangement, green cards and diary entries." Thus Haji held court in a corner of Cannon Square.

Salty skeptics watched him transacting business and said, "The man is a public nuisance. One cannot cross the square safely anymore." Haughty gossips said, "We hear that he consorts with all sorts of evil creatures." Cucumber-fingered cynics said, "God willing, rivals will trim that malicious tongue of his."

Indeed, Haji's was a competitive calling. In the narrow square professionals of all arts vied for attention. Vendors of bitter almonds, tire thieves, and junk sellers hawked their wares. Liver cooks and beet merchants praised their produce. Bankers, bakers, and butchers jostled one another. Also a typist hovered about, hiding in dark corners, ready to spring forth and set up shop the minute Haji averted his head.

Amidst this melee, Haji crouched, observing the bustle with that yearning look of a camel upon cotton seeds. If shoppers snubbed him, if regulars slighted him, if the typist snatched a customer, and settled down to punch his machine, Haji appealed to the store owners directly. "Brother vendors. Neighbor businessmen. I ask of you, is there room for more than one author in this square? Instruct your patrons to frequent my establishment."

He raised prices and reduced them, he cursed and cajoled, he hurled unsolicited advice in the general direction of onlookers, until, cornering some hesitant customer, coercing the fellow to sit cross-legged on the ground, he said, "Enunciate properly. Who is to receive this letter?" This was just the first in a series of questions. For half an hour he interrogated his patron on the content and purpose of the piece, the desired tone, diction, style, and format. Then he licked his pen, raised his brow, blew *Allah Akbar* in the air, and wrote, "May I be your slave and servant, the carpet beneath your feet. Allow me to forward my salaam and prayers. My father forwards his salaam and prayers. My mother forwards her salaam and prayers. My other kith and kin forward their salaam and prayers." Later he ended a letter in a similar vein. "May your shadow never diminish. May I make a balcony from my head for your steps. This green leaf is from your slave and servant." Between these ceremonial introductions and conclusions, space permitting, he squeezed in a word or two uttered by the client.

Question the soul, however, who requested a slight alteration, abbreviation, or rephrasing. Pity the person who protested that he had no father or brother. Such impertinence angered Haji. He cast pen and paper aside and roared, "Why, sir, you know better? Take your business elsewhere. Find that typist. He has operated a grocery, dabbled in gynecology, proceeded to geographical astrology, and is now a writer of mail. Save for a few flowery maxims he is practically illiterate. But he will suit you better."

Now Haji neglected his customer. He chewed a *nabat* and gurgled. He cleaned his nails, scrubbed his feet. He napped; he drank a tumbler of tea. Now, abruptly, eyeing the letter seeker, he said, "Sir. You are still here? I ask of you, if a man lets his donkey to graze on the land of a friend and pays for this service, and it so happens that his donkey becomes pregnant, who, sir, does the offspring belong to—the owner of the animal or the proprietor of the land? You do not know? May I suggest to you, then, to leave important matters to your elders." With half a dozen riddles of this nature he thoroughly cowed the customer. Then he licked his pen, raised his brow, blew *Allah Akbar,* and said, "Tell me, who is this to be sent to and what do you propose to say?"

The inquisitive asked him, "Haji, why bother asking folks what they want said?"

"Your excellencies," he responded. "These are uneducated people. They tell me what they generally feel and I fashion that into acceptable prose."

His reasoning confounded friends, but it scarcely convinced foes. Arm-in-arm cucumber cynics and salty skeptics paced the square and said, "The blackguard robs simple, poor villagers. His whole family ought to find themselves honorable professions." Damning information had it that an elder brother of Haji's, a self-proclaimed ninety-nine-year-old who led a flourishing practice in the main mosque feigning epileptic seizures.

Glib rumors of this sort pained him. "How do I know who goes where masquerading as my brother?" he remarked. "I have no kith or kin. Probably the man is cross-eyed and cannot see straight. Why else would he be sitting in a house of worship pleading for alms? I assure you, mosque beggars are the most suspicious personalities."

He marked time by the movement of school children. They passed him on their way to the Dabestan at eight, taunted him during recess, and raced home after four. By then he had exhausted his clientele, collected various copper coins, and stuffed them in his socks.

In due course the din of Cannon Square subsided. Shopkeepers closed their *megazehs*. Beggars, vendors, hired hands went their separate ways. Haji followed suit, assembled his apparatus, and found shelter in the doorway of a house or the threshold of a shop.

No doubt he conducted a valuable service. No doubt he enjoyed wooing patrons, sparring with foes. No doubt he would have continued, to the hour when milk sprouts in the nipples of eunuchs.

One day, a day neither hot nor cold, at the most ordinary hour, the appointed hour, as the horizon resembled a sheet of charcoal dotted by camphor, Rostam Abbad discovered the Revolution. Word hummed down the dusty Tehran Road. Wise beards and white beards heard it. The local pundit heard it. In the shade of walnut trees, playing backgammon, reciting Ferdousi, men heard it. Soaking their hot feet in cool streams, children heard it.

Certain citizens feared the whole affair. Half a dozen sold their belongings and emigrated to Cleveland. Others appointed themselves Revolutionary Guards. They patrolled streets; they stopped cars; they searched houses. Also they liberated Shady Palace. This caused much commotion. Some folks organized an expedition and toured the property, noting watery gardens of *maryam* and narcissus, and many columns, and many rooms. They rushed home and said,

"There are many things to see." The next day a larger crowd scaled the mountain and sought entry. An old officer wearing a new khaki stopped them at the gates and shouted, "Go back." For the guards had bolted the windows, wired the walls, inaugurating Rostam Ab-bad's Revolutionary Committee for Public Grievances.

Perched in his usual corner in Cannon Square, Haji witnessed the twists and turns of history. He wrote his letters. He kept to his own affairs.

A fortnight after that ordinary day, uniformed guards seized him and said, "Haji, Haji, what have you done?"

"What have I done, sirs?"

"Do not be coy with us, Haji. Your brother spied for the anti-Revolution."

"Brother? I have no brother."

"He printed all sorts of leaflets in the main mosque and God knows what else. Do you know him?"

"That beggar? I have heard of him. What of it? For the past fifteen years he has claimed kinship to me."

"Come with us."

"Why, sirs? Just because some rabble calls himself my relative? Besides, I never saw the man."

"Enough, Haji. Provide evidence and you will be freed."

Meekly he followed them. The palace brimmed with people. Guards ran to and fro. Relatives of detainees cried here and there. "Sit," the guards ordered. He sat and marveled, a finger of amazement in his mouth. Even the most exaggerated accounts left him ill-prepared for this. A chandelier hung in every room. Oak doors connected room to room. While the authorities rushed back and forth, opening, shutting doors, Haji counted forty chandeliers above forty carpets smooth as a woman's moustache. These luxuries he saw on the first floor. Perhaps there was a second, he reasoned, a third and a fourth, since the winding staircase that linked floor to floor spiraled to the sky.

Hours later the guards returned and dragged him to a hall where thousands of books lay in glass shelves. There the authorities dared him. There they blamed him. Again and again he said, "I am no traitor. That man is not my brother." He spent the night in a cellar alongside communists and pickpockets.

In the succeeding months he maintained his innocence. He cursed. He reeled. He swore. He petitioned the Municipality, the different Committees, the President of the Republic. Each and every time the authorities informed him, "Your brother has confessed and is serving time in Tehran."

"That good for nothing character is not my brother."

"You are implicated in his affairs."

"Gentlemen, do not believe him. Mosque beggars are highly unreliable."

"Either admit to your crimes or show us proof."

"How am I to do that? Am I a biographer or a writer of birth certificates?"

"Take this fool away," they said.

Date-eyed and afraid, every day, handcuffed Loyalists, Royalists, and other assorted anit-Revolutionaries marched forth and met their colleagues in the cellars of Shady Palace. These suspects the authorities processed swiftly. A few were flogged. A few were freed. Crammed in trucks the rest were forwarded to Tehran. None remained incarcerated longer than Haji. The authorities told him, "We have not harmed you, not sent you to the capital where you could be tortured. Come. Come. Tell us what you know."

"I know nothing," he said. "Nothing." He clamored. He complained. A year or two passed. He said nothing. As the carpets wore thin, he said, "I know nothing." As the grass, *maryam,* and narcissus grew waist high in the untended garden, he said, "I know nothing." As the roof leaked and the tiled columns dulled, he said, "Nothing. Nothing." As the palace, trampled by numerous feet, prey to the dust and the wind, adapted a less splendorous look, he said, "That man is not my brother. I know nothing." And he clamored. And he complained.

The authorities sympathized with his predicament. "Haji," they said. "Stop this racket. There is no peace in this compound because of you." They transferred him to a spacious room on the second floor and said, "Now be content. You have your very own room, table, chair, and view of the garden."

"Pray, how long?" he asked. "How long?"

"It is not in our hands. Tehran demands a confession from all political prisoners. Ages ago you should have repented."

A friendly official hit upon an ingenious idea. He ordered a stack of magazines brought up to Haji's room from the library and said, "Haji, look here. There are pictures of women in these pages. American women. English women. They are misled, misinformed. Their hair is uncovered. They wear sleeveless shirts and low-cut dresses. Make good use of your time. Cover their nakedness. We plan to distribute these papers to the public."

"Am I a painter?" he retorted. But his days were long, his nights dreary. Presently he picked a pen, chose a magazine, and sat by the window. Glossy pictures filled this foreign text; not a word could he decipher. There were so many pictures though. Most required prompt attention. From cover to cover he searched the paper, applying the ink at necessary junctures, draping exposed knees and bare arms. Something in the act soothed him. He moved to another text. When he had sorted through the whole bundle he called on the guards for a second supply.

Late spring the buffalo gazed westward, hiding one foot, hoping for rain. Midsummer the grape burned bright as a lamp; on strings spiders seemed too hot to hunt. Autumn arrived heavily, fattened like a persimmon, riper and riper, then retreated, ushering in the winter snow. Beyond the windowpanes the years breezed away and Haji worked.

He woke at dawn and toiled past dusk. To the authorities he said, "I have fallen behind. Do not expect to distribute these papers yet. I am working night and day to finish." He worked slowly. Each paper, each page, every photograph, posed a new problem, a fresh challenge.

He found women in a variety of positions, in all shapes and sizes. Some reclined on cars. Some rested on cushions. Some held objects and grinned. Some grimaced. Some were sweet as *halva*. Some sour as a saw. Some looked plump. Some looked thin. Some young. Some old. Some felt smooth to the touch. Some tough and taut.

Before tackling the task at hand, Haji examined his subjects, considered their flaws. Then he licked his pen and wove his veils. He clothed their sinewy legs and dyed nails. He blotted their necks. He covered their wrists and exposed chests. With the tip of his pen he stroked them, shaded their naked limbs from strange and shameless eyes. Those he liked he treated this way. But those whom he judged disreputable, he attacked and tore apart.

The authorities visited him once a month. Each and every time he shuddered and said, "I am yet to finish. I am a few weeks behind and am working night and day."

One day they told him, "Your brother has died."

"He was not my brother."

"Nevertheless, we will plead your case with Tehran." He nodded. They returned and said, "A recalcitrant lot. But do not despair. We have other means."

Nowadays he wandered around the palace freely. There were few prisoners left. The building was in desperate need of repair. Plaster flaked off the ceiling. Walls sagged. Columns cracked. "This place is uninhabitable," the authorities argued. They built a modern facility nearby and told Haji, "Tehran is adamant. They want a confession."

"Stranger things, I hear," Haji said. "I hear that typist fellow went out of business because masons, vendors, villagers all have learned to read and write. Anyway I have much to do."

When the authorities prepared to evacuate the palace they explained, "We will contact them once more, Haji. Do not lose hope. In the meantime we will take you to our new facilities."

"Why, sirs? Are you dissatisfied with my performance? I will work harder. Only allow me to stay. The books, the papers are here."

In this manner Haji and an old Revolutionary Guard became the sole occupants of Shady Palace. His jailer cooked for Haji, did his wash, and every morning hauled a bundle of magazines to the second floor. Pen in hand Haji greeted him and said, "Am I to go to the well and return thirsty again? If the authorities so inquire, inform them that I am working ceaselessly."

Snowy seasons, he toiled indoors. The yellowed worm-eaten pages crumbled in his hands. The mold and the dust irritated his eyes, itched his nails. He worked and worked. For after he clothed them, after he draped, after he veiled, traced their every curve, suddenly, their withered faces shone, their eyes loomed larger, and their lips quivered, promising perpetual enchantment.

Melon days and summer nights, his jailer placed a chair on one of the numerous balconies and there too Haji labored. Sometimes old salty skeptics and cucumber cynics saw him on these crumbling *eivans,* pointed him out to their grandchildren, and said, "During the Revolution, it is recorded, he was a spy and killed many. The Revolution, dear ones, have you heard of it? Do you know about that great turmoil?"

THE SUTTON PIE SAFE
by Pinckney Benedict
(Princeton University)

A blacksnake lay stretched out on the cracked slab of concrete near the diesel tank. It kept still in a spot of sun. It had drawn clear membranes across its eyes, had puffed its glistening scales a little, soaking up the heat of the day. It must have been three feet long.

"There's one, Dad," I said, pointing at it. My father was staring at the old pole barn, listening to the birds in the loft as they chattered and swooped from one sagging rafter to another. The pole barn was leaning hard to one side, the west wall buckling under. The next big summer storm would probably knock it down. The winter had been hard, the snows heavy, and the weight had snapped the ridgepole. I wondered where we would put that summer's hay.

"Where is he?" my dad asked. He held the cut-down .410 in one hand, the short barrel cradled in the crook of his elbow, stock tight against his bare ribs. We were looking for copperheads to kill, but I thought maybe I could coax my dad into shooting the sleeping blacksnake. I loved the crack of the gun, the smell of sulphur from the opened breech. Again I pointed to the snake.

"Whew," he said, "that's a big one there. What do you figure, two, two and a half feet?'' ''Three,'' I said. ''Three at least.'' He grunted.

''You gonna kill it?'' I asked.

''Boys want to kill everything, don't they?'' he said to me, grinning. Then, more seriously, ''Not too good an idea to kill a blacksnake. They keep the mice down, the rats. Better than a cat, really, a good-sized blacksnake.''

He stood, considering the unmoving snake, his lips pursed. He tapped the stock of the gun against his forearm. Behind us, past the line of willow trees near the house, I heard the crunch of gravel in the driveway. Somebody was driving up. We both turned to watch as the car stopped next to the smokehouse. It was a big car, Buick Riviera, and I could see that the metallic flake finish had taken a beating on the way up our lane.

My father started forward, then stopped. A woman got out of the car, a tall woman in a blue sundress. She looked over the car at us, half waved. She had honey-colored hair that hung to her shoulders, and beautiful, well-muscled arms. Her wave was uncertain. When I looked at my dad, he seemed embarrassed to have been caught without a shirt. He raised the gun in a salute, decided that wasn't right, lowered the gun, and waved his other hand instead.

It was too far to talk without shouting, so we didn't say anything, and neither did the woman. We all stood there a minute longer. Then I started over toward her.

''Boy,'' my dad said. I stopped. ''Don't you want to get that snake?'' he said.

''Thought it wasn't good to kill blacksnakes,'' I said. I gestured toward the house. ''Who is she?'' I asked.

''Friend of your mother's,'' he said. His eyes were on her. She had turned from us, was at the screen porch. I could see her talking through the mesh to my mother, nodding her head. She had a purse in her hand, waved it to emphasize something she was saying. ''Your mom'll take care of her,'' my dad said. The woman opened the porch door, entered. The blue sundress was pretty much backless, and I watched her go. Once she was on the porch, she was no more than a silhouette.

''Sure is pretty,'' I said to my father. ''Yeah,'' he said. He snapped the .410's safety off, stepped over to the diesel pump. The snake sensed his coming, turned hooded eyes on him. The sensitive tongue flicked from the curved mouth, testing the air, the warm concrete. For just a second, I saw the pink inner lining of the mouth, saw the rows of tiny, backward-curving fangs. "When I was ten, just about your age," my dad said, levelling the gun at the snake, "my daddy killed a big old blacksnake out in our backyard."

The snake, with reluctance, started to crawl from the spot of sun. My dad steadied the gun on it with both hands. It was a short weapon, the barrel and stock both cut down. It couldn't have measured more than twenty inches overall. Easy to carry, quick to use: perfect for snake. "He killed that blacksnake, pegged the skin out, and give it to me for a belt," my dad said. He closed one eye, squeezed the trigger.

The shot tore the head off the snake. At the sound, a couple of barn swallows flew from the haymow, streaked around the barn, swept back into the dark loft. I watched the body of the snake vibrate and twitch, watched it crawl rapidly away from the place where it had died. It moved more quickly than I'd seen it move that afternoon. The blood was dark, darker than beets or raspberry juice. My dad snapped the bolt of the gun open, and the spent cartridge bounced on the concrete. When the snake's body twisted toward me, I stepped away from it.

My dad picked the snake up from the mess of its head. The dead snake, long and heavy, threw a couple of coils over his wrist. He shook them off, shook the body of the snake out straight, let it hang down from his hand. It was longer than one of his legs. "Wore that belt for a lot of years," he said, and I noticed that my ears were ringing. It took me a second to understand what he was talking about. "Wore it 'til it fell apart." He offered the snake to me, but I didn't want to touch it. He laughed.

"Let's go show your mother," he said, walking past me toward the house. I thought of the woman in the sundress, wondered what she would think of the blacksnake. I followed my dad, watching the snake. Its movements were slowing now, lapsing into a rhythmic twitching along the whole length of its body.

As we passed the smokehouse and the parked Riviera, I asked him, "What's her name?" He looked at the car, back at me. I could hear my mother's voice, and the voice of the other woman, couldn't hear what they were saying.

"Hanson," he said. "Mrs. Hanson. Judge Hanson's wife." Judge

Hanson was a circuit court judge in the county seat; he'd talked at my school once, a big man wearing a three-piece suit, even though the day had been hot. It seemed to me that his wife must be a good deal younger than he was.

The snake in my father's hand was motionless now, hung straight down toward the earth. His fingers were smeared with gore, and a line of blood streaked his chest.

"Why'd you kill the blacksnake?" I asked him. "After what you said, about rats and all?" I was still surprised he'd done it. He looked at me, and for a moment I didn't think he was going to answer me.

He reached for the doorknob with his free hand, twisted it. "Thought you'd know," he said. "My daddy made a belt for me. I'm gonna make one for you."

The woman in the sundress, Mrs. Hanson, was talking to my mother when we entered the porch. "I was talking to Karen Spangler the other day," she said. My mother, sitting at the other end of the screen porch, nodded. Mrs. Spangler was one of our regular egg customers, came out about once every two weeks, just for a minute. Mrs. Hanson continued. "She says that you all have just the best eggs, and the Judge and I wondered if you might possibly . . ." She let the sentence trail off, turned to my father.

"Why, hello, Mr. Albright," she said. She saw the snake, but she had poise: she didn't react. My father nodded at her. "Mrs. Hanson," he said. He held the snake up for my mother to see. "Look here, Sara," he said. "Found this one sunning himself out near the diesel pump."

My mother stood. "You don't want to bring that thing on the porch, Jack," she said. She was a small woman, my mother, with quick movements, deft reactions. There was anger in her eyes.

"Thought I'd make a belt out of it for the boy," my dad said, ignoring her. He waved the snake, and a drop of blood fell from his hand to the floor. "You remember that old snakeskin belt I had?"

Mrs. Hanson came over to me, and I could smell her perfume. Her skin was tan, lightly freckled. "I don't think we've met," she said to me, like I was a man, and not just a boy. I tried to look her straight in the eye, found I couldn't. "No'm," I said. "Don't think we have."

"His name's Cates," my mother said. "He's ten." I didn't like

it that she answered for me. Mrs. Hanson nodded, held out her hand.
"Pleased to meet you, Cates," she said. I took her hand, shook it,
realized I probably wasn't supposed to shake a lady's hand. I pulled
back, noticed the grime under my fingernails, the dust on the backs
of my hands. "Pleased," I said, and Mrs. Hanson gave out a laugh
that was like nothing I'd ever heard from a woman before, loud and
happy.

"You've a fine boy there," she said to my dad. I bent my head.
To my father, my mother said, "Why don't you take that snake out
of here, Jack. And get a shirt on. We've got company."

He darted a look at her. Then he waved the snake in the air, to
point out to everybody what a fine, big blacksnake it was. He opened
the screen door, leaned out, and dropped the snake in a coiled heap
next to the steps. It looked almost alive lying there, the sheen of the
sun still on the dark scales. "Mrs. Hanson," he said, and went on
into the house. He let the door slam behind him, and I could hear
him as he climbed the stairs inside.

Once he was gone, Mrs. Hanson seemed to settle back, to become
more businesslike. "The Judge and I certainly would appreciate the
opportunity to buy some of your eggs." She sat down in one of the
cane bottom chairs we kept on the porch in summer, set her purse
down beside her. "But Sara—may I call you Sara?" she asked, and
my mother nodded. "Something else has brought me here as well."
My mother sat forward in her chair, interested to hear. I leaned
forward too, and Mrs. Hanson shot a glance my way. I could tell
she wasn't sure she wanted me there.

"Sara," she said, "you have a Sutton pie safe." She pointed
across the porch, and at first I thought she meant the upright freezer
that stood there. Then I saw she was pointing at the old breadbox.

My mother looked at it. "Well, it's a pie safe," she said. "Sutton,
I don't know—"

"Oh, yes, it's a Sutton," Mrs. Hanson said. "Mrs. Spangler told
me so, and I can tell she was right." Mrs. Spangler, so far as I knew,
had never said anything to us about a pie safe. Mrs. Hanson rose, knelt
in front of the thing, touched first one part of it and then another.

"Here, you see," she said, pointing to the lower right corner of
one of the pie safe's doors. We'd always called it a breadbox, kept
all kinds of things in it: canned goods, my dad's ammunition and
his reloading kit, things that needed to be kept cool in winter. The

pie safe was made of cherry wood—you could tell even through the paint—with a pair of doors on the front. The doors had tin panels, and there were designs punched in the tin, swirls and circles and I don't know what all. I looked at the place where she was pointing. "SS" I saw, stamped into the wood. The letters were mostly filled with paint; I'd never noticed them before.

Mrs. Hanson patted the thing, picked a chip of paint off it. My mother and I watched her. "Of course," Mrs. Hanson said, "this paint will have to come off. Oh, a complete refinishing job, I imagine. How lovely!" She sounded thrilled. She ran her hands down the tin, feeling the holes where the metal-punch had gone through.

"Damn," she said, and I was surprised to hear her curse. "What's the matter?" my mother asked. Mrs. Hanson looked closely at the tin on the front of the pie safe. "It's been reversed," she said. "The tin panels on the front, you see how the holes were punched in? It wasn't put together that way, you know. When they punched this design in the tin, they poked it through from the back to the front, so the points were outside the pie safe."

"Oh," my mother said, sounding deflated. It sounded ridiculous to me. I couldn't figure why anyone would care which way the tin was put on the thing.

"Sometimes country people do that, reverse the tin panels," Mrs. Hanson said in a low voice, as if she weren't talking to country people. My mother didn't disagree. "Still, though," Mrs. Hanson said, "it is a Sutton, and I must have it. What will you take for it?"

I guess I should have known that she was angling to buy the thing all along, but still it surprised me. It surprised my mother too. "Take for it?" she said.

"Yes," Mrs. Hanson said, "it's our anniversary next week—mine and the Judge's—and I just know he would be thrilled with a Sutton piece. Especially one of the pie safes. Of course, I don't think it'll be possible to have it refinished by then, but he'll see the possibilities."

"I don't know," my mother said, and I couldn't believe she was considering the idea. "Is it worth a lot?" It was an odd way to arrive at a price, and I laughed. Both women looked at me as if they had forgotten that I was on the porch with them. I wondered what my father would say when he came down from putting on a shirt.

Mrs. Hanson turned back to my mother. "Oh, yes," she said.

"Samuel Sutton was quite a workman, very famous throughout the Valley. People are vying to buy his pieces. And here I've found one all for myself. And the Judge." Then, as if understanding that she wasn't being wise, she said, "Of course, the damage to it, the tin and all, that does lower the value a great deal. And the paint." My father had painted the breadbox, the pie safe, when it had been in the kitchen years ago, to match the walls. We'd since moved it out to the porch, when my mother picked up a free-standing cupboard she liked better.

"I don't know," my mother said. "After all, we don't use it much anymore, just let it sit out here. And if you really want it . . ." She sounded worried. She knew my father wasn't going to be pleased with the idea. "We should wait, ask my husband." Mrs. Hanson reached into her handbag, looking for her checkbook. I knew it wasn't going to be that easy.

"Didn't that belong to Granddad?" I asked my mother. She looked at me, didn't answer. "Dad's dad?" I said, pressing.

"It was in my husband's family," my mother said to Mrs. Hanson. "He might not like it."

"Could we say, then, three hundred dollars? Would that be possible?" Mrs. Hanson asked. She wasn't going to give up. Just then, my father opened the door and stepped out of the house onto the porch. He had washed his hands, put on a blue chambray shirt, one I'd given him for Christmas.

"Three hundred dollars?" my father said. "Three hundred dollars for what?" I saw my mother's face set into hard lines; she was determined to oppose him.

"She wants to buy the pie safe," my mother said. Her voice was soft, but not afraid.

My father walked over to the breadbox, struck the tin with two fingers. "This?" he said. "You're going to pay three hundred for this?" Both my mother and Mrs. Hanson nodded. "I think that's a fair enough price, Mr. Albright," Mrs. Hanson said. I noticed she didn't call him Jack.

"You could use it to get someone over to help you work on the barn," my mother said. My father didn't even look at her. I moved to his side.

"Didn't know the breadbox was for sale," he said. "Didn't know that it would be worth that much if it was for sale.

"My father owned that," he said. "Bought it for my mother, for this house, when they were first married." He turned to my mother. "You know that," he said.

"But what do we use it for, Jack?" she asked. "We use the barn. We need the barn. More than some pie safe."

My father put his hand on my shoulder. "You're not going to leave me anything, are you?" he said to my mother. She flushed, gestured at Mrs. Hanson. Mrs. Hanson managed to look unflustered.

My dad looked at Mrs. Hanson. Her calm seemed to infuriate him. "We aren't merchants," he said. "And this isn't a furniture shop." He turned to me. "Is it, boy?" I nodded, then shook my head no, not sure which was the correct response. "Mrs. Hanson," my mother began. You could tell she didn't like my father talking like that to Mrs. Hanson, who was a guest in her home.

"Don't apologize for me, Sara," my dad said. "Go ahead and sell the damn breadbox if you want, but just don't apologize for me." My mother opened her mouth, shut it again.

"Boy," he said to me, "you want a snakeskin belt like I was talking about? Like my daddy made?" He gestured out the porch door, to where the headless snake lay. A big fly, colored like blue glass, was crawling on the body.

"Yes, sir," I said, glad not to have to look at the high color rising in Mrs. Hanson's cheeks.

"You come out back with me, then, and I'll show you how to skin it, how to stretch the hide. How'd that be?" Neither my mother nor Mrs. Hanson said a word. My dad pushed me ahead of him, and I headed out the door.

As he came after me, he turned and spoke through the screen. "I'll tell you something, Mrs. Hanson," he said. "You ought not to try to buy what hasn't been put up for sale."

Outside, my father groped in his pocket for a second, came up with his old Barlow knife, flicked the blade out. "You hold the snake for me," he said. "We'll take that skin right off him." He held out the body to me. I hesitated, reached out and took it.

It was heavy and ropelike, cool and limp in my hands. The scales were dry as sand. "Set it down there," my dad said, "and hold it stretched out tight." I set the snake down.

"Belly up," my dad said. "We don't want to mess up the scales on his back. That's what makes a snakeskin belt so nice, so shiny, them back scales." I rolled the snake. The scales on the sausagelike belly were light-colored, looked soft, and I prodded them with a forefinger. The skin rasped against my fingernail.

"Here we go," my father said, and pressed the blade of the knife against the belly of the snake. He always kept the knife razor-sharp, had a whetstone at the house he kept specially for it. I looked away. The knife made a sound as it went in; I thought I could hear him slicing through muscle, thought I could hear the small, cartilaginous ribs giving way under the blade.

Mrs. Hanson left the porch, and I could tell from the way she was walking that she must have gotten what she wanted. She moved with a bounce in her step. She looked over at us where we were kneeling, shook her hair back out of her face, smiled. My father paused in his cutting for a second when he heard the car door open. Mrs. Hanson backed the Buick around, headed back down the lane, toward the highway. A couple of low-hanging branches lashed the windshield as she went.

My mother stood on the porch, an outline behind the mesh of the screen, watching her go. When the car was out of sight, she turned and went back into the house.

My father gave a low laugh. When I looked at him, he was holding something gray between two fingers, dangled it back and forth in front of my face. "I'll be damned," he said. I looked down at the snake, the open stomach cavity, realized that he was holding a dead mouse by its tail. "No wonder that snake was so sleepy," my dad said. "He just ate." I stood, turned away from him.

"What's the matter?" he asked. I didn't answer. "You aren't gonna let that bother you," he said, and there was disdain in his voice. I put my arms over the top rail of the board fence around our yard, leaned my weight on it. I closed my eyes, saying nothing.

My father lowered his voice. "Thought you wanted that belt," he said. I wanted to turn to him, tell him that I did want the belt, just to give me a minute. I wasn't sure I could trust my voice not to break. "Guess not," he said.

Once again, I heard the sound of the knife, two quick cuts. I turned to look, saw that he had deftly sliced the body of the snake, had carved it into three nearly equal sections. It looked like pieces of bicycle tire lying there, bloody bicycle tire. My father rose, wiped his hands on his jeans.

"You think about that, boy," he said. "You think about that, next time you decide you want something." He walked past me, not toward the house, but toward the ruined barn.

HIGH BRIDGE
by Fenton Johnson
(Stanford University)

On his workshop bench, Thomas Hardin Masterson lines up the woods he has chosen, his favorites: chocolate brown walnut; ruddy cedar he had cut and cured himself; bleached white cypress, salvaged from the mash tubs at the old distillery and smelling faintly of young whiskey. To these he adds newcomers: gingko, buttery smooth and yellow; wild cherry, deep red, from a tree he'd planted himself, forty years before.

Rose Ella, his wife, is dead. Before himself—who would have thought it? A year ago she'd helped shovel him into an ambulance, to take him to a Louisville hospital where they'd removed most of his cancerous gut. He'd recovered, to stand half-hollowed out and hear the doctor give him a year to live. Across the next months he and Rose Ella talked very little and thought a great deal about what was to come of her after his death.

Now she has been dead four months, while he stands among the antique tools and stacked woods and power saws of his shop, assembling woods for a lamp for Miss Camilla Perkins, his next-door neighbor and in forty-seven years of marriage the only woman he has kissed besides his wife. "Forty-seven years and one other woman," he says to himself. "And that just a kiss." He is astonished by his own loyalty. If on his wedding day someone had predicted this, he would have laughed out loud.

Since his wife's death, he has kept all but one of his children at bay. They have asked to come; he has managed to hold them to weekend visits, not by words—he avoids talking of his illness—but by his plain refusal to be cared for. They have their own lives, and he is careful to remind them of this: his sons have jobs, his daughters have children.

But now his youngest son Ravenel pushes open the door, carrying two cups of coffee. At thirty-four, Ravenel is not married, has never had so much as a girlfriend. Instead he brings home men from San Francisco, where he lives—a different man every summer. With those visitors, Rose Ella was civil, even flirtatious. Tom Hardin stayed in the shop.

This time Ravenel has come home alone. He has left a job in San Francisco, God knows what; Tom Hardin keeps Ravenel's jobs in mind no more than the names of that stream of summertime men. In Tom Hardin's day jobs were tied to something. He knew who a man was by what he did and what he turned out: furniture, or plumbing, or (in Tom Hardin's case) bourbon. As far as Tom Hardin could tell, Ravenel turned out paper.

"I brought your coffee, Father."

"I can see that." Tom Hardin points with his plane, the old-fashioned kind with the knob and the crossblade, that requires muscle and a good eye. "Set it there."

Ravenel sets the coffee down. "So how are you feeling."

"Not bad." How good can a dying man feel? Tom Hardin holds his tongue.

"Mind if I look on?"

"No, not at all." All through his childhood, Ravenel never set foot in the shop, except under threat of a whipping. Now he wants to look on. It is this, the changing of things, that angers Tom Hardin. For all their lives he and Ravenel have hardly spoken to each other, except to snap and back off. Now Tom Hardin is dying and they are supposed to get along, here is Ravenel asking to be taught in a month what it took Tom Hardin himself a lifetime to learn. "What kind of wood is that?" Ravenel says, pointing.

"Gingko. Came from the monastery walk. You remember those big trees where you used to be able to park for midnight Mass."

Ravenel shakes his head. "I guess that was before my time."

Tom Hardin puts on his glasses and holds the wood to the window. Ravenel flips on the overhead fluorescent. With the board Tom Hardin swats the switch off. "I need the sun to look at this." He turns the plank back and forth in the window's square of light.

"Well." Ravenel stands and brushes his jeans of wood shavings. "You want your coffee? It's cold."

"Leave it. I'll drink it."

Ravenel shuts the door behind him with a careful click.

The last time Tom Hardin drank coffee his stomach seized up in knots, but he has not said a word of this to anyone except Miss Camilla. When he hears the house door slam, he takes the coffee, opens the door, and pours it on the ground.

In 1950, when Camilla Perkins was forty years old, the parish board asked her to teach penmanship and English in the Catholic grade school. Hiring her was a radical step: she was their first lay teacher. Tom Hardin, who was on the parish board, knew they chose her because they believed her safely into spinsterhood, no temptation for the high school boys or the men of the parish.

She was tall, thin, *arch:* curlicues of dyed black hair dangled over her arching forehead, pencilled eyebrows arched over deep-socketed, protruding eyes. In her marriageable years she had been thought plain, Tom Hardin himself had said so.

Then their generation aged. The married women wrinkled and sagged from childbearing. Weighted down with kids, laundry, groceries, they slowed their steps and words and thoughts.

At forty Miss Camilla was plain as ever, but with her years her blanched skin stretched tight. She came to speak and walk with a forward-moving intensity that commanded attention: she was a teacher.

At forty-two, Tom Hardin had too many children and a life that was slipping through his hands. Ravenel, number six, was due that December. Tom Hardin watched Rose Ella swell and his wallet shrink. He felt trapped. When in November friends asked him to go deer hunting in upstate New York, he fled, leaving Rose Ella a three-word note: "I'll be back." In it he folded two crisp one-hundred-dollar bills.

"Guilt money," Miss Camilla told him later, on their first drive to High Bridge. She was blunt about this, like everything else; it was another reason Tom Hardin liked her. Women in New Hope were not raised to be blunt. Camilla Perkins had not been raised to be blunt, but she was plain and came to understand this early on. "What have I to lose," she'd said to Tom Hardin.

Rose Ella, who was married and not plain, could not bring herself to voice her anger. She took the two hundred dollars, which Tom Hardin left to buy food and Christmas presents for the children, and bought herself a new coat. In 1950 two hundred dollars bought a very nice coat indeed, a scarlet wool knee-length affair with a real mink collar. Miss Camilla learned all this because five days after Tom Hardin left to hunt deer, Rose Ella crossed the yard, swollen with Ravenel and wearing her scarlet knee-length fur-collared coat, to beg for money to buy groceries until Tom Hardin returned. Miss Camilla had just bought a new car and was none too well off herself, and so for the next two weeks the five Masterson children ate supper crammed around Miss Camilla's walnut gateleg table, with Patsy K., the youngest, perched on a stack of the complete Shakespeare.

Tom Hardin looks up from his workbench, to see Miss Camilla hobbling across the yard. She has had two heart attacks; she has been told she will not survive the third, and that it may come at any time. Weather permitting, she comes over daily to his shop. On this cold December day, weather most certainly should not be permitting, but she is coming, Tom Hardin likes her for that.

He pulls up stools by the stove, pours them both a finger of whiskey in plastic cups. Miss Camilla raises hers to the rafters. "So the meeting of the Mostly Alive is called to order," she says gaily. He raises his cup. He touches it to his lips and sets it down with a grimace. "Forty years of making this stuff and all of a sudden I can't stand the taste of it."

"I saw Ravenel leave," Miss Camilla says. "I saw you pour out your coffee. You really think it's important to hide that from him. He's a grown man, you know, he left a job to be with you."

"Any job that he can just up and leave can't be much of a job," Tom Hardin says.

"Ravenel ran a library in San Francisco. A *big* library, which you know perfectly well. A fine job, I might add."

"How do you know what I know," Tom Hardin says, but he grins at her impertinence.

"Between teaching your children, knowing you for thirty-five years, and listening to Rose Ella complain about your faults, I think I have a good idea of what you know. A better idea, I think, than yourself, sometimes."

Tom Hardin takes up his glue bottle and finds it clogged. He tries to squeeze it open by force of strength, but he cannot squeeze hard enough to clear up the spout. He takes out a knife and carves away the dried glue. "Everything is so goddamn slow," he says.

Miss Camilla touches her whiskey to her lips.

Live dangerously: he scrabbles among the litter on the workbench until he finds the prime block of his best walnut. To its four sides he glues thin planks of pale gingko. He clamps this work in a vise, then sits heavily, breathing hard. "You watched through all that. Ravenel would have asked five questions, not one of them worth the time it took to spit it out."

"And he would know more than I do."

"He would know the names of things, but he wouldn't know how to *do* them. I'll bet you could come back here tomorrow and do what I just did in the same amount of time and do it good."

" 'Well,' " Miss Camilla says. "Do it well, and I would do it well, I will be happy to do it well." She stands and picks up her cane. "It was *good* to talk to you. Try to remember: you work *well*; you do *good* work."

Tom Hardin returned from that upstate New York hunting trip with a magnificent eight-point rack. Ravenel was born a week later. In that week, Rose Ella did not speak a word to him. In the evenings she lay in bed, swollen and waiting, while he went to the shop to mount the antlers on a plaque of worm-eaten chestnut he'd saved for a special occasion.

One by one his sons had earned the right to enter his shop. Excepting his oldest friends, the men of the town stood outside unless invited in. On his second night back from New York, Miss Camilla strode in, refusing him so much as a knock. She planted her squat black pumps on the poplar planks. Burned by the heat of her arching gaze, Tom Hardin saw her for the first time as something other than plain. "You have abused your wife," she said. "You must apologize."

"Apologize, hell. She's got her coat." Fresh from a hunt, an eight-point rack on the bench before him, Tom Hardin was feeling rambunctious. He was sanding the chestnut plaque. He shook it at her, not meaning to threaten, only wanting to make clear who here was boss.

She jerked the wood from his hands and slammed it to the floor. It split along the grain. "I have no desire to lecture you on things you already know. You know what is good and what is evil. One way to know evil is that those who commit it hide from what they have done. You are hiding, here, from what you have done." She left, walking sweaterless into the December night. Standing in the light from the doorway, Tom Hardin watched her cross the yard, her pumps leaving dark circles in the frosted grass.

He was at the distillery when Rose Ella went into labor. She did not call him but drove herself to the hospital. When after work he found the house empty, he called Miss Camilla to drive him over. At the hospital, he had her wait, while he bought roses for Rose Ella from the florist in the lobby, the first flowers he'd ever bought. As he left the florist's shop, he held them extravagantly high: December roses! Miss Camilla gave him not so much as a nod.

Ravenel was a difficult birth. Tom Hardin and Miss Camilla waited together, well into the night. In the stuffy hospital heat the roses wilted. When the nurse called his name, Tom Hardin took Miss Camilla's hand, pulled her along; he wanted her to witness this gift.

Rose Ella lay spent, black circles under her eyes, hollow-cheeked. Ravenel lay in a crook of her arm, unmoving. The last two or three babies had come so easy, Tom Hardin had forgotten that birth could be this hard. He lay the roses on the bed. "Dead flowers," Rose Ella said, her face turning to the wall.

These nights Tom Hardin sleeps not at all. How can he sleep, with no guts to anchor his body to its bed? If his problem were only the pain, he would have no problem. But each day he leaves a little more of his life behind. In the mornings, crossing the flagstone patio (stones he had hoisted and prodded and cursed into place), he is sapped of a half-hour's strength. He sits in the shop, breathing heavy and shallow, until he hears Ravenel open the back door to bring coffee. Then he stands and picks up a piece of wood, or an awl, or an oil can, anything to look busy. "It's not like Ravenel would know what goes with wood and what doesn't," he grumbles to Miss Camilla, one morning after Ravenel has come and gone.

" 'As if,' please, introduces a comparative clause. 'It's not *as if* Ravenel would know the difference.' Which is to say you've scared him away from asking questions?"

"He hangs around. He's persistent, I'll give him that much."

"What he wants is important. Otherwise he could bring himself to speak." She takes up the glue. "How many more layers are you planning to have me stick on this thing?"

"It's nearly done. The hard part comes next, the turning on the lathe." He hands over the planks of sweet-scented cedar. "You still drive," he says. "I see you take your car out."

Miss Camilla glues each plank in place, and sets and clamps the block. "Just for trips to the store, or to church."

"What say you and me take a little spin some sunny afternoon." From his perch near the stove he tosses her a rag to wipe the glue from the bottle spout. He can see her hesitating; probably she knows where he will want to go. "A dying man's last request," he says. "That's a joke."

"I suppose I owe you something for all this woodworking education," she says. "As long as it's sunny."

By February, things come to the point where Tom Hardin cannot work at his bench. Something new is happening here—he feels the cancer growing. At night he places his hand on his side, feeling the cancer pulse with a life of its own, its beat a half-beat behind the beat of his own heart. He cannot escape the notion that he is doing this to himself—the cancer is a part of himself, after all, that is killing him, and taking its time in getting around to it.

He has given over the gluing and clamping to Miss Camilla, in the hope that once this is done he will recover the strength to mount the layered block on the lathe and turn it into a lamp. He has not told her that it will be a lamp, nor that it will be his gift to her.

These mornings Ravenel still brings coffee, but he cuts short his hanging around to imply questions. Instead he crosses the yard to Miss Camilla's, where he sometimes stays for more than an hour. This delays her arrival at the shop. Tom Hardin finds himself getting irritated with Ravenel, though he knows he has no reason; it's not as if Ravenel is holding something up. Miss Camilla will work her way across the yard in her own good time.

"What do you *do* over there anyway," Tom Hardin says to Ravenel one snowy morning, when it is clear that Miss Camilla will not make it across the yard.

"Nothing, really. We talk about books, mostly. Miss Camilla taught me English, you know. She doesn't get much chance to talk about that kind of thing."

"Do you talk about her heart? How is her heart?"

"She never says. She won't talk about it."

"You talk about me?"

Against the window's glare Tom Hardin sees the outline of his son's chin, identical to his own: cut with a T-square, nicked at its corners. He watches Ravenel study a cardinal in the barren dogwood branches, a bloody tear against the gray-sheeted sky. "Once or twice," Ravenel says.

"You're hogging her time." Tom Hardin speaks sharply, then regrets his words: not their sharpness, but the showing forth.

Ravenel picks up both cups, still full. "I'm here now, dammit. What more do you want." He kicks open the door and dumps the coffee in the snow. He crosses the yard to Miss Camilla's, leaving the shop door open. From his seat Tom Hardin watches the brown stain, until the falling snow covers it over.

The snow has not completely melted when Miss Camilla next crosses the yard. Tom Hardin opens the door, but she does not come in. "Why can't you acknowledge that he is here?" she asks. "And what he is here for?"

Tom Hardin turns away to pick up the laminated wood, still clamped. His fingers test its seams. "It's trying to warp. That could be a problem."

"Is it because he used to avoid your shop? He is trying to learn. He wants to learn."

"In three months. Four months."

"Do you think he gave up a job and came back only for that? He knows he can't learn wood in that little time."

He turns to her then. "Ravenel hasn't said a word to me. If he wants something, let him ask."

"He is too much like you to ask."

"He is *not* like me," Tom Hardin growls. "Let him get a woman.

He's never had a woman. He's never even mentioned a girlfriend. He's not married. He has no family.''

Miss Camilla's face tightens, bitter and narrow. "Neither have I, old man.'' She turns and stumps across the snow-puddled yard.

A month after Ravenel was born, Tom Hardin drove Miss Camilla in her brand-new DeSoto on their first trip to High Bridge. By then Rose Ella was speaking to him, to ask him to chop more wood or to see to the leaky faucet in the outbuilding where they'd rigged up a bathroom. That was all she was saying; no gossip, no jokes, no flirting.

One February day, snow closed the schools, but by noon the sun emerged and the main roads were clear. Tom Hardin left the distillery to visit Miss Camilla.

He asked her to go for a drive, asked if he could drive the brand-new DeSoto. She must have wondered when he drove on and on without turning back but she said nothing. He was on the parish board, after all. He had voted to hire her; Rose Ella had seen fit to remind Miss Camilla of as much, across those ten days of feeding the Masterson children.

They reached High Bridge at three, with the sun low in the sky. Built over the Kentucky River gorge, it was Andrew Carnegie's proof that the impossible could be done. At the time he built it, High Bridge was the world's highest bridge, carrying the Illinois Central south from Lexington to the coal mines of Kentucky and Tennessee. Three years later someone built a higher bridge, and someone else built still higher bridges after that.

Tom Hardin and Miss Camilla walked on the pedestrian catwalk to the middle of the bridge. Tom Hardin stole sips from a half-pint tucked in his coat pocket. Far below, in the long winter shadows, the cornstalk-stubbled bottomland was dusted with white. From a tiny farmhouse a single trail of smoke rose to spread flat, a thin gray tablecloth of haze covering the bottoms.

"Wait,'' Miss Camilla said, touching his arm. "I can feel the bridge shaking. A train must be coming.''

In a moment they heard its whistle, in another moment they saw it round the bend. The engineer blew his horn in short, angry blasts. They were close enough to see him shake his fist. The bridge vibrated and hummed, its webbing of girders swaying in harmony with the train's speeding mass. Miss Camilla's eyes narrowed with alarm. He cupped his hand to her ear. "It's OK!" he shouted. "It's built to do that!"

It seemed natural then to slip his arm around her shoulder and press his mouth against hers. For the long minute of the train's passing he kissed her. She neither resisted nor kissed him back. Then the caboose passed, sucking up the train's roar and leaving behind only the jeering shouts of the brakemen.

She pulled away. They stood until the last echoes tangled themselves in the trees' bare limbs. Then she spoke, still looking out over the valley. "Is this a bribe?" She plunged on, not waiting for his answer. "I know your kind. You think any flat-chested woman should faint in your arms and be grateful for the chance. I've known your kind for years. I've fought them for years. Don't think you're any different, just because you gave me a job." She turned away, to step smartly along the catwalk in her neat black pumps. In shame and anger, Tom Hardin trailed behind.

On an indifferently sunny day in late March, Miss Camilla and Tom Hardin take their last drive, with Miss Camilla peering through the steering wheel of her 1950 DeSoto. Ravenel waves them off. "Have a safe trip," he says. Tom Hardin feels like giving him the finger, but out of deference to Miss Camilla he keeps his hands in his lap.

They are hardly out of the drive before Tom Hardin turns to Miss Camilla. "How about driving to High Bridge."

"I knew you would ask that. That's an hour or more away, and I've seen better roads."

"We'll go slow. What have we got but time."

"Why do you want to go back there, of all places."

"You know why I want to go back there."

She does not answer, but she turns in the right direction. Tom Hardin settles back in his seat.

It takes two winding hours. They pass landmarks: Saint Joe's Cathedral, where Dutch Master paintings donated by a grateful Louis Philippe were discovered to be imitations; Perryville Battlefield, where on a hot, drought-ridden September day, eight thousand Union and Confederate soldiers died in a fight for a drink from the only running spring.

They reach High Bridge at noon. Miss Camilla parks in the gravel lot, under the historical marker. Hers is the only car. Tom Hardin climbs the small stoop to the bridge catwalk.

At the top of the steps he stops, wheezing and panting. Under his shirt, his right side hangs heavy, his swollen liver pressing against his belt. Spring is early. Redbud and white and pink dogwood bloom against the limestone palisades.

Tom Hardin takes Miss Camilla's arm. "I was going to make a lamp from that block of wood." He chooses his words carefully. He does not want to misspeak now.

"I know."

"I was going to give it to you."

"I thought as much."

"I'll never finish it. Turning it takes a good eye and a steady hand. I've lost that. But I thought you would want to know. I was making it for you."

"You're very kind." With her cane she points to the blooming redbud. "It's greener now than it was then," she says. "Really, this is a better time of year to come."

"Miss Camilla." He is afraid to form the question, his words come out flat and hard. "Can I kiss you."

She laughs, short and harsh. " 'May,' " she says. "*May* I kiss you. No, you may not."

His disappointment is too great not to give it voice. "My God, Camilla, why are you saying no now? What difference does it make?"

"Before, Rose Ella lived, and you took what you wanted. Now she is dead, and suddenly you ask."

"I couldn't ask, then." He forces himself to find and say the words. "I didn't know how. Things are different, now. I'm older."

"Old enough that even I look good."

"You looked good to me then."

"Anyone would have looked good to you then. Any*thing* would have looked good to you then. I was available, with a new car and a school holiday." She plants her cane, covers one mottled hand with another, stares over the valley. "Tom Hardin. You seem to think I have never known love." She speaks in a voice determined to convince. She might be lecturing herself. "I have known love. I have been lucky in love."

"Who has loved you."

For a long moment she says nothing. Then, "My students." She pauses. Her voice falters, uncertain. "My neighbors. Your son."

Tom Hardin drops her elbow. "I should tell that boy to leave." He walks to the car. Along the catwalk, he listens for her voice. He hears only the rush of the wind through the girders and the chatterings of the swallows.

When finally she reaches the car, he holds the door for her, but does not shut it once she has climbed in.

"Tom Hardin," Miss Camilla says gently. "You have been looking in the wrong places."

He does not move. "Do you think she ever forgave me?"

She says nothing. He knows she is turning her answer over in her head, an answer she is sure of but uncertain whether to present. "No," she says finally. "No, I don't think she ever did."

They arrive home as it is getting dark. Ravenel bounds across the yard, full of noise and concern. Miss Camilla leans across the seat to plant a kiss, her lips cool and paper dry on Tom Hardin's cheek. "You're persistent," she says. "I'll give you that much." She climbs from the car and shuts the door.

That night is a bad one, brought on, Tom Hardin knows, by the sitting and riding, and by Miss Camilla's words. The next morning he is in the shop before Ravenel is out of bed. He can do no more than sit, now, but he prefers sitting here, among his tools, to sitting in the house, where Rose Ella reigned.

At ten Ravenel comes to the shop. He no longer brings coffee but he comes and sits on the stool near the stove. Some mornings he has sat for a half-hour, and they have said nothing.

This morning Tom Hardin waves Ravenel away from the stool. "I want you to do me a favor."

"Sir?"

"I want you to take this package over to your friend next door." He has wrapped the block in brown paper grocery sacks. He waves Ravenel at it. "Tell her I thought she might use it to fuel her stove." Ravenel lifts the sack, feels its weight, hesitates. "Go on!" Tom Hardin says.

He watches his son cross the yard. In Ravenel's walk he sees his own walk, that bow-legged strut peculiar to the Masterson men.

He sits for a few minutes, then Ravenel returns. He comes in without knocking, and places the unwrapped block of wood on Tom Hardin's workbench. "She thanks you," Ravenel says, "but she insists that it be finished, and says to tell you that she does not want to see it otherwise. She tells me that I am to finish it. You are to show me how. She says."

"She does." Tom Hardin takes the block of wood and holds it to the light. It is not a good gluing job, even for a beginner. "It can't be done," he says. "It won't hold up to the lathe." Ravenel moves to the doorway, staring out at the newly greened lawn.

From across the yard Tom Hardin hears Miss Camilla's door open, and he lifts his head. Ravenel steps out and crosses to offer his arm, which she accepts. For a moment they talk, then they turn away, to return to Miss Camilla's house.

Tom Hardin studies her three-legged walk, as she pulls herself to her door with the help of her cane. I am too old, he thinks. I have too little time left to change. If that is stupid and narrow, so be it. I have earned that privilege.

Yet he watches Miss Camilla poling away from him, his son at her side. He hefts the wood in his hands, turning it over in the window's light, his unthinking fingers testing its strength against the turning on the lathe.

PIE DANCE
by Molly Giles
(San Francisco State University)

I don't know what to do about my husband's new wife. She won't come in. She sits on the front porch and smokes. She won't knock or ring the bell, and the only way I know she's there at all is because the dog points in the living room. The minute I see Stray standing with one paw up and his tail straight out I say, "Shhh. It's Pauline." I stroke his coarse fur and lean on the broom and we wait. We hear the creak of a board, the click of a purse, a cigarette being lit, a sad, tiny cough. At last I give up and open the door. "Pauline?" The afternoon light hurts my eyes. "Would you like to come in?"

"No," says Pauline.

Sometimes she sits on the stoop, picking at the paint, and sometimes she sits on the edge of an empty planter box. Today she's perched on the railing. She frowns when she sees me and lifts her small chin. She wears the same black velvet jacket she always wears, the same formal silk blouse, the same huge dark glasses. "Just passing by," she explains.

I nod. Pauline lives thirty miles to the east, in the city, with Konrad. "Passing by" would take her one toll bridge, one freeway, and two backcountry roads from their flat. But lies are the least of our problems, Pauline's and mine, so I nod again, bunch my bathrobe a little tighter around my waist, try to cover one bare foot with the other, and repeat my invitation. She shakes her head so vigorously the railing lurches. "Konrad," she says in her high young voice, "expects me. You know how he is."

I do, or I did—I'm not sure I know now—but I nod, and she flushes, staring so hard at something right behind me that I turn too and tell Stray, who is still posing in the doorway, to cancel the act and come say hello. Stray drops his front paw and pads forward, nose to the ground. Pauline blows cigarette smoke into the wisteria vine and draws her feet close to the railing. "What kind is it?" she asks, looking down.

I tell her we don't know, we think he's part Irish setter and part golden retriever; what happened was someone drove him out here to the country and abandoned him and he howled outside our house until one of the children let him come in. Pauline nods as if this were very interesting and says, "Oh really?" but I stop abruptly; I know I am boring. I am growing dull as Mrs. Dixon, Konrad's mother, who goes on and on about her poodle and who, for a time, actually sent us birthday cards and Christmas presents signed with a poodle paw print. I clasp the broom with both hands and gaze fondly at Stray. I am too young to love a dog; at the same time I am beginning to realize there isn't that much to love in this world. So when Pauline says, "Can it do tricks?" I try to keep the rush of passion from my eyes; I try to keep my voice down.

"He can dance," I admit.

"How great," she says, swaying on the railing. "Truly great."

"Yes," I agree. I do not elaborate. I do not tell Pauline that at night, when the children are asleep, I often dance with him. Nor do I confess that the two of us, Stray and I, have outgrown the waltz and are deep into reggae. Stray is a gay and affable partner, willing to learn, delighted to lead. I could boast about him forever, but Pauline, I see, already looks tired. "And you?" I ask. "How have you been?"

For answer she coughs, flexing her small hand so the big gold wedding ring flashes a lot in the sun; she smiles for the first time and makes a great show of pounding her heart as she coughs. She doesn't look well. She's lost weight since the marriage and seems far too pale. "Water?" I ask. "Or how about tea? We have peppermint, jasmine, mocha, and lemon."

"Oh, no!" she cries, choking.

"We've honey. We've cream."

"Oh no! But thank you! So much!"

After a bit she stops coughing and resumes smoking and I realize we both are staring at Stray again. "People," Pauline says with a sigh, "are so cruel. Don't you think?"

I do; I think yes. I tell her Stray was half-starved and mangy when we found him; he had been beaten and kicked, but we gave him raw eggs and corn oil for his coat and had his ear sewn up and took him to the vet's for all the right shots and look at him now. We continue to look at him now. Stray, glad to be noticed, and flattered, immediately trots to the driveway and pees on the wheel of Pauline's new Mustang. "Of course," I complain, "he's worse than a child."

Pauline bows her head and picks one of Stray's hairs off her black velvet jacket. "I guess," she says. She smiles. She really has a very nice smile. It was the first thing I noticed when Konrad introduced us; it's a wide smile, glamorous and trembly, like a movie star's. I once dreamt I had to kiss her and it wasn't bad, I didn't mind. In the dream Konrad held us by the hair with our faces shoved together. It was claustrophobic but not at all disgusting. I remember thinking, when I awoke: Poor Konrad, he doesn't even know how to punish people, and it's a shame, because he wants to so much. Later I noticed that Pauline's lips, when she's not smiling, are exactly like Konrad's, full and loose and purplish, sad. I wonder if when they kiss they feel they're making a mirror; I would. Whether the rest of Pauline mirrors Konrad is anyone's guess. I have never seen her eyes, of course, because of the dark glasses. Her hair is blonde and so fine that the tips of her ears poke through. She is scarcely taller than one of the children, and it is difficult to think of her as Konrad's "executive assistant"; she seems a child, dressed up. She favors what the magazines call the "layered look"—I suspect because she is ashamed of her bottom. She has thin shoulders but a heavy bottom. Well, I want to tell her, who is not ashamed of their bottom. If not their bottom their thighs or their breasts or their wobbly female bellies; who among us is perfect, Pauline.

Instead of saying a word of this, of course, I sigh and say, "Some days it seems all I do is sweep up after that dog.'' Stray, good boy, rolls in dry leaves and vomits some grass. As if more were needed, as if Stray and I together are conducting an illustrated lecture, I swish the broom several times on the painted porch floor. The straw scrapes my toes. What Pauline doesn't know—because I haven't told her and because she won't come inside—is that I keep the broom by the front door for show. I keep it to show the Moonies, Mormons, and Jehovah's Witnesses who stop by the house that I've no time to be saved, can't be converted. I use it to lean on when I'm listening, lean on when I'm not; I use it to convince prowlers of my prowess and neighbors of my virtue; I use it for everything, in fact, but cleaning house. I feel no need to clean house, and certainly not with a broom. The rooms at my back are stacked to the rafters with dead flowers and song sheets, stuffed bears and bird nests, junk mail and seashells, but to Pauline, perhaps, my house is vast, scoured, and full of light—to Pauline, perhaps, my house is in order. But who knows, with Pauline. She gives me her beautiful smile, then drops her eyes to my bathrobe hem and gives me her faint, formal frown. She pinches the dog hair between her fingers and tries to wipe it behind a leaf on the yellowing vein.

"I don't know how you manage" is what she says. She shakes her head. "Between the dog," she says, grinding her cigarette out on the railing, "and the children . . ." She sits huddled in the wan freckled sunlight with the dead cigarette curled in the palm of her hand, and after a minute, during which neither of us can think of one more thing to say, she lights up another. "It was the children," she says at last, "I really wanted to see."

"They'll be sorry they missed you," I tell her politely.

"Yes," Pauline says. "I'd hoped . . ."

"Had you but phoned," I add, just as politely, dropping my eyes and sweeping my toes. The children are not far away. They said they were going to the end of the lane to pick blackberries for pie, but what they are actually doing is showing their bare bottoms to passing cars and screaming "Hooey hooey." I know this because little Dixie Steadman, who used to baby-sit before she got her master's degree in Female Processes, saw them and called me. "Why are you letting your daughters celebrate their femininity in this burlesque?" Dixie asked. Her voice was calm and reasonable and I wanted to answer, but before I could there was a brisk papery rustle and she began to read rape statistics to me, and I had to hold the phone at arm's length and finally I put it to Stray's ear and even he yawned, showing all his large yellow teeth, and then I put the receiver down, very gently, and we tiptoed away. What I'm wondering now is what "hooey" means. I'd ask Pauline, who would be only too glad to look it up for me (her curiosity and industry made her, Konrad said, an invaluable assistant, right from the start), but I'm afraid she'd mention it to Konrad and then he would start threatening to take the children away; he does that; he can't help it; it's like a nervous tic. He loves to go to court. Of course he's a lawyer, he has to. Even so, I think he overdoes it. I never understood the rush to divorce me and marry Pauline; we were fine as we were, but he says my problem is that I have no morals and perhaps he's right, perhaps I don't. Both my divorce and Pauline's wedding were executed in court, and I think both by Judge Benson. The marriage couldn't have been statelier than the dissolution, and if I were Pauline, only twenty-four and getting married for the very first time, I would have been bitter. I would have insisted on white lace or beige anyway and candles and lots of fresh flowers, but Pauline is not one to complain. Perhaps she feels lucky to be married at all; perhaps she feels lucky to be married to Konrad. Her shoulders always droop a little when she's with him, I've noticed, and she listens to him with her chin tucked in and her wrists poised, as if she were waiting to take dictation. Maybe she adores him. But if she does she must learn not to take him too seriously or treat him as if he matters; he hates that; he can't deal with that at all. I should tell her this, but there are some things she'll have to find out for herself. All I tell her is that the girls are gone, up the lane, picking berries.

"How wonderful," she says, exhaling. "Berries."

"Blackberries," I tell her. "They grow wild here. They grow all over."

"In the city," she says, making an effort, "a dinky little carton costs eighty-nine cents." She smiles. "Say you needed three cartons to make one pie," she asks me, "how much would that cost?"

I blink, one hand on my bathrobe collar.

"Two-sixty-seven." Her smile deepens, dimples. "Two-sixty-seven plus tax when you can buy a whole frozen pie for one-fifty-six, giving you a savings of one-eleven at least. They don't call them convenience foods," Pauline says, "for nothing."

"Are you sure," I ask, after a minute, "you don't want some tea?"

"Oh no!"

"Some coffee?"

"Oh no!"

"A fast glass of wine?"

She chuckles, cheerful, but will not answer. I scan the sky. It's close, but cloudless. If there were to be a thunderstorm—and we often have thunderstorms this time of year—Pauline would have to come in. Or would she? I see her, erect and dripping, defiant.

"Mrs. Dixon," I offer, "had a wonderful recipe for blackber—"

"Mrs. Dixon?"

For a second I almost see Pauline's eyes. They are small and tired and very angry. Then she tips her head to the sun and the glasses cloud over again.

"Konrad's mother."

"Yes," she says. She lights another cigarette, shakes the match out slowly. "I know."

"A wonderful recipe for blackberry cake. She used to say that Konrad never liked pie."

"I know."

"Just cake."

"I know."

"What I found out, Pauline, is that he likes both."

"We never eat dessert," Pauline says, her lips small and sad again. "It isn't good for us and we just don't have it."

Stray begins to bark and wheel around the garden and a second later the children appear, Letty first, her blonde hair tangled and brambly like mine, then Alicia, brown-eyed like Konrad, and then Sophie, who looks like no one unless—yes—with her small proud head, a bit like Pauline. The children are giggling and they deliberately smash into each other as they zigzag down the driveway. "Oops," they cry, with elaborate formality, "do forgive me. My mistake." As they come closer we see that all three are scratched and bloody with berry juice. One holds a Mason jar half-full and one has a leaky colander and one boasts a ruined pocket. Pauline closes her eyes tight behind her dark glasses and holds out her arms. The girls, giggling, jostle toward her. They're wild for Pauline. She tells them stories about kidnappers and lets them use her calculator.

With each kiss the wooden railing rocks and lurches; if these visits keep up I will have to rebuild the porch, renew the insurance. I carry the berries into the kitchen, rinse them off, and set them to drain. When I come back outside Pauline stands alone on the porch. Stains bloom on her blouse and along her outthrust chin.

"Come in," I urge, "and wash yourself off."

She shakes her head very fast and smiles at the floor. "No," she says. "You see, I have to go."

The children are turning handsprings on the lawn, calling, "Watch me! me! me!" as Stray dashes between them, licking their faces. I walk down the driveway to see Pauline off. As I lift my hand to wave she turns and stares past me, toward the house. I turn too, see nothing, no one, only an old wooden homestead, covered with yellowing vines, a curtain aflutter in an upstairs window, a red door ajar on a dark brown room.

"Thank you," she cries. Then she throws her last cigarette onto the gravel and grinds it out and gets into her car and backs out the driveway and down to the street and away.

Once she turns the corner I drop my hand and bite the knuckles, hard. Then I look back at the house. Konrad steps out, a towel gripped to his waist. He is scowling; angry, I know, because he's spent the last half hour hiding in the shower with the cat litter box and the tortoise. He shouts for his shoes. I find them toed out in flight, one in the bedroom, one down the hall. As he hurries to tie them I tell him a strange thing has happened: it seems I've grown morals.

"What?" Konrad snaps. He combs his hair with his fingers when he can't find my brush.

"Us," I say. "You. Me. Pauline. It's a lot of hooey," I tell Konrad. "It is."

Konrad turns his face this way, that way, scrubs a space clear in the mirror. "Do you know what you're saying?" he says to the mirror.

I think. I think, Yes. I know what I'm saying. I'm saying good-bye. I'm saying, Go home.

And when he has gone and the girls are asleep and the house is night-still, I remember the pie. I roll out the rich dough, flute it, and fill it with berries and sugar, lemons and spice. We'll have it for breakfast, the children and I; we'll share it with Stray. "Would you like that?'' I ask him. Stray thumps his tail, but he's not looking at me; his head is cocked, he's listening to something else. I listen too. A faint beat comes from the radio on the kitchen counter. Even before I turn it up I can tell it's a reggae beat, strong and sassy. I'm not sure I can catch it. Not sure I should try. Still, when Stray bows, I curtsy. And when the song starts, we dance.

NOTES ON CONTRIBUTORS

JONATHAN AMES grew up in New Jersey and graduated from Princeton University in 1987. His first novel, *I Pass Like Night*, was published by William Morrow and Co.

STEVEN BARTHELME studied at Boston College, the University of Texas at Austin, and Johns Hopkins University, worked as a taxi driver, apartment manager, advertising and P.R. copywriter, and now teaches English at the University of Southern Mississippi in Hattiesburg. His stories have won the PEN Syndicated Fiction Project Competition, the Texas Institute of Letters Short Story Award, and the Ernest Hemingway Short Story Award. His short-story collection, *And He Tells the Little Horse the Whole Story*, was published by Johns Hopkins University Press in 1987 and is being reissued by Vintage. He recently completed a novel, to be published by Random House.

LAUREN BELFER attended Swarthmore College and the M.F.A. writing program at Columbia University. She lives in New York City with her husband and son. "Trainscapes" is her first published fiction.

PINCKNEY BENEDICT lives with his wife Laura on his family's dairy farm north of Lewisburg, West Virginia. He studied at Princeton University and the University of Iowa Writers Workshop. He has published two collections of stories, *Town Smokes* (Ontario Review Press) and *The Wrecking Yard* (Doubleday).

ETHAN CANIN is the author of a collection of short stories, *Emperor of the Air,* and a novel, *Blue River,* both published by Houghton Mifflin. He attended the University of Iowa Writers Workshop and has taught writing at the University of Michigan and San Francisco State University. A recent graduate of Harvard Medical School, he now lives in San Francisco.

JENNIFER COKE was born in Black River, Jamaica. A graduate of Sarah Lawrence College, she received an award for poetry from the Academy of American Poets. She currently works as a free-lance business writer in New York City. "Eye Water" is a chapter from an unpublished novel.

MARK DEWEY is a native of Wisconsin who now lives in Charlottesville, Virginia, with his wife and two children. He was a Henry Hoyns Fellow in Creative Writing at the University of Virginia in 1989–90.

HARRIET DOERR was born in Pasadena, California, in 1910. She attended Smith College in 1927, but received her B.A. from Stanford University in 1977, where she later took part in the graduate fiction program. Her first novel, *Stones for Ibarra,* won the National Book Award. She is completing a second novel, to be published by Harcourt Brace Jovanovich. Portions of it have appeared in *The Atlantic* and *The New Yorker*.

MICHAEL DRINKARD grew up in Redlands, California, was educated at the University of California at Santa Cruz and Columbia University, and now lives in New York City. Alfred A. Knopf published his novel, *Green Bananas,* in 1989. He is a recipient of the Ingram Merrill Foundation Award.

MOLLY GILES studied at San Francisco State University, where she is now an assistant professor in Creative Writing. Her collection of short stories, *Rough Translations* (University of Georgia Press), won the Flannery O'Connor Award, the Bay Area Book Reviewers Award, the Boston Globe Award, and was nominated for a Pulitzer Prize. She is working on a new collection, entitled *Survival in the Wilderness*, and a novel.

EMILY HAMMOND, received an M.F.A. from the University of Arizona, has published in *Crazyhorse, Fiction, Prism International*, and other magazines, including *Nimrod,* which awarded her the Katherine Anne Porter Prize. She won first place in the 1992 *American Fiction* anthology. A fifth-generation Californian, she is working on a novel.

A. M. HOMES is the author of *Jack,* a novel, and *The Safety of Objects,* a collection of short stories. Stories from the collection have appeared in *Story, Mirabella, Between C & D, Christopher Street, New York Woman, The Quarterly,* and *Bomb.* A graduate of Sarah Lawrence College, the University of Iowa Writers Workshop, and the Whitney Museum Independent Study Program, A. M. Homes has been the recipient of a New York Foundation for the Arts Fellowship and a James Michener Fellowship.

FENTON JOHNSON is the author of *Crossing the River*, as well as widely published short stories and essays. His fiction has won a National Endowment for the Arts Fellowship in Literature, a Stegner Fellowship in Fiction at Stanford University, and a James Michener Fellowship from the University of Iowa Writers Workshop. "High Bridge" is adapted from a chapter of *Scissors, Paper, Rock,* a novel in progress. A frequent contributor to *The New York Times Magazine,* he divides his time between Kentucky, where he was born, and San Francisco. He teaches creative writing at San Francisco State University.

SUZANNE JUERGENSEN is a native of New Hartford, New York. Now living in San Francisco, she studies creative writing at San Francisco State University and is working on a collection of short stories. "Physics" is her first published fiction.

DAVID LIPSKY was born in 1965. A graduate of Brown University, he received an M.A. in creative writing from Johns Hopkins. His fiction has appeared in *The New Yorker* and other magazines, and has been anthologized in *The Best American Short Stories*. His collection, *Three Thousand Dollars*, was published by Summit Books in 1989. His novel, *Triangle*, will be published in the spring of 1992. He lives in New York City.

SUE MILLER is the author of three books: *Inventing the Abbotts*, a collection of short stories, and *The Good Mother* and *Family Pictures*, both novels. She studied in the Creative Writing Program at Boston University, where she now teaches. She lives in Boston with her family.

WALTER MOSLEY went to Goddard College in 1971, but spent most of his trimesters hitchhiking around America, and was asked to leave the school after one year. After that, he became a computer programmer, attended Johnson State College in Vermont, and then studied political theory at the University of Massachusetts. In 1981, he moved to New York. One day at Mobil Oil headquarters, where he was supposed to be writing a computer program, he wrote this sentence: "On hot sticky days in southern Louisiana the fire ants swarmed." That led him to enter the writing program at City College of New York. Since 1990, he has published two novels, *Devil in a Blue Dress* and *A Red Death*. His third novel, *White Butterfly*, will be published this year by W. W. Norton.

DANIEL MUELLER grew up in a suburb of Minneapolis, butchered salmon on Kodiak Island, Alaska, taught high school English in Tamil Nadu, India, and in Wausau, Wisconsin, and has attended writing programs at the University of Virginia in Charlottesville and at Hollins College in Roanoke, Virginia. His short story "The Night My Brother Worked the Header" won the 1990 Playboy College Fiction Contest. He has also published stories in *The Crescent Review* and *Timbuktu*.

BRAD OWENS, a native Texan, attended the graduate writing workshop at Stanford University, where he has been a Jones Lecturer in Creative Writing. His work has appeared in *Threepenny Review*. He is currently a fellow at the Cité Internationale des Arts in Paris.

ANN PATCHETT has published short stories in *The Paris Review, The Iowa Review, The Southern Review, Epoch,* and *20 Under 30*. A graduate of Sarah Lawrence College, she received the James A. Michener/Copernicus Society Award for a novel in progress, which she completed at the Fine Arts Work Center in Provincetown. Her novel, *The Patron Saint of Liars,* will be published in the spring by Houghton Mifflin.

M. T. SHARIF studied creative writing at Boston University. His works have appeared in *Agni, The Antioch Review,* and *The Best American Short Stories of 1989*.

MONA SIMPSON is the author of *Anywhere But Here,* which has been translated into fourteen languages, and of *The Lost Father,* forthcoming from Knopf. She attended the writing program at Columbia University, has received grants from the National Endowment for the Arts and the Guggenheim Foundation, and currently is a Bard Center Fellow at Bard College.

CHRIS SPAIN grew up in South America. His collection of short stories, *Praying for Rain,* was published by Capra Press in 1990. A graduate of Columbia University's writing program, he also has a degree in agriculture from Colorado State and was awarded a Stegner Fellowship at Stanford University. His stories have appeared in *The Antioch Review, Story, The Quarterly, Story Quarterly,* and the *Pushcart Prize Anthology*. He lives in California.

THE EDITORS

JOHN BIRMINGHAM, a vice-president of the Henfield Foundation, is formerly an associate editor of the *Transatlantic Review*. He has published two books, *Our Time Is Now* and *The Vancouver Split*. A free-lance journalist, he has written for *The New York Times, Esquire,* and *Premiere*.

LAURA GILPIN attended Sarah Lawrence College and the writing program at Columbia University. Her book of poems, *The Hocus Pocus of the Universe,* won the Walt Whitman Award, sponsored by the Academy of American Poets. She was awarded the Transatlantic Review Fellowship to Breadloaf Writers' Conference and has received a grant from the National Endowment for the Arts. A registered nurse, she is associate director of Planetree, a nonprofit consumer health-care organization based in San Francisco, which is working to humanize hospitals.

JOSEPH F. McCRINDLE is president of the Henfield Foundation, which he set up in 1958. Born in New York, he was educated at Harvard University and Yale Law School, spent two years in the U.S. Army, mostly in London, and then escaped a Wall Street law firm in less than a year. After working in one London and two New York publishing firms, he became a literary agent, but enjoyed reading manuscripts more than trying to sell them. In 1959, he helped found the *Transatlantic Review,* and remained its editor and publisher until it ceased publication, after sixty issues, in 1977. He lives in London, New York, and Princeton.